STOW AWAY

By Dr. Lee H. Campbell

SECOND EDITION

(First edition: ebook ISBN# 9781626754348)

Cover: based on a photo of the author at the age her memories came back

Artist: Bill Cassa

For permissions or to comment, contact the author at lee.stowaway@gmail .

TABLE OF CONTENTS

DEDICATION

DEDICATION

I dedicate STOW AWAY to those mothers who, in the 1970s, ended a silence that had been imposed on them for decades. Terminating their zipped-lip service to the American adoption system put them more at risk than they had been since their initial loss. Under threat now was their rehabbed social standing, the "normal" family they were promised as compensation for their loss, and even, in some cases, their careers and livelihood. Though their renewed labor helped to reform adoption for generations to come, these women have gone unheralded. This book sounds an opening note on their behalf.

I also dedicate this work to these mothers for a personal reason. They mentored me, taught me how to mentor them, and along the way they encouraged me to be the best possible "dangerous woman" I could be.

And I especially dedicate this work to Gail Hanssen Perry, who has always been quietly yet powerfully indispensable to the Cause and to me.

- Lee Campbell

Why I Wrote This Book

2013

AGE: 68

FLORIDA

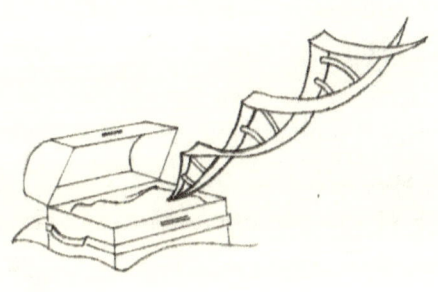

I'm 68 years old. Although I'm now retired, for more than 30 years I was called "Doc C" around my college campus. Students in my courses on Psychology, Human Development, Sociology, Marriage and the Family (and more) also called me "fun but firm."

Another rumor about my courses was the way I ignored my podium. Though a standard issue podium inspires hope and fear in students and professors alike, my podium was no altar. It was something I mostly breezed by. I was a pacer, always stirring up connections between some new perspective and a student nearby, then between that student and another in a back corner.

My course material was as theoretical as you might expect a college course to be. But the concepts also applied to students' lives. Sometimes light bulbs switched on, only to quickly turn off when unexpected insights about personal situations hit students over the head. That can get pretty threatening. So I sometimes compared and contrasted text concepts to myself.[1] This gave students the guts to more deeply and publically examine—and affirm—their own lives. Soon, my students were teaching each other and me more than standardized tests could ever prove.

Trust bloomed between us. If the classroom grew into a safe enough place for *me*, I sometimes took a big breath and exhaled my deepest and once most well-guarded secret about an experience I had in the hush-hush early 1960s. Some of my colleagues could argue I "should" have continued to keep it private. I couldn't agree.

Keeping my Google-able secrets wouldn't have done my students or me any good. Just the opposite. Outing myself preemptively was consistent with my goal to be open and accessible to my students. Airing this particular experience also had the potential to model one way students could survive and thrive and help others along the way.

Even so, there is one part of my life I never turned into a teachable moment. There's no science to back it up. During my walks around the proverbial block, more often than not I was ushered by serendipity. Although we typically think of destiny as the thing that points us upward and onward, that wasn't true for me. Instead, my serendipity, my destiny, my fate, my fill-in-the-blank was retro. It pointed me back in time. Though I always found it eyes-rubbingly hard to believe, I was shown again and again there was yet one more thing from 1963 I needed to fix.

Take, for example, my encounter with E. Wayne Carp. A historian at Pacific Lutheran University in Tacoma, Washington, Wayne emailed me a few years ago. He was writing a biography, he said, about someone I once knew.[2] Wayne's subject, Jean Paton, had been a colleague of mine in the '70s and '80's.

Jean was an adopted woman and an adoption reformer. She led a national group she called "Orphan Voyage." I was Jean's counterpart. In 1963 I surrendered a child to adoption, which is, as you guessed, the experience I mentioned above. Thirteen years later, in 1976, I founded the first support and advocacy group in the world for mothers like me. It was tricky to find an identity that captured our experience, its fall-out, and whatever our new role would turn out to be. For starters, I needed to settle on one word among the many that others tossed around for us. I ended up inventing a new one: "birthmother." I called my organization "Concerned United Birthparents" —"CUB."

Birthing CUB wasn't easy labor. It was more like being bled with primitive tools in the 18th century from three carotid arteries! I had to straighten myself out. At the same time, I had to reach out to others. Meanwhile, I had to muster our personal-works-in-progress to challenge the socially-sacred institution of adoption. It all seemed worth it.

But most of the old guard (and they're still around) called our work a disaster. They even called me a "dangerous woman." Fortunately for me, Jean wasn't one of them.

With Jean's books, *The Adopted Break Silence* (1954) and *Orphan Voyage* (1968), her newsletters called *The Log*, and her mighty typewriter on which she wrote me very long letters, Jean became one of my mentors and, later, a colleague. I wasn't the only one who thought highly of Jean. By the time she died at 93, she held the distinction of being the earliest and among the longest-lasting adoption reformers in the United States.

Wayne told me he wanted to re-trace the ties between Jean and me. He asked if I would fact-check chapters that described the work I did with CUB. His wasn't an unusual request. Over the years, I had vetted several such books. It would be my privilege, I told him.

About a year later, Wayne sent me his draft. As it happened, I was finishing the last semester before I retired. Much as I loved teaching, there were other things I now wanted to do. Like, for my first time ever, next to nothing.

I relished my vision of retirement. My next-to-nothings would blithely loop through three "B"s: Body (diet, yoga); Books (finally, my fill of fiction); and Bon-bons (lots of chocolate, which would bring me back to Body). Those B's would help me rest up for my next phase of retirement, when my energetic husband would join me.

Imagine my surprise, then, when Wayne's book became a speed bump, then a detour. Serendipity was up to her old tricks, although I didn't recognize the signs at first.

In reading the draft of Jean's biography, I was stunned to see Jean had kept every piece of paper that ever crossed her palm, whether incoming or outgoing. The difference between Jean and me unseated my cross-legged yoga pose. There was Jean, a historian's dream; alongside her, there was I, a historian's nightmare. I pushed "Pause" on *Namaste* to ask myself: And, just what papers did you save, Missy?

It wasn't that I didn't write anything to keep. I wrote my heart out, as did others who involved me as co-author, editor, publisher or sounding board. But, except for my personal journals, I kept none of it. Kicked everything to the curb, I did.

Soon I remembered I was responsible for more than I first thought. I recalled the way I'd blown a second chance. When another birthmother wanted me to take CUB materials off her hands, I told her she should recycle it all instead—the kind of recycling where stuff goes into a city truck and gets shredded into meaningless cardboard that stores hamburger or something. As a social scientist, I should have known better. My answer to my friend, in effect, trashed my own history and that of many others.

Around the same time, Steve Jobs died. Hitting the heel of my hand to my head, I recalled I even threw away his letter to me about searching for his birthfamily. At the time, his letter was like a riddle I didn't have time to solve. I only recently realized I shouldn't have taken his letter personally; it reflected his characteristic rude and abrasive self. [3]

Yet, with my own papers, I had been just as flippant, just as rash, and even perhaps callous. But, I wondered, what could I do about it now? Could I go back in time, contact some of the many thousands of other mothers I had once known and re-assemble at least some CUB materials from others' attics, basement boxes, or bottom file drawers? Musing, I began to think maybe I could.

Unlike me, others keep stuff. Maybe they save it for sentimental reasons or for no reason except they hate to get rid of anything. The more I thought about it, the greater my respect grew for these blessed hoarders.

Contacting CUB's current Board of Directors with my recent thoughts, I learned that, even as I was realizing the gap I'd left behind, so were they. They had lamented at a recent Board meeting that new members kept trying to re-invent the wheel; they didn't know about the wars fought by earlier CUB veterans.

The CUB Board and I had come to the same question: what could be done about CUB's missing history? Now, we came to the same answer: I would become CUB's Curator. Tapping technology that hadn't been available during early CUB, I would use emails, Skype, and free smart phone minutes to locate old CUB stuff. But then what?

Tracing an old rumor, I learned Radcliffe's Schlesinger Library at Harvard already housed some CUB materials in their center for women activists. They were excited by my project, saying they wanted whatever I could collect. And Harvard isn't exactly a recycling truck! About then I recognized serendipity's handiwork. I now faced for the umpteenth time my latest mission for my longest challenge.

I would need to act fast, though. I was a member of the first generation of adoption reformists and we were dying off (see "Afterword"). Not to be morbid about it but lately I even read the Obits. My once skeptical eyes have now seen proof that people my age die unexpectedly every day. Since I knew I was the best person to gather CUB's history—if only to redeem myself—I got to work.

As Fed Ex and UPS delivered boxes from veteran CUBers, I began to unpack, store, and inventory the materials in my home library. Soon I realized something else. It seemed to me if I was going to collect CUB's history, I might as well narrate it. But how could I tease out CUB's story from my own? Early CUB and I were barnacled together.

My mission got bigger. I began to narrate both CUB's story and mine. Soon I realized the volume of material would require two books. The first—the one you are reading now— is *STOW AWAY*. Primarily my story, it is also CUB's back story. My upcoming book, *CAST OFF*, broadens the scope. It shows how other mothers also came out of hiding to finally honor their instincts, and how we, laboring together, squared off against a one-sided system that was (and largely still is) stacked against us (see "Afterword").

I completed my CUB collection. To my surprise, I pretty much found everything there was to find. I digitized a lot of it for CUB's website (www.cubirthparents.org). Then I shipped a disk and the hard copies to Harvard.

My three "B"s still wait patiently around the next corner of my life. And when I get there, if serendipity tries to pivot me backward with any more ways to make peace with my past…well, I have my trigger finger poised on a stun gun and it is already twitching.

Namaste.

Lee Campbell,
Florida

CHAPTER ONE

1 9 6 3

AGE: 18

NEW HAMPSHIRE

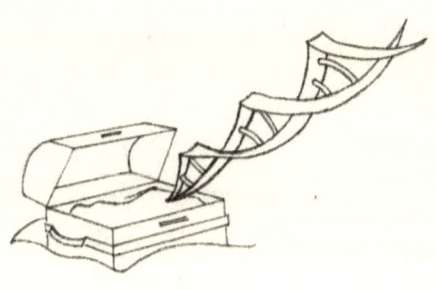

I was a good girl who went bad. I was new at being bad—this bad. I didn't have enough experience to know what to do.

I was newly knocked up and mentally knocked out. But the state of New Hampshire said they would put me in good hands. My new social worker would know how to iron out everything.

Yet, I had a problem the first time I sat in her office. According to the name plate on her heavy oak desk, she was "Miss" followed by a last name with four-syllables. It ended with a vowel. Italian.

My very-ex-boyfriend, Tom, and his family had Italian last names that ended with a vowel. As one united block, they had responded to the paternity suit my family filed against Tom after he said he wasn't the father of my baby. Dad told me he had filed the suit to get enough money to send me away. I was about as okay with that as I could be under the circumstances. I still hoped that after Tom saw me again, he would drop his denial right then and there in the courtroom.

Tom's family wasn't about to take that chance. They started to dicker. After a few short blasts of offers and counteroffers, Dad finally settled out of court. Their settlement of $900 was a respectable sum for 1962 and I was desperate for some respect. But with the family's check, Tom had also entered a plea of *Nolo Contendre*. This was like grinding another filthy cigarette stub into the heaping ashtray that stunk up my mind.

My mind wasn't the only thing that was trashed. At 17, my heart was a tender thing. For weeks, it had felt as if a wash-woman with lye-coarsened hands had been wringing it out. With Tom's plea, I felt one last twist and then the wad was unceremoniously dumped in my chest. My heart now slumped in a corner, limp and musty, detached from its own beat.

I didn't need to learn how Tom's legal plea translated into teen talk[4]; I capital-K-Knew and felt its meaning.

I had taken all the lumps I could. Now all I wanted was to follow Dad's plan, to be sent away—away from the rumors the court case had stirred up. Which was probably part of Tom's family's plan in the first place: to get rid of me.

Now another Italian last name was staring me in the face and it belonged to the only person who knew how to help. Yet, with Tom's betrayal flashing like neon, she was caught in the same spooky light. I tried to overlook that glare, to keep the promise of her separate from the promises Tom hadn't delivered.

Then a new flare shot across my brow. For my social worker's first step in my rescue, she told me to call her by her first name: "Carole." *Carol* was the name of the traitor who had taken Tom away—after she had heard the rumors about the court case and after she had phoned me to act all nicey-nice, no doubt looking for more gossip she could use against me.

Connecting my social worker's last name with her first name was like a one-two punch.

As I tried to rebound, I saw another complication. I had never before used a first name for anyone who was years older than I. First names were for friends. Since most of my friends had taken sides against me, I could have used a fresh supply. But it seemed to me as if Carole was trying to force-feed our relationship. I didn't have enough energy for more phony friends.

I tried to re-arrange words to avoid calling her by any name. Each unlabeled sentence helped me feel as if I had a little control over something. Still, Carole was more powerful than I in ways that were beyond me.

I was a five-foot-two, 90-pounder whose high school had kicked out like a contaminant. Carole was a bigger-than-life college graduate. She loomed over me at six-feet-something and had a voice so loud she could have preached without a podium. It hurts my ears even now to remember it.

I soon learned, though, that if I gritted my back teeth hard enough when she talked, the buffeting in my ears would muffle the sound. I could listen to her that way. I knew listening was the polite thing to do but there was an even better reason. She was the professional who knew better and I was the client who had screwed things up.

* * *

Months later, I left the Florence Crittenton Hastings House—Flo Crit—the home for unwed mothers that Carole had found for me. Now I needed her permission. I wanted her to allow me to visit my son in foster care. She told me that wasn't what I was supposed to do. In reply, I stared at the hands in my lap until the silence stretched uncomfortably for both of us. With a "TSK," she agreed.

Obviously, I was still a trouble-maker, since I went on the visit anyway. During the visit, I tried to assume the perfect pose with my baby: not too desperate, not too eager. When I inhaled his delicious baby scent, when he curved his little hand around my finger, I measured out the visceral thrill—so much for this moment, so much for the next. I kept a little thrill for later, for after I left.

I sensed Carole waiting for my next mistake. She shot glances at me when she and the foster mother paused in their conversation. Her quizzical expression was like a mirror. I could imagine what she saw. Before, I had insisted on visiting my baby; now, I seemed detached. Still, I couldn't worry about what she thought she saw. I had to be with my son in my own way—a way that kept my feelings sacred, just between him and me.

Later, when I asked for more visits, Carole resisted more strenuously. I claimed it was helping me make up my mind. I offered her words she wanted to hear and she condescended to allow more visits. It bought me some time.

I needed to try to penetrate the wall Dad and Mom had erected to keep out the mother in me and the grandparents in them. Their wall was guarded better than Berlin. I had named my son after Dad, giving him another boy in the family to help balance his four daughters and one son. It hadn't won Dad over. He was worried about his other children's reputations, saying they were already tripping over my dirty laundry. My sisters' friends weren't allowed to hang out with them. On street corners, my brother was fighting his friends' taunts about me.

For my mother's part, she knew her place: she had to stand by her husband. And anyway she was afraid of taking more licks from our neighbors' wagging tongues. Even more, mom was afraid of the tongue lashing she knew she would receive from her own mother. So far, she told me, she had been able to keep my *MaMere* in the dark.

I suspected there must be other support out there, but I didn't know where to look. Not yet. Meanwhile, suspecting there was support wasn't evidence I could get some of it even if it did exist. Without some help, I couldn't make the plan I needed to counter Carole's.

* * *

I didn't know how to put Carole off any longer. I had to keep my next appointment with her. I reasoned she knew stuff she was holding back. I just hadn't found the right way to ask. When I had used the words I knew, she told me that, unless there was an adoption, I would have to pay for foster care and for the time in the maternity home that wasn't covered by the settlement I received from the paternity suit. I had tried to apply for jobs, but I was so nervous I flunked typing tests. I couldn't imagine how I could afford to reimburse anyone anything. I needed to find new and better words to use with Carole. I knew I had to find a way to get a handle on stuff.

I took the bus to her office building. Holding onto the banister, I shuffled up the wooden staircase to the second floor. I tracked the shellacked wood baseboard as if it were an arrow to her office, second door on the right. There, with supremely primed patience, she "should" on me again. I should understand, Carole said, she couldn't continue to work with me. I should know things had gone on too long and her superiors wondered about the delay. My relationship with her *should* have come to a close by now.

Then, like a medieval artist in short supply of canvas, she used broad brush strokes to paint over my sketch of a promising future. Any hope she might help me keep my child vanished under that brush. From a faraway place, I tried to voice my potential. But my uncertainty made my promise sound hollow, even to me.

I couldn't compete with her rat-a-tat delivery. She turned on her good cop. She turned on her bad cop. She sometimes channeled the two in the same long breath. She was too fast for me. I couldn't freeze-frame her. She was a moving target. It was never a fair match.

She replayed the facts of the situation I had created for myself. She knew I wanted to redeem what I had done and to prove I was no longer the selfish girl I had been. She knew I surely could see the need for that. She also knew I didn't really mean to pass along my mistakes to my son. She asked a rhetorical question and confirmed that I did not want to saddle him forever with the labels *illegitimate* or *bastard*. She knew I wanted him to have a better life.

About then, Carole abruptly tore the top sheet from a legal-sized pad of yellow-lined paper. With her pen, she carved a bold line down its center. At the top of the left column, she wrote "Things I can give my son."At the top of the right column, she wrote "Things adoptive parents can give him." She left me alone with the paper, expecting me to fill it. I was eager for the task. I wanted to excel.

But my column stumped me. At that time, I didn't know for certain what I could give my son. After the hollowness of my earlier attempts, I knew I had to be concrete. Still, if I had learned anything from my experience, it was the importance of being fair. I turned to the other column. I listed items I had been told adoptive parents could supply. When I returned to my column, I perked up. I suddenly knew how to win. I could offer him "love." To me, love was a solid override; it trumped everything. I passed the paper back to Carole.

She went straight to my long list for adoptive parents. She applauded it. When she returned to my column, my spine collapsed; she was not impressed. I protested that no one would love him the way I did. She said the people who wanted to adopt him had already seen him. They already loved him.

Clearly, I was in the way. I had sensed it before. Now I was left with no more arguments. Stressing the words she wanted me to absorb, her megaphone voice added an echo to **redeem**, **release**, and **free**. Her words covered my current of thought like an oil slick.

Sensing her advantage, Carole drew my attention to the "X" on a line of the same paper she had shipped across her desk to me over the previous two and a half months. In the margin near that "X," her nail, filed to a point and polished a spooky white, played Taps. I noticed that the white of her nail matched the white in the angle of her fingertip as it slowly completed each downward stroke. She was pressing hard. Her intention was clear. Her finger would stay put; she wasn't going anywhere. Neither, apparently, was I. She would not let me slip out her office, not again. Not until I gave her what she wanted. Exhausted, I allowed my chin to drop in a nod.

Carole then opened a side door in her office, which led to another. She beckoned to someone waiting there. A new woman entered. She was a notary, I was told, a witness. Both women stood above me. Now there were two agents of the state bulwarked on one side of the desk, the two of them sending me a signal to get on with it.

I looked up at them. As if they suddenly realized that hovering went too far outside their moral code, they quickly sat down.

After the notary left, Carole fixed her eyes[5] on the prized signature, an official seal stamped beside it. She avoided looking at me. She didn't see my eyes' tear-slicked surface. She didn't see hardening begin at their corners.

Her business done, the Amazon rose from her chair. I knew I should follow suit but my arms felt too heavy to raise me. They felt what my mind had not yet grasped: I would never again hold my baby.

I had been told, often—by many more than Carole—that my surrender was inevitable. Yet I throbbed with disbelief. I couldn't understand how any of this could have happened.

Carole crossed the floor to roll back my chair. I ignored the hands she offered to help me stand. Summoning some energy, I pushed onto my own two feet. She transferred her hands to my shoulders, rotated me on my heels, and walked me to the door.

The door had an upper panel with a pebbled surface that made my reflection look as distorted as I felt. Overwriting the pebbly surface were some painted letters I couldn't read from my side.

Apparently, my mother's love wasn't the only thing that wasn't good enough. My brain still wasn't up to par. I was too dumb to find the right words for Carole and I couldn't read stenciling on a door. Agents of the state—including the family I trusted—had driven home their point.

When Carole opened the door to usher me out, I was finally able to turn my back on her. Then she stabbed me with one last round of advice, "After you go out that door, make a new life for yourself. Forget this happened. Don't tell anyone about it." As if in after-thought, she added: "except your future husband."

MORE

* * *

Dr. Kate Waller Barrett and Charles Crittenton co-founded the Florence Crittenton maternity homes with the tenet of "keeping mother and child together." But in 1947, the National Florence Crittenton Mission surrendered this policy, a victory for social workers who used the ideology of professionalism to carve out creative careers for themselves. — Karen Wilson-Buterbaugh. *Adoption Induced Post Traumatic Stress Disorder in Mothers of the Baby Scoop Era* .Yahoo! News. Mar 30, 2010.

*

In 1955, seven social work organizations merged to form the National Association of Social Workers. One of the first areas of concern for the new organization was establishing standards for social work practice.

According to Article 2 of the NASW bylaws, a main purpose of the association is "to provide opportunity for the social work profession to work in unity toward maintaining and promoting high standards of practice." — The National Association of Social Workers (NASW). 13 February 2013. Web.

*

The "Baby Scoop Era" was a period in history starting after the end of World War II and ending in the 1970s. It was characterized by a high rate of newborn adoptions, two million in the 1960s alone. —-The Baby Scoop Research and Initiative: *Research and Inquiry into Adoption Practice 1945-1972. Web. 13 February 2013. Web.*

*

Beginning in the 1940s and 1950s and continuing into the '70s, illegitimacy was defined in terms of psychological deficits on the part of the mother. The dominant psychological and social work view was that most unmarried mothers were better off separated by adoption from their newborn babies. In most cases, adoption was presented to the mothers as the only option and little or no effort was made to help the mothers keep and raise the children. — Wikipedia, sources include historians Rickie Solinger, author of *Wake Up Little Susie* and *Beggars and Choosers* and Ann Fessler, author/producer of *The Girls Who Went Away* and author/producer of *A Girls Like Her.* 5 January, 2013. Web.

CHAPTER TWO

1 9 6 5 – 1 9 7 2

AGE: 20-27

CAPE COD

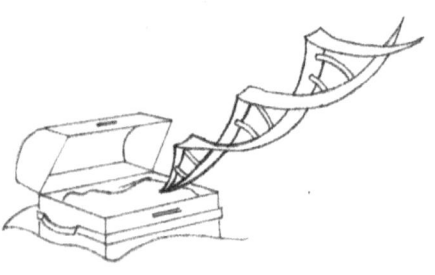

I found my husband, Dave, at a New Hampshire bank. I was their "New Accounts Girl" and he was my boss, seven years my senior. Everyone liked Dave. He had a great sense of humor that tickled my love for word play. And that, along with his rock-solid integrity made him irresistible. As a bonus, he was also handsome as the Dickens with soft blue eyes.

As we dated, I learned his mother, Elsie, had been 44 when she had him; his three brothers and one sister were much older. His sister had never married and she took over a lot of his care. Since he was born early, she decided he needed to continue to incubate. During his early months, she kept him bundled near the steam radiator. When Dave was 15, his father suffered a stroke that kept him bed-bound for 12 years. Knowing Elsie, as became my privilege, she cared for Dave's father lovingly and patiently, and with very little money.

Dave's and my goals were in the same ballpark: we would do better. He wanted prestige; I wanted respect. Together, we could move up the ladder of success. We married within a year.

We continued to live in New Hampshire for a while, Dave working at the bank. But when we vacationed one summer on Cape Cod and ran out of money, he went into a local bank to cash a check. Just before he closed the car door, I joked "Ask them for a job!" He did. They hired him, but not before they interviewed me to make sure I would be acceptable. For the interview, I dressed in a classy gray dress with a dropped waist and pleated skirt. I looked as wholesome as Marlo Thomas on "That Girl."

From the boss' twice-over, I knew he liked what he saw. Our two year old son, Scott, was his usual polite and charming self, so he, too, passed. The bank paid for our move and rented us a house until we bought one in Harwich a few months later. After our second son, Todd, was born in Hyannis, we found in Brewster what we saw as our perfect permanent home. We settled down to raise our family.

About three years later, we received great news from Dave's boss, George. He told Dave that, from among all his employees, he had selected our family to represent the bank in a five week all-expenses-paid trip to Sweden. We wouldn't depart for months, which was good because I was making a long list of things to do. Meanwhile, Dave had his proof of prestige, and I had mine of respect.

As Dave and I chatted happily about our windfall, the phone clattered. Walking on air, I answered with an upbeat "hello." I was surprised to hear my father's voice at the other end. Call it intuition or call it my sense that things had been going too well. Somehow I knew my rosy situation was about to change.

As if to confirm this sixth sense, Dad delivered shocking news: "Your baby sister is pregnant."

Baby sister? That would be Donna. How old was she? Nineteen? Twenty? Pregnant? Had she gotten married? Had I been told but somehow forgotten? It was possible.

26

Unless something in my original family directly affected me—like: when will you come for a visit?—their news earned at best my divided attention. If I were going to give full attention to anything, it would be to my little slice of heaven on Cape Cod—with my loving husband and two small boys. If I wanted to say anything to my father it would be to brag about our astonishing news of Sweden, letting him know in the telling how well regarded I had become.

"Are you still there?" Dad asked.

When I exhaled "Yes" I realized I had been holding my breath. I set my golden news on an upper shelf, out of reach of the tarnish Dad was about to set loose. It had come to me that, no, Donna wasn't married. And now she was pregnant. As I tied these two thoughts together, my stomach grew oily.

I tried to think of ways to tie up—or tidy up—the conversation with Dad. Maybe I could bolt if I said "Congratulations. Thanks for the news. Bye." Or maybe I could put the receiver back in its cradle after an "Oh no! That's awful. Bye." But I didn't take time to weigh the pros and cons of either. I already knew Dad would usher me to an exit of his choice.

Even so, I didn't expect him to be so blatant, to say as he did: "We think she should give the baby up for adoption."

I drew a ragged breath. How could Dad be so . . . so tone deaf? So oblivious? How could he use *that* word with me?

27

"You still there?" he repeated.

I murmured, wondering for a second if I really was there. Maybe I was having a dream? A nightmare.

Dad continued:"Your life has turned out pretty good, Lee. Great husband. Kids. House. Right?"

This conversation had to end.

But he continued to talk, my reaction not registering on him. His words thumped along an unyielding father-daughter floor, like bowling balls on hardwood. Its echo blocked my ears. I wanted to howl a mouthy roar to clear the tubes, but like a sick singer, I couldn't warm up. And, after all, he was my father. While I had back-talked Mom a few times, I had never dared to approach, never mind cross, any boundaries with Dad.

Dad assumed we "had a bad connection."

"I can...hear...you."

"Anyway, we wondered if you would tell Donna that."

I managed to push out "Tell Donna...what?"

"That adoption was good for you. That you don't even remember... it."

Words crisscrossed aimlessly in my mind. Remember... it? Not until you, *Dad*, betrayed our agreement to never talk about *it*. Painfully roaming also was: Why have you—again—put your concern for your other kids above concern for me?

I was tapped out. Dad had said too much. I hadn't said enough. Meanwhile, Dave stood in the doorway, his fine brows creased in question. When I got off the phone, I would have to tap dance my way to a nap and cheerfully invite him to join me.

Now, though, I learned my father wanted me to tell Donna I had a good life, and that I no longer remembered what had happened to me. Before his call, those two things had been true enough: good life, no memories.

A half-thought skittered like spidery legs across my mind. If I didn't remember what had happened, then it didn't exist. So how could something that didn't exist lead to a good life, something that, in fact, did exist? But those flimsy legs slipped into a groove and disappeared.

I told myself I wouldn't talk *with* Donna. I would talk *to* her. We wouldn't have a conversation; I would have a monologue. That much I could control.

When I checked my memory for this book, I asked Donna what she recalled about the phone call I later had with her. It seemed to me I must have been adamant she give up her baby. But as Donna remembers it, I quickly repeated what our parents told her I would say. But whether I was adamant or a mere echo, I did care how her pregnancy turned out. For reasons of my own, I wanted her to surrender.

If Donna surrendered her baby, then I wouldn't have the contrast between her ability to keep hers and my inability to keep mine. Without that contrast between Donna and me, there would be no reminders for either of us. If we both had lives without our babies, we could each reinforce for the other that neither event happened.

* * *

Just before I napped, I must have told my mind to scrub itself clean of my conversation with Dad. Then for double-insurance, after I napped I got out of bed on the side opposite the one I had used that morning, something I occasionally do when I need to re-set a day gone wrong.

A new woman again, I fed my family a typical fall New England supper. A rib-sticking traditional meal of smoked brisket, cabbage, carrots, small round potatoes and onions reinforced my priorities. Now it seemed to me a little twilight game of croquet would be the perfect end to the day I had refreshed. Dave and the boys were more than game.

The recently hung wooden storm door slapped behind me as I headed to the garage to retrieve the wickets, balls and mallets. While our evenings of croquet would soon give way to winter, for now the heat that Cape Cod bay had absorbed all summer was being carried off-shore to our light-dappled acre of land. The feel of the air on my face was more delicious than dessert.

With the front of the house facing west, the waning sun caught the natural shingles just so, turning their wet-look-brown to a warm shade of honey. Dave and I were proud of our little half-Cape, an architectural style in Cape Cod villages that had served as a starter home for early settlers. If the sea yielded a generous bounty, a settler would have tacked on the missing half of the house.

Ours was a typical half-Cape. A low slung roof capped a front door and, on one side of the door, two multi-paned windows. White muslin curtains discreetly hinted at the country décor within. We had also added touches to the outside of our house so authentically "old-Cape" that a member of the Brewster Historical Society wanted to put it on their roster. I apologized when I told her our home was only circa 1947.

Probably the setting contributed to her mistake. The house sat on a busy street off what native Cape Codders call King's Highway. Low irregularly-laid rock walls marked the perimeter of our property. To the right of the front door, an American flag waved a greeting.

The flag didn't reflect my political leanings. I voted in whatever way Dave did. He joked I made decisions about our family while he made decisions about the world. He explained that Republicans believed it was wrong to lean on others, that you should make your own way. That made sense to me since that's what we were doing. I did admit, though, to mixed feelings about Vietnam.

While the peaceniks appalled me, I wasn't a fan of war. I actively dissuaded my boys from war play. Violence or even meanness made me uncomfortable. I never spanked and, since I made the day-to-day decisions about the boys, Dave didn't either.

I could be marginally patriotic, though, which fell under the "right thing to do" category. When my brother re-upped twice during Vietnam, and even though I wasn't that emotionally close to my original family any more, I baked him many care packages.

To me, the flag by our door was mostly for show. Displaying a flag was a thing most fine people did and I put my refinement out front when I could. The flag was also just the right touch for the look we wanted.

As Dave and the boys saw me wheel our croquet set to the front yard, they caught up with me to help me lay out the court between the house and the rock wall that separated us from the street. We could have laid it out blindfolded.

Dave, Scott and I strategically smacked our mallets against our colored balls. When it was Todd's turn, he swung his mallet wherever it was inspired to go. Between his turns, he ran around the wickets, his mallet poised high on a shoulder like a baseball bat, an adjustment I made after he shouldered it soldier-style. I knew we were like a Norman Rockwell scene that flashed to passers-by as if on a drive-in screen. That night, as usual, drivers honked and waved as they glimpsed our regularly scheduled broadcast of a contented family.

* * *

The next weekend, I readied our house for a little celebration with Dave's boss, George, and his wife, Mary.

We were going to thank them for selecting our family for the trip to Sweden. After the plans for the celebration got underway, I returned to my kitchen desk to work on a job for my at-home secretarial service. But that didn't last long. I was soon interrupted by the need to settle a little skirmish. "Ma-ah" Todd cried as he scooted into the kitchen as if on roller skates. "Scott just drooled on me."

I stopped typing and shifted in my chair toward Todd. As a toddler, he was so beautiful he was too often mistaken for my daughter. It didn't even work to dress him all in brown. And, despite cutting his chin-length curly locks, he remained a cutie-pie. His eye colors—plural—were unique. They didn't change from baby-blue until he was more than a year, and, even now the color was indecisive. One eye was light butterscotch; the other, milk chocolate. Tears clung to his lower lashes.

Scott had drooled on him? As the oldest of five, I knew about sibling rivalry, but Scott had been smitten by his little brother from the get-go. Scott had never one-upped Todd before. Surprised, I stood and yanked down the scrunched back hem of my mini-skort. Then, smoothing its front panel, I called for Scott, drawing out the vowel so it sounded "Sco-ott," a pronunciation that announced we needed to have a "conversation." But my voice didn't need to carry. Scott had arrived right behind his brother.

Scott's eyes also misted sadness, with a little worry thrown in. There was nothing indecisive about his eye color, singular. They were 100% dark chocolate, like my

33

own, as my high school friend, Sandi, had reminded me when she took her first look at him.

Genes had parceled things out between my boys. Where Todd had my naturally curly hair, Scott's was Beatle-straight. When Scott scowled in concentration, as he did now, his long bangs fell past his brows, accenting super-sized lashes that were the envy of my friends; and, heck, I wouldn't have minded the extra mileage myself. Dave was somewhere in the boys, but we were still trying to find it. For consolation, I reminded him they had his type of equipment.

"I didn't mean to, Momma," Scott quickly apologized. He looked earnestly at me, tugging on my heart as surely as I had the hem of my skort. "I was wrestling with him and I told him if he didn't say 'uncle,' I'd drool on him, and I let a little goo get in my mouth . . . but I didn't mean for the goo to really fall. I . . . I didn't," he concluded, the last few words directed at Todd.

As I stood to comfort both my treasures, Todd wrapped his arms around one of my legs. Uncertainly, he pivoted to return Scott's look. I ruffled Todd's curly head to assure him that life with his brother would return to normal. "What do you say, Todd? Do you forgive him?"

Todd had to think about that; he hadn't had to forgive Scott for much before and the possibility took a moment to get used to.

After the apology was accepted, I told them: "Come on. Let's go into the family room and practice a little Swedish, shall we?"

Before we left the kitchen, I glanced at the transcription I had been working on. I had a deadline on that job, and I still had to finish fixing dinner. After I quickly tallied the time I needed for each, I knew I wouldn't have a problem. And if time did turn a little crunchy, I knew I could ask my friend, Marie, to do some typing for me. As my typing business grew, I had begun to pass jobs her way. She understood. Like me, and like all of our friends, our kids came first.

My business had begun with a rental real estate lady who had posted a "Help Wanted" ad in the "Women's Jobs" section of our local paper. For her correspondence, I used a business course in speedwriting to take dictation from her over the phone. Then I delivered her letters to her home, a stack at a time. She signed each letter with "Mrs." and her husband's first and last name, as if she didn't have a first name of her own. Such closings flowed smoothly from my fingertips, since all stories and photos of women in newspapers were referenced and captioned that way. After I got my business going with her, I added more clients. Although I took one-time jobs, I preferred books-in-progress so I could count on that income a little longer. Those authors spoke into a tape recorder, dropped off their tapes to me, and I transcribed them using a Dictaphone that one writer had given me.

Before the boys' drooling episode, I had been working on a book about a local guy who pursued a panda over and through the mountains of China by following its scat. After I looked up "scat" in the dictionary, I found his whole "adventure" rather unappealing. But, while the typing didn't fascinate, Dave and I needed the extra cash to rehab our home.

The boys and I headed for the TV room. We picked our way through their obstacle course, sidestepping the matchbox cars lined along the floral design of the hooked rug in the dining room. After that successful negotiation, we made ourselves comfortable at their Formica play table where we began our new game. I pointed above their heads to the ceiling molding on which I had tacked colored construction paper. There, Swedish numbers one through ten displayed in large print: *EN: 1. TVA: 2. TRE: 3* . . . . These were oversized flash cards the boys and I had made together so we could learn some Swedish. To show George our whole family was invested in making the bank proud, the boys planned to perform a few numbers after dinner.

We had help on how to pronounce the numbers. Dave's mother, Elsie, was a second generation Swedish immigrant. Over the phone she had tutored me. Having learned some French from my grandmother, my *MaMere*, the numbers of a foreign language had come fairly easy to me. That is, except for the number seven, which could only leave the throat when gargled. As the boys and I giggled about that, we returned to the kitchen.

From a shelf above my secretarial desk, I pulled my favorite book, "The Joy of Cooking." I had already turned back corners of the pages I wanted for our special meal. This celebration would be a cake walk. Some prep had been done beforehand, with Scott and Todd serving as my "helper-men." To continue their involvement in our joint project, I now gave them a few more tasks. That done, I affectionately patted their little butts and sent them back to the "zoom" and "boink" of their car crashes.

With such an important meal coming up, I could have been a nervous wreck. But I was sure of myself as a hostess. I knew I was a good cook and I had already set the dining table in a whimsical theme of Swedish blue and yellow. Elsie had helped me plan the meal.

For an appetizer, she had suggested smoked salmon with sour cream on toast points. She had also suggested I serve a Swedish sweet bread with cardamom called *vitteber*, which she had years before taught me how to bake. For the main course, she thought we could get away with cheap but authentic Swedish meatballs.

For that, I had already soaked stale bread in nutmeg-seasoned milk, hand-squeezed the bread "dry," and folded the pulp into a couple of pounds of hamburger. The boys and I had then rolled the meat mixture into balls that were "not too big," as Scott had tutored Todd, "and not too small." After I sautéed the meatballs in butter, I removed them to my new Corning Ware casserole dish so I could scrape the scraps in the bottom of the frying pan into a white sauce to add to the meatball casserole.

As my helper-men and I worked together, we sang songs from *Sesame Street* and *Mr. Rogers' Neighborhood*. As usual, I had as much fun getting ready to entertain as I did during it.

MORE

Nana Elsie's Swedish Meatballs

Sauté in large skillet one small diced onion until golden brown; set aside. Toast 2.5 slices of *stale* bread. Soak bread in cinnamon-seasoned milk; set aside. Put one pound loosened hamburger in large bowl. Drop one cracked egg atop meat. Squeeze moisture from soaked bread; plop with onion atop meat/egg. Mush layers till evenly mixed.

Reheat skillet, adding butter. Roll meatball-size globs between floured hands till rounded and add to skillet. As meatballs brown, remove from skillet and set aside. Leave any meatball scraps in skillet.

Add 2 T of flour to 1.5 cups of cinnamon-seasoned, watered-down milk in a cup. Over low heat, stir and press flour against sides of cup to remove lumps. Add more watery milk, continuing to stir so lumps don't form. Slowly stir flour mixture into skillet, scraping up remaining bits of meatball. Add more water and/or cinnamon, as desired.

Return meatballs to gravy in skillet. Allow meatballs to cook throughout. Due to milk content, don't allow to fully bubble. Serve with egg noodles or mashed potatoes. Elsie preferred the potatoes.

Today's Shortcut for Toasty Cheesums

Dump one bag of shredded parmesan cheese (only parmesan and not canister) into a medium size bowl. Liberally sprinkle dehydrated instant minced onion on cheese. Grind pepper atop onion. Stir in heaping tablespoons of mayonnaise (Hellmann's only) bit by bit until "gloppy" but "firm." Mound on rounds of Pepperidge Farm pumpernickel party bread (only). Broil till golden and puffy. Transfer to warmed, not hot, plate and serve immediately.

Marie's Pineapple Bread

Assemble on countertop: 6 sticks butter; 3 boxes confectionery sugar; 12 eggs; 2 tsp vanilla; 2 tsp lemon juice; 2 "confectionery sugar boxes" of flour (which is tricky now that manufacturers tend to use plastic bags, so when you find boxes, hold onto them); 2 lg cans crushed pineapple, drained.

Cream butter. Add sugar. Add eggs one at a time. Beat between additions. Add vanilla and lemon juice. Stir in flour and mix (great cardio workout). Add pineapple. Use 4 GREASED loaf pans. Bake at 325 degrees for 1.5 hours or until done.

CHAPTER THREE

1 9 72 - 19 7 4

AGE: 27-29

SWEDEN

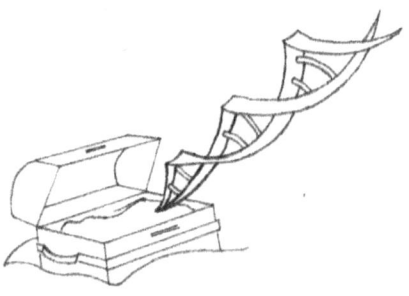

T hree weeks before our trip to Sweden, Scott got the chicken pox; then Todd; and, finally, Dave. Dave's spots cleared only a couple of days before we took off.

My nursing a success, we were able to present a picture-perfect family of good health to our Swedish hosts. After greeting us at the airport – the four of them waving tiny American flags – they ushered us into a waiting limousine. As we wound through immaculate Stockholm streets to the outlying suburb of Lidingo, I discovered they spoke English very well. Once in a while they hunted for words, which we supplied in a kind of bonding ritual. When we arrived at Hotel Foresta, we were shown the suite of rooms they had reserved for us.

A large bouquet of flowers stood on a round table in the middle of the living room. As if the foliage doubled as a Christmas tree, small wrapped gifts were stacked nearby for Scott and Todd. Even the refrigerator was stocked with special cheeses, *vitteber*, orange juice and milk. Later, David and I tried to outdo each other in translating the Swedish labels.

The hotel maid tidied up every day and took our laundry to the hotel cleaners. Some days David hopped into the car our hosts provided and drove to the bank. On those days, I took the boys for long walks, stopping at a small store nearby to choose new foods to try. Most days, though, our hosts chauffeured us around Stockholm.

On our first trip into the city, we stopped by the bank where Dave proudly introduced us to his new colleagues. Then we visited the rest of Stockholm. Often called "Venice of the North," Stockholm is made of fourteen islands connected by a series of bridges. Stockholm's center island, *Gamla Stan*, meaning "old town," was stunning. As we were escorted down its cobblestoned streets, I was awed by *Gamla Stan*'s contrast with the glass and steel of Stockholm's other islands. As wide-eyed as a child, I entered its central square. And then I braked.

Like a dog brought to heel by a high-pitched command others can't hear, I was suddenly on alert. I felt strangely unsettled. I told myself it was because everything was different in *Gamla Stan*. In my experience, its closest cousin was the arch and slope of the cobblestoned streets in Boston's Federal Hill. But, where the homes in Federal Hill were cleanly rectangular, each of them faced in dignified brick with dark-green or black shutters, the rooflines of the homes in *Gamla Stan* were instead scalloped, each building painted a different pastel shade.

The buildings that lined *Gamla Stan's* central square were as mesmerizing as classic works of art in a foreign gallery. At the hub of the square a huge fountain reigned. Around the fountain, florists offered flowers of every color and description from buckets at their feet. Of course, I had seen vendors hawk their wares around fountains before— in Boston, England, Scotland, and France—but for reasons I couldn't explain, I found this particular scene arresting. My sixth sense tingled.

Did that gauzy curtain move at that fourth story window? What was behind it? A spirit from Stockholm's past? Picking up my pace to keep up with our hosts, I rounded a corner. I was surprised no one collided into me from the opposite direction. Sensing a stranger in my space wasn't an altogether odd sensation. I had felt this way many times before, when someone stared at me from *behind*. But this time I felt as if someone was *ahead* of me, just on the other side of that corner, walking purposefully toward me as if to gently chide me for not predicting its vibes more quickly. I couldn't account for the prickling on my arms. The feeling of being tracked from ahead, as if I followed breadcrumbs, persisted. Every time I rounded a street corner, my pulse quickened again. I didn't label the feeling as fear. If anything, I was intrigued. I joked to myself I must have had a past life in *Gamla Stan*.

The Lutheran churches did nothing to break the spell. Funded by the state, each church looked similar to the next. In the nave, stained glass windows towered on my left and right. Chandeliers that gleamed like gold hung above me, suspended from long thick chains. So far, things seemed normal enough. But as I walked down the wide aisles, the thick, old-red bricked walls seemed to softly vibrate, as if hordes of bats were fluttering in the cantilevered ceilings. I was reminded of Alfred Hitchcock's movie, *The Birds*. I began to feel disconcerted.

Between tours of churches, I felt normal. But every new church put me out of alignment again. By the time we reached the last church on our agenda, the walls seemed to close around me as if its grandeur was reduced to the intimacy of a chapel. I felt compelled to make some kind of vigil. I fought it, knowing that suddenly falling to my knees would look bizarre to our hosts. I couldn't think of anything important to pray for anyway.

On another day trip, we visited castles. There, I felt divided in a different way. Sweden's castles were unlike any I had seen when I visited England and Scotland. There, the castles were sterile-cold and rock-hard forbidding. But, in Sweden, they were friendly places. The low ceilings were painted in colorful scenes, and in at least one corner of each room, a columnar fireplace of glazed blue and white tiles stood ready to warm.

I was so at home in these castles that I felt as if I was being inspired by something inside me, like I was in the middle of a lucid daydream. Although I normally don't realize I'm daydreaming until I snap out of it, I was aware of this one. It was easy to imagine heat blazing from the core of the fireplaces. It was hard to resist the impulse to lean over the heavy-planked tables and adjust their centerpieces. At the same time, I wanted to be *part* of the lush settings beyond the windows, not to visit the outdoors but to spring from them, like a tree or, better still, a doe. Equally attached to the interior and the exterior of the castles, I felt as if I were divided on a split screen. In one corner I was a serving wench tending to the castle; in another, a doe deciding whether to munch on garden or moss.

Feeling compartmentalized wherever I went was perplexing. I had been divided by present time and the past, by contentment with my life and the need for a vigil, and by the vision of me as both a servant and a deer. I continued to wonder why. Since the sensations felt new, I wondered if I was being drawn to do something novel with my life. Maybe there was some new opportunity I should check out? Maybe the wench and doe symbolized I should do some new decorating or gardening when I got back home. Maybe I should juxtapose a row of old-fashioned hollyhocks with a row of hybrid roses? Maybe I should be on my knees, weeding? Yet, none of the roles I tossed around in my mind seemed like the right key to fit the lock the feeling had on me.

I began to wonder in a new way. Was it instead possible that something *inside* me wanted to be drawn out? As a kid, I had written poetry and I vaguely recalled a similar feeling before I purged a poem. Maybe I should try writing again? Maybe I had a poem or story inside me about Sweden? When I played out the role of writer in my mind, a tumbler on the lock turned.

A few days later, while Dave was at work and after the boys and I had had our usual long walk and nap, I settled them in the living room. I knew they would play quietly as they usually did, especially with the new Swedish toys we bought for them. I reacquainted them with the *Matryoshka* dolls, rounded wood figurines gaily painted in red, orange, and yellow. I reminded the boys how they could untwist one doll to reveal another nested inside. I realized I paused during my demonstration every time a new doll was revealed. There was something poignant about these nested dolls. I wondered if that was because I was being inspired to include *Matryoshka* in the poem I planned. I couldn't imagine how that unpronounceable multiple-syllable word could work in a poem, but I knew including it on a potential word list couldn't hurt. As the boys reached instead for their decorated wooden Gotland horses, I gratefully smiled at how predictable they were. For good measure, I also made sure their Tonka trucks were on hand.

On the way to the back bedroom Dave and I shared, I grabbed the shorthand notebook and pen I had packed for our trip. Sitting on the edge of the bed, I turned the cardboard cover of the notebook over its top wire loops and looked at a fresh page. Staring back at me was a narrow pale green sheet with darker green lines running horizontally and one single darker line running vertically down its middle. I waited for inspiration. None came. I was surprised. I was sure a poem was scratching to be let out.

I jumped to the next step. I made a word list. For the header of the left column, I wrote *Swede*; for the right column, I wrote *Sweden*. There was something about the way the columns were structured that made me uncomfortable. I shrugged it off and got busy. Under Swede I wrote: bleed, creed, deed, feed, mead, need, peed, reed, seed, weed. *Sweden* was trickier: freedom? two-ton? What about using the "den", then? Fen, men, friend, lend, mend, tend, wend?

After looking them over, I asterisked some that resonated: bleed, creed, mead, seed, weed, mend, tend. Only one word had real potential—mead—a warm Swedish beer made from honey that I had found revolting. To tease more inspiration, I began to doodle. I got lost in the scribbles. After a few strokes, I broke from my reverie. On the page I realized I had scribbled a word: *It*.

While only two letters, *It* covered subtext that bled like old print wallpaper under a fresh coat of white paint. *It* was code for . . . .

How had *It* gotten there? The subtext needed more paint. Energetically, I scribbled over and over *It*. When *It* had been thoroughly hidden, I saw it as the doodle it must have always been.

I tried again. I flipped the doodled page over the wire binding and looked at a fresh page. But that empty space now seemed like a calling card. I flashed on a scene in a book I once read. From that scene, I knew it was common for guests in Victorian times to leave their calling cards in elegant bowls on tables in hallways. The guests' cards reminded their hosts they were etiquette-bound to return the guests' visit. When I looked at the blank space on the shorthand page, I felt a host's similar commitment. Within a second, that commitment grew to compulsion. I needed to visit with that page, to have a conversation with it, now.

Then two things happened at the same time. Even as part of me insisted I ignore the compulsion, another part of me began to write. The part that needed to write had won. All my energies converged upon my pen like cannons on a captain during a mutiny.

I don't know how much time passed. It seemed like minutes; it seemed like hours. But page after page in the notebook became filled with random scenes of history. Not Sweden's. My own. Bug-eyed, heart pounding, I transcribed the notes. I saw they bore a name: "Michael." And a birth month: December. The date, I couldn't decipher: 20-something? the 20th? the 21st?

Here was evidence I had lost my mind. *How could I have allowed this to happen?* I closed the notebook and stared at the cover. In yellow and green, it announced that the notebook contained the 500 most frequently misspelled words in a business office. Words beginning with the letter "A" were printed along the edge of the outer cover; the rest continued on the inside cover. I began to read the words to myself: "Absence, Accommodate, Accrual...."

As my breathing slowed, I knew I had to learn exactly how I had failed. Looking inside myself, I discovered ... layers. There were layers to me. This sort of surprise discovery about myself had occurred before. For example, when I first realized emotional pain could also be physical; a loss could register in my arms and legs, and my gut.

A few years later, I had also realized there were layers of intellectual curiosity in me, and mine was shallower than others.' When I had visited London as the 21-year-old guest of a Brit who took me to meet her friends, they asked me why the "cowboys shot the Indians on American television." Although I had never before given those military charges a second thought, their question penetrated some intellectual cavity in me that had somehow been closed off.

But what did this more recent sense of layers mean? And how could I have so much stuff inside me and not know it?

Now that I remembered my earlier discoveries of layers, I wondered something else. Not how it was I had found them before, but how I had successfully ignored them afterward. I needed a refresher course.

I realized I didn't want to learn more about layers. I didn't want to go mining for trouble. I wanted to continue to live as I had been—on the surface where I could see and control what I did.

I shifted to the business of prevention. I tried to recall what triggered the episode. I realized the episode began when I looked at an empty page. It continued when I paid too much attention to that space. To prevent future episodes, then, I could not allow my attention to have a vacancy. I needed to redouble my effort to be busy.

First, though, I needed to shut down the evidence—the site of the episode. I returned to the pages I had written on. Without re-reading a word, I quickly tore those pages from the notebook's wire binding, ripping out some loops as if to reinforce my intent. I shredded the pages in one direction, then another. As the shreds fell to the bottom of the wastebasket, the shards took form: a social worker's last letter to me…a baby's hospital picture. Some memories still trailed, like rogue cancer cells after surgery.

Spooked, I bolted for the living room where Scott and Todd innocently zoomed around their trucks. I gathered them to me, inhaled their little-boy smells, read them a story, asked questions, answered theirs, and tried to return to their safe, trusting world.

When Dave came home, I rushed to him, wrapping my arms around his waist. "Whoa," he teased, "and I haven't even told you my good news yet!"

More good news? I felt as guilty and undeserving as if I had been unfaithful to him. Still, I threw a bright smile his way. "Tell me about it!"

The bank had made all the arrangements. We would join the upper management of *Sparbanken* on their annual voyage to Helsinki, Finland. We would party with their Finnish counterparts. We were booked into Cabin Number One on the cruise ship.

The cabin was beautifully appointed; the smorgasbord on deck, lavish; our new Swedish friends, riotous; the toasting, to the limit of endurance; the slot machines, inviting; the nursery, equipped beyond imagination for Scott and Todd; the Helsinki people, delightfully crazy – one dancing on a table, another pounding a shoe in imitation of Krushchev. And I laughed, danced, ate, and made love with my devoted husband. Through it all I carried an imposter's fear of discovery.

But there was hope. Once we got back to our Cape Cod home and friends, to my average and normal life, I could return to my old self.

MORE

* **

"…what it really means is that the parent cares for her child so much she will give up her desire to have her own offspring with her, if others have convinced her it will benefit the child.

These are the real moralists of our day. They are people who sacrifice in a way most of us don't know how to sacrifice. There is a tremendous humanity there which can be used to serve the child and to serve us too." —John L. Brown. *Rootedness.* Family Involvement. Ma/Jn 1974. Print.

*

Through our culture we acquire a set of **feeling rules** for a given role or specific situation. These rules include how, where, when, and with whom an emotion should be expressed. Such rules can estrange you from your true self. —Arlie Hochschild. In: Diana Kendall. *Sociology in Our Times.* Cengage Learning. 2011. Print.

*

In psychology, "repressed memory" is an event that occurred in a subject's past, the memory of which was actively repressed, often because of the psychologically devastating impact of that memory. —The *McGraw-Hill Concise Dictionary of Modern Medicine*. The McGraw-Hill Companies, Inc. 2002. 20 February 2013.Web.

*

In 2000, the American Psychiatric Association's Diagnostic and Statistical Manual of Mental Disorders (DSM-IV-TR) defined Post-Traumatic Stress Disorder (PTSD) as a disorder linked to a traumatic event. Symptoms included hyper-vigilance, flashbacks, emotional numbness, (and) avoidance of stimuli associated with the trauma.

Even though a current criterion of PTSD says the trauma must threaten one's physical integrity, Weathers and Keane in 2007 called for more studies on stressors that "elicit PTSD symptoms ….Many mothers who experienced the loss of a child to adoption have described these symptoms. — Karen Wilson-Buterbaugh. *Adoption Induced Post Traumatic Stress Disorder in Mothers of the Baby Scoop Era.* Web. Yahoo! Contributor Network. March 30, 2010.

CHAPTER FOUR

1 9 7 3

AGE: 28

CAPE COD

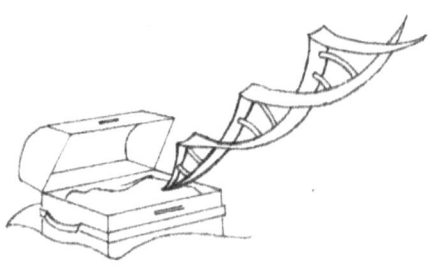

A letter from my father waited for me at home. "Any more news about Sweden?" he wrote. "We loved your last letter with the vivid description of all you saw there. Send more details soon.

> . . . Mom and I are both well, as
> are Donna and Heather. Heather is
> getting cuter by the day and although
> she talks a mile a minute, it's in her
> own language. I'm convinced she
> knows what she is saying and thinks
> we are stupid not to understand her.

> She is reaching the age I enjoy. I
> take her paddling with me in the lake
> behind the house. I also hold her in
> my lap so we can swing together
> in the backyard....

My single sister? The child she was able to keep? My father enjoyed spending time with her swinging on a tree? Before I could blink, I thought: How is it that when my child's cradle had rocked his bough, my father had turned his back?

I dashed out of the kitchen. Dave was swearing under his breath, screwdriver in hand. The screen door had blown off its hinges while we were away. He wasn't very handy so I wished him good luck. To avoid talking, I quickly turned toward the vegetable garden I had started before we left for Sweden. I was relieved to see it was overgrown with weeds. I knew I was looking at a lot of work. I also knew I could call the owner of the vegetable stand around the corner who rototilled gardens as a sideline. But rousting spiky intruders with my own hands appealed to me.

After I yanked out weeds, I grabbed trash bags, got the boys in the car, and we went to the bay. The tide was way out, headed to West Dennis. A ton of black seaweed baked in stinky clumps on the beige strip of beach, free for the picking. The boys and I scooped seaweed by the bags-full and toted them home. I was slimy and pungent by the time I finished mounding the seaweed between the rows of bush beans, kohlrabi and peppers and around the dirt walls that corralled tomatoes and cucumbers. After I assured myself all weed seeds had been snuffed, I restrung the sunflowers to the bunny-fence that surrounded the garden. As I headed to the shower I smiled with satisfaction; the deed was done. Everything was back in order.

* * *

The small talk was so boring, part of me fell asleep. Usually, the bank's annual summer outing at the Christopher Ryder House in Chatham was a treat. I always loved talking with the other bankers' wives, sharing news about our kids, our newest recipes, and such. With Sweden a recent news flash, I should have been tickled to tell them funny stories about the bankers we met. I wondered where my sense of humor had gone.

But the wait staff's usual eruption in show tunes roused my mood. Their rendition of "The Age of Aquarius" rocked the timbers. By the end of the evening I was able to strum an enthusiastic invitation to George and Mary for dinner the following Friday night. We wanted to thank them again for the trip. Dave and I had agreed beforehand on the day. For them, we would give up the Friday night candlelight dinner I always prepared for the two of us. The Saturday night alternative was out. We wanted to preserve our time in front of the TV for our Saturday sitcoms. Time away from the *Mary Tyler Moore Show*, the *Bob Newhart show, M.A.S.H.* and *All in the Family* was not an option.

The next Friday, as we sat in our living room—surrounded by souvenirs of crystal, of decorated wooden Gotland horses, and of prints of *Gamla Stan*—we watched slides of Sweden snap onto a projection screen. Every scene was free of shadows. I was now able to reflect with unreserved delight on our trip. The stories about Sweden I had mentally rehearsed drew their intended chuckles. Afterward, I presented a typical Friday meal in Sweden. Heaping bowls of hot, thick pea soup were followed by pancakes *med* lingonberry sauce. For dessert, we offered ponies of Mesimaria, a sweet sherry-like liquor we had bought on the cruise ship to Finland. All was light and friendly.

Light didn't last. The next night as Dave and I watched *All in the Family*, I did not laugh with him as usual when Archie ordered Edith to "stifle herself." Instead, my spotlight slid from Archie to Edith. I looked for comparisons and contrasts between her and me. To me, her eyes looked like vacant lots, and that made me feel uncomfortable. But I didn't identify with the terrible slouch of her shoulders under her aproned housedress. My mother had made me walk too many miles from room-to-room and even up and down stairways with a book on my head for me to cave on posture. No housedress hung in my closet either. Dressing well was high on Dave's list of wifely to-dos. But I wasn't off the hook quite yet. There was a stab of recognition as I watched Edith scurry around––making things right over here, doing busy work over there. Edith was like an ant in search of a sugar cube. It hit me that I might have the same goal she did: others' approval.

During the singsong of "Don't get mad, get Glad," a commercial for plastic sandwich bags, Dave observed, "You seem quiet."

He did have pretty good radar where my moods were concerned, so I admitted I was a little thoughtful. "Don't you think Archie is mean to talk to Edith like that?" I asked. "You never talk like that to me."

His thoughtful blue eyes pinned me. "No, why would I? Archie is only a fictional character. It's supposed to be a spoof. You know that. You've always laughed at him before."

I persisted, "But, Dave, are people laughing at Archie or at Edith because she's such a dimwit?"

"What does it matter? You know…" he paused as if looking for the right words "…I've noticed you have been pretty serious lately. Is everything okay?"

Dave liked me sunny, not surly. I liked me sunny, not surly, too. "Well," I said in a huff, abruptly standing. "I don't have to be 'up' all the time, you know. I can have some normal moods once in a while."

As soon as I left the room, I regretted my outburst. But Dave would want me to explain, and I really had no idea what had set me off. I thought a night of the silent treatment might help. During my time-off I would either find an answer to pass along to him or he would back off. I was betting on him backing-off; he hated conflict even more than I did.

* * *

Like many residents of vacation spots whose old friends and distant relatives descend on them, I complained. But deep down, I liked showing how smart we were to live in a place others wanted to be. If I had taken anything away from my large family, it was the pleasure of entertaining. That summer, such pleasure took a needy note. Company-coming became synonymous with welcome-distraction. I went a step further than usual. I issued invitations to a slew of people and insisted they take advantage.

We had a Cape-flavored itinerary for each round of visitors. Clamming headed this list. At twilight during low tide, we would go to the bay with buckets and clawed garden tools. Looking for air holes in the muddy flats, we would bend over to scoop gunky dollops of sand-embedded, soft-shelled clams. We'd separate clams from mud, toss out any that were partially opened, rinse the others at water's edge, and bring them back home. There, the clams would be scrubbed, then plunged in boiling water. In our huge, well-pitted aluminum kettle, the clam shells would open. For our hors d'oeuvres, we'd crack open the shells. With two fingers we'd pinch out the meat, swish each in hot water to remove any leftover sand, dunk them in warm butter, and to complete the process, swallow the delectables whole. Meanwhile, the barbecue sizzled with steaks and the steamer worked on veggies picked from the garden.

* * *

Thanks to a full dance card, the summer of 1973 scooted by. The sole speed bump had been when my high school buddy, Sandi, called me. She was the only friend with whom I had kept in touch. In a breathy Marilyn Monroe voice tinged with a Boston accent, she mentioned in passing that she had gone to the tenth high school reunion for our class. My sudden silence must have spoken for me. I could tell she didn't know if she should apologize for the slip. Having been kicked out of high school because I was pregnant, I had not received an invitation.

"Who was there?" I covered, aiming for a light tone. Trying to read between my lines, she volunteered, "Tom's band was hired for the gig." The photo of him that had been in the high school year book flashed like heat lightning behind my eyes. The slogan under his photo read: "Boys will be boys." I excused myself from Sandi's call and withdrew to my garden. There, I yanked more weeds.

* * *

Soon Scott was in second grade, leaving Todd and me to enjoy special time together. Together we'd ready that day's craft, like blowing out eggs to later paint the shells or rooting through crayons to find old ones to later melt as candles. After the school bus returned Scott home, I greeted him in our ritual hug-sway. Then the three of us either completed the crafts Todd and I had prepared or we read and colored together. When David arrived home, we'd rush to him like he was Robert Young on the old "Father Knows Best" television show. Then the boys would go into the TV room to play, while Dave and I caught up on each other's day over hors d'oeuvres I made special for the two of us. This time I tried another of Marie's recipes: Toasty Cheesums.

As I often did, I had enlisted my helper-men. After I scraped a block of parmesan cheese against the sides of a grater into a bowl, I had handed the manila shavings to Todd. I supervised while he added instant minced onion and pepper. Then Scott took over, mixing in the mayonnaise until it was, as he called it, "gloppy." After a quick demonstration of mounding the glop on slices of party bread, the boys followed my lead. Then we placed the cookie sheet of mounded squares into the oven. I would broil these until they puffed nice and brown.

Toasty Cheesums would become comfort food to Scott and Todd, something they have asked all their lives for me to make for them. As much as they like the taste of the Toasties, I think they like more that this is one hors d'oeuvre I serve like a maid, unlike other dips and spreads they get on their own. I like it for the same reason.

* * *

The fall gave way to wintry beginnings and plans for Christmas. When it was time to buy our tree, Dave cleared the snow off the car, emptied the backmost section of the Pinto wagon and hunted for twine. Meanwhile I bundled five year old Todd. I knelt at Todd's eye level to put newspaper on his heels and ease on his boots; then, I slipped the laces through the grommets and tied them up. As I made a knot and bow, I winked at Todd and he tried to wink back, closing both eyes. I allowed myself to kiss his perky little nose. After the zippering, I wrapped the scarf I had knit for him around his neck. With the scarf, I could have drawn him to me and noisily smooched all over his apple round cheeks. But because it was easy to be distracted by Todd's deliciousness, I reminded myself to stick to business.

Scott had waited patiently for his turn. Now seven, he had put on his own boots but lacing was still a little tricky. He could have zipped up his own jacket but he instead only slipped one set of teeth into the parallel stop and waited for me to finish the job. He still liked me to make the zzzzzip noise as I tugged the pulley along the chain to its top. I was happy to provide the sound effects and when I got to the top, he winked to show he knew more than his brother. Winding the hand knit scarf around Scott's neck was no less an exercise in hug-resistance than it had been with Todd. For the final touch, I capped both their heads with twin hand knit toques, turned up the brims and, for Todd, fastened the ear muffs under his chin. Mittens came last.

Then it was my turn. Most every spring I cut my hair really short and most every fall I grew it really long. At this

60

point, the dark wavy mop kept getting caught in the collar of a yellow parka I had bought the year before when we went on a family ski trip. As we three walked to the car to join Dave, I satisfied my kiddie-hug-deprivation by gathering the boys to me—one still a little baby-fat sturdy, the other a set of jacketed bones, the way I had been until my pregnancy with Todd finally rounded me out a little.

Our snow tires crunched the newly plowed white stuff that had come early that year. We traveled along Brewster's Route 6A toward Orleans. But we didn't have to go that far. Colby's, where in the summer you could place a window order for the Cape's best hot dog, now hawked a stand of Balsams firs. When Todd climbed out of the car, he sucked on the strong pine aroma as if through a straw. Scott, taking a cue from his younger brother, as he often did, also inhaled noisily. Not to be outdone, Dave and I sighed "Ahh" in unison. We all laughed little cold puffs of breath, then laughed some more at our chorus.

Pulling out first one tree, then another, Dave asked Scott and Todd, "How do you like this one, guys?" They gawked gravely, considering.

"Turn it around," I suggested to Dave, fluffing up some branches as he pivoted the leading candidate. "We're kind of spare on this side" I pointed out to the boys. "This would have to go against the wall. Otherwise, it looks pretty good to me. What do you think?"

Jumping from one foot to the other to keep warm, the boys nodded enthusiastically. On our way back to the car, I playfully yanked Scott's cap over one eye and he peered up at me through the other. Not to ignore Todd, I did the same and he rewarded me with a gap-toothed smile. We stuffed the base of the tree into the back of the wagon and tied the tree top to the wagon's back door. We reversed the process after we pulled up to our house at the end of our long driveway.

We each took part of the tree to collectively march it into the house. Along the way we passed the large boulder between the garage and the house that served in the summer as backdrop for a rock garden. I noticed that the bird bath cemented on the boulder's summit was now stacked with four inches of snow, an unusual amount for the Cape. I suggested to Scott and Todd they come back later to swipe it off. The birds wouldn't take baths any time soon but I knew the boys would have fun scooting up the shoulders of their "mountain" and putting their mittens to work.

Scott noticed the landscape too. Pointing to the scrub pines dotting the backyard, Scott realized our new tree wasn't Cape material. "Where did our Christmas tree come from, Dad?" Scott asked.

"Maine, maybe. Or maybe it came from New Hampshire, where you were born."

Scott smiled, proud to have been born the same place as the tree.

I let go of my part of the tree to unlock the back door. Standing on a back step, I held the door open so they could march on. They clomped through the kitchen, past the dining room, and into the family room. As I closed the door behind them, I groaned to see the kitchen floor and its braided rug were now littered with pine needles. It reminded me again how hard Dave and I had worked on that floor. We had poured a solution that included boiling water on the previous linoleum to loosen it; then, we scraped it up, inch by horrible inch. Planks of yellow pine had been unearthed, which we sanded and urethaned until it gleamed.

Among my friends, I was known for my "spotless but cozy" kitchen. If my friends had seen it that day, they would have had to edit "spotless." "Cozy," though, would have still worked.

In pursuit of our homey look, Dave and I had sanded the varnish on the wood cabinets and painted them a mustard color, which the paint chip certified was a true Colonial shade. The two wide windows, which overlooked the winter wonderland of our side yard, created a backdrop for our round dark-pine table with captain's chairs. Small antique cookie cutters paraded along the window sills, a showcase I repeated with old cobblers' tools on the window sill above the white porcelain sink. With every gust from our forced air furnace, valances of homemade red-print calico danced like frilly mini-skirts on the three upper windows.

Our kitchen was a space I so loved that for the previous three years, I hadn't bought one loaf of bread. I wanted to pound the dough myself so I could inhale its yummy, yeasty smell as it rose round and domed in the oven. But at that moment, the rich aroma in the house was now a blend of *boeuf bourguignon* as it re-heated in the crock pot and the piney Christmas tree wafting from the TV room.

In the middle of the TV room, the tree stand, pulled from attic storage earlier in the day, stood waiting. Dave inserted the tree trunk in the stand and twisted its long thick screws to hold the tree upright. We walked around it to confirm the side that would back into the corner. I put strings of colored lights on the tree, looping them generously on the front and sides. Wanting to help, the boys took a gold garland from a box. Scott took one end and Todd, the other. They went in opposite directions to wind it around the tree. I pointed out it would look nicer if it scalloped around the branches; a little higher here, a little lower there. They didn't much care and their attention span was just about shot. It was time for dinner. Then, they shared a bath with water toys, including a yellow rubber ducky for Todd. Afterward, I wrapped them in towels I had pre-heated in the dryer, throwing a section over their head so I could play "Where did Scotty (or Toddy) go?"

Bedtime stories followed: *Little Toot* for Scott; *The Little Engine That Could* for Todd. To send them into good dreams, I leaned over each boy to plant a kiss on their eye lids, a familiar rite of nightly passage. As their lids fluttered like the wings of baby birds, I smiled knowing the send-off was already working its mommy-magic.

With the boys properly bedded, I re-joined Dave downstairs. We took our spiked eggnog into the TV room.

We wanted to finish decorating the tree. The pine aroma was more intoxicating than the eggnog. I appreciated the finery we placed on the branches, each bauble reminding me of past Christmases and how we had added to our collection. Filled to the brim with love for my family, I couldn't imagine how life could get any better.

It was right about then my life grotesquely tilted again; this time, in front of a witness. I turned to Dave, pointed to the box of glass ornaments near him, and said: "Michael is celebrating a birthday somewhere. Please pass me the silver ball over there."

I have since learned that sound can last four seconds. In the first second, I noticed Dave was immobilized. In the next, I thought I hadn't been clear about the color ornament I wanted. But the expected quizzical look about color wasn't a match for the shock on Dave's face. By the third second, my words rained on me, shattering my contentment as if it had been a fragile family heirloom.

It was awful enough I had ghost-written words in Sweden. Now my tongue was beyond my control. On my own, I would never have hung words like that in the air where they could swing like some kind of noose. I moaned to myself. *"What is going on?"*

Dave knew what I meant. When he had first said he loved me, I answered him by telling him about "the child," as my social worker had instructed me to do four years before. I had replied in one long exhale: "IhadachildwhenIwas17andsurrenderedhimforadoption." I had then firmly declared: "I don't ever want to talk about it again." I had meant it through and through.

For proof, when we moved into our first apartment, I unpacked a baby picture. It was of Michael. Power emanated from the picture that I knew had no place in my new life. I asked Dave what I should do with it and he told me I should do whatever I wanted to do. Looking intently at Dave, I tore it up. During the years since then, neither of us said another word about any of it. Didn't have to. Didn't want to. There was nothing to say. The experience didn't exist. Consciously.

But now? Like a skywriter noticing her plane had scripted the wrong ad, I tried to overwrite my words with new ones. I hadn't yet breathed, so I exhaled, hoping masking words would flow in its current. I heard myself politely tell David, "The silver one. The one your mother gave us . . . when Todd was born."

Though the cover-up was a fumble, I had somehow pushed the right button. Michael's birthday became Todd's, who had also been a December baby. These new words had what sociolinguists call a leak-back effect; they revised previous words that no longer fit. Many years later, Dave told me he didn't remember the incident. He must have seized the opportunity to tell himself he initially misunderstood. The new words were what he really wanted to hear. And they gave me what I wished I'd really said.

* * *

I had gotten away with it, but now I walked on eggshells. Like the childhood game of sidestepping cracks in sidewalks to avoid breaking a mother's back, I previewed my moves. I didn't want another Swedish episode where my pen moved across a page like the planchette of a Ouija board. I didn't want to open my fat mouth and hear the death knell of forbidden words.

Then months passed without another slip and my happy life returned as if it had never left.

MORE

Events that trigger trauma can include a birth ordeal, forced separation, mis-attunement by a parent to an offspring's grief, hearing about the loss of someone close, and more.

People can experience similar trauma differently. Differences may result from the larger meaning the event represents for the individual (which may not be immediately evident); diverse coping skills, values and beliefs (some of which may have never been identified); and the reactions and support from family, friends, and/or professionals.

Sometimes feelings associated with a trauma can be delayed, for even years after the event. To suspend feelings, a person may have dissociative symptoms ("splitting off" parts of the self), experience memory lapses, and avoid situations that resemble the initial event. When trauma is belatedly recognized, there may be a delayed reaction, such as mentally re-experiencing or having intrusive thoughts about the trauma. —Santa Barbara Graduate Institute Center for Clinical Studies and Research and L.A. County Early Identification and Intervention Group. With information from Helpguide.org. 2005. *Emotional and Psychological Trauma: Causes and Effects, Symptoms and Treatment.* Web.

*

Slips of the tongue are almost inevitable. Sigmund Freud, whose name is indelibly linked with such gaffes, called them *Fehlleistungen* (faulty actions). He deemed them notable for revealing an unconscious thought, belief, wish, or motive. —Jena Pincott. *Slips of the Tongue.* Psychology Today. Web.

*

Did you ever have someone tell you something while you were distracted, turn to them and say 'excuse me?' only to then 'hear' what they said? That's echoic memory."— Dr. C. George Boeree. *Memory.* webspace.ship.edu . Web.

*

Cecile Brennan, coordinator of the counseling program at John Carroll University in University Heights, Ohio, says she often tells her students that a person in crisis does not have the mental state to reflect on their emotions. They're trying to survive. It may be important for someone in a crisis NOT to feel things intensely at the time. To postpone feelings until later can be an important defense mechanism that shouldn't be undermined. —Lynne Shallcross. *A Calming Presence.* Counseling Today. February 1, 2012. Web

CHAPTER FIVE

1 9 7 4

AGE: 29

CAPE COD

- A N D -

1 9 5 8 – 1 9 5 9

AGE: 13-14

NEW HAMPSHIRE

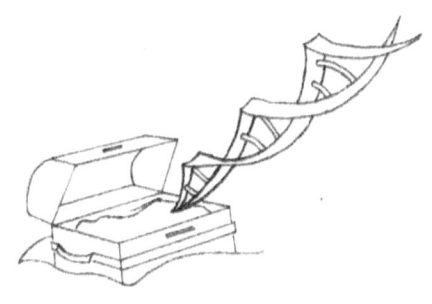

One comfortable evening, while Dave attended a meeting and Scott and Todd slept, I turned on the television. I moved to the couch, curled my legs to one side, and picked up my needlepoint. I was eager to claim some time for myself. I began to work the stitches for the slogan on the needlepoint: "As Ye Sow, So Shall Ye Reap." I slipped the needle through the small "x" printed on the linen, and, by the time the needle emerged from the underside, the thrust of the movie had emerged.

I didn't realize I had driven the needle into a finger until a drop of blood appeared on the fabric. I asked myself: *What on earth am I watching?* Soon, an ad for the network announced that the scheduled broadcast of "A Stranger Who Looks Like Me" would return after a few messages. Quickly, I thumbed through the listings in the *TV Guide*. I found I had inadvertently tuned to a story about an adoptee's search for the mother who had given her up for adoption.

I couldn't move.

In the next scene, an adoptee—played by Meredith Baxter—and her new friend—played by Beau Bridges—were in a group session with others who had experienced adoption in some way. In the group were two adoptive parent couples and one mother who had surrendered; the rest were adoptees. The surrendering mother said she knew she had done the right thing. The adoptive parents agreed. But the adoptees did not toe that party line. I flinched when they described their pain. "I need to know where I came from," one said. Another declared she had the "right" to know and had every intention of exercising that right. An adoptive mother hedged. "Well, we are coming into a time when things are changing. Everything is opening up."

My God!

In another scene in the movie, Meredith approached a social worker who, from behind her desk, made clear that things had not opened up in her agency. "We promised our mothers confidentiality," she crowed. In dismissal, she answered her ringing black phone, twining its cord around her finger. As Meredith left the office, she noticed a staff member in the hallway exit a room labeled "Records." Before the door could lock behind him, she glanced around her to make sure no one was looking. Then she slipped into the room like a burglar. But, just as she began to scan the labels on storage boxes, she was caught red-handed.

Her next step was the hospital where she had been born. Again she was refused information. She and Beau retreated to the hospital cafeteria. As nurses in starched uniforms walked by, Meredith befriended a staff member who was finishing his lunch. Making up a story, she cajoled him into securing her mother's name. With the name in hand, Meredith was able to locate her mother's address. Shaking, she approached her mother's front door.

It felt urgent to learn what happened next: What would this mother do! What *could* she do?

To my surprise, she allowed Meredith into her house. She gave her the time of day, just barely. "I don't want my kids to know" she told Meredith, gesturing at photos lining a fireplace mantel. When Meredith asked about her father, the woman winced—a gesture I automatically mimicked. The mother reported, with a faraway look: "I have forgotten about it."

Later, I sat as still as if I had been handcuffed to medieval stocks. Could it be true? Did some adoptees want to *know*? Was it idle interest or were they as driven as the movie portrayed? Meredith's surrendering mother had been asked about the father. She replied she had forgotten. I could strongly identify with that mother.

Today, I have a distinct memory of my reaction. I got up from the couch. I turned my hands over each other, compulsively wringing them. I walked through the dining room to the kitchen. I pressed my forehead to the cool window of the back door. Looking at the black sky beyond, I felt like an insect caught in an overturned bowl. No matter which direction I scurried, I would crash into something hard. For now I could breathe under the dome, but how long would air last?

* * *

Like a woman who feels it is time to become pregnant, I began to notice pregnancies everywhere. Clouds were pregnant with rain. My garden did not grow, it gestated. My life felt suspended. As in Sweden, I was aware of layers within. I could feel answers throb there, like the echo of a baby's kick. But what was I supposed to do with these sensations? They seemed demanding, as if I should tap into them. How? Where were the tools? And, just as quickly came the opposite command, again like Sweden: stop that… ***shut down, now***!

I began to notice other things. Old songs on the radio: when did songs from the late 50s and early 60s return to the airwaves? When did they begin to be called "Golden Oldies?" How long had that phrase been around? Why didn't I notice any of this before? I found I knew most of the words in those songs. The few words I forgot were like blanks to fill in. When I was able to retrieve missing words from my mind, I hunted, like a schizophrenic, for messages in the lyrics. What clues were there? Why did this song play? Why that? I seemed powerless to turn the knob of the radio to the left and reduce the volume or, better still, to turn it off. My choices seemed to be to either leave the volume as it was and stay preoccupied, or to turn up the volume. I learned that if the volume was loud enough, the static rendered the lyrics so garbled, I couldn't focus on them. And the static had a bonus effect: it subsumed the noisy questions in my mind, quieting them like a mother might do with a child's backtalk.

One day I heard the lyrics: "Walk on by, wait on the corner. I still love you but we're strangers when we meet."

"GEEZ-US!" On automatic now, I cranked the volume. Heart thumping, I backed into a chair. As if I had time-traveled, I agonized: *"Why, Tom? Why?"* On that heel, another thought kicked in: *"Why do I care?!* That had been—what?—ten years ago? A dozen? I didn't want to do the math. Before, life had been simple. Clear. I loved my

73

husband, my kids, my life. Now, I needed to know: where was this sabotage coming from?

I didn't realize I was doubled over, my eyes trained on the floor, until the music abruptly stopped, deafening the room with silence. Dave had arrived home, opened the back door, entered the kitchen, and turned the knob to *Off*.

"What's wrong?" he asked. "Are you alright? Are you going deaf?"

I relaxed as if a grip had released me. But I must have continued to look wild-eyed. Dave took my hands in his. "Tell me," he urged.

I couldn't find words or sentences, never mind paragraphs. I threw out whatever disjointed thoughts came to mind. He caught them and pieced them together. I trailed: "Now I can't think of anything else."

He went quiet, looking for the solution. Coming up empty, he asked: "What can I do?"

I could see he was worried about me. I hated to distress him. But his face showed he was worried about more than just me. If the past returned to my life, there would be complications for our boys, himself, and even his career. After all, I had been interviewed for the job as much as he had; I had played a role in our selection for the trip to Sweden. I knew he was already thinking ahead to what this could mean to the respect and prestige we had earned together.

"Nothing," I finally answered. There was nothing he could do. At his crestfallen look, I amended: "I don't know." It was too convoluted to think through. I shared his concerns. And, for me, there was still more: What if Michael searched? What about Tom? How could I tell Michael what Tom did? What about my family—Michael's aunts, uncle, grandparents—whom I had pushed to the margins of my life? Wouldn't I want them to welcome Michael? But did *I* want to welcome Michael? And how could I backtrack from the secrets I had kept from Dave's family and from our friends?

David thought further, settled his concern on me, and asked: "What do *you* want to do?"

I could only tell him I didn't know that either. How could I even begin to figure out something I didn't want to think twice about, but which was taking over my mind.

* * *

Now that I was aware that some adoptees were searching, I began to notice newspaper articles about them. Looking for answers in radio airwaves had not helped; maybe music was too compelling? Instead, I began to turn my attention to the more stable black-and-white of printed words.

I began to clip articles about adoption. I scissored guiltily, with one eye looking out the window to the driveway. I didn't want Dave to discover what I was doing. He had begun to come home at odd times of the day to make sure I was alright. I didn't want him to worry. I didn't want to hear him continue to question what he should do or what I wanted to do. I did not believe I could ever learn what our options were. What *my* options were. For, I knew I had created this mess and was even now compounding the mess on a daily, sometimes hourly, basis. Not only was I clipping articles but I was squirreling the clippings out of sight. Every time I added a clipping to my cache, I wondered what I hoped to gain. Perhaps I thought if I could just gather enough clippings, the right letter—in whatever size or font—would randomly pop from pages and magically re-arrange into a message I might be able to decode. With increasing desperation, I wanted to know why I was so fixated on impossibilities. But messages and answers did not appear.

During stolen moments, I was a secret news clipper and hoarder. But other times, I tried to iron out David's worries. As best I could, I intensified my devotion to him and to our boys. When school ended that summer, I applied for a job as the secretary to the principal of the boys' elementary school. Now that Todd was enrolled for the Fall, the blank spaces of time at home were not something I wanted to face alone. My school job would keep me busy, controlling my spare time in ways I was apparently unable to do on my own. Meanwhile, my work schedule could parallel the boys' school time. I could touch base with them during the day, be at home when they were, and I could bring in some income that would ease at least one of Dave's concerns.

Such was my latest hope and plan.

* * *

In the meantime, there was the summer to get through. It was off to a good start. My garden began to sprout. The boys and I began to spend our usual summer-stoked days on the bay with my friends and their kids. And, I decided to try to bridge the gap with my family. I would host a family reunion, visit with all of them at the same time.

I developed menus for each meal of the three days we would be together. I drafted shopping lists, equipment lists, and lists of lists. As reunion day drew near, the boys and I picked blueberries from the orchard owned by our neighbor across the street, who had also volunteered a couple of his bedrooms. I froze some blueberries for pancakes, using the remainder in muffins. I made extra loaves of white bread, quick breads, and stacks of cookies. I needled a reluctant David— an isolationist when in the midst of my noisy "overly" affectionate family— into setting up two tents in the backyard. I scooted about collecting mattresses, rollaway cots and cooking equipment from friends.

I also prayed for sunshine. Anticipating this petition would be granted because I was overdue for some petition to be granted, I bought a second croquet set and a badminton set and I borrowed horseshoes and stakes from my neighbor. On the first morning of our reunion, a bright blue sky signaled "reprieve." There would be plenty of outdoor cooking and activities. We'd all keep as busy as my one body could make it.

The clan began arriving. Each sibling came with contributions I had assigned to them for the food table. I checked off their contributions on my master list in the chronological order of my siblings' ages: Brenda, her husband and five kids—check—more cookies, soft drinks, cereal variety packs; Sandi and her husband—check—for a light touch, the family joke: her "barrels" of macaroni salad; Richard, his wife and their two kid—check—cases of beer. Mom and Dad who had flown up from Florida were exempt, as was Donna who arrived with the child she had been able to keep.

Their arrival was a speed bump. I had been able to avoid drawing a contrast between my situation and Donna's when she lived 1500 miles away. Recently, though, Donna had returned to Manchester. Before, it had also helped that Donna's child was a daughter. Now the difference between our children's gender was the only thing I had left that I could use to wall off a comparison. I tried to focus on that, and on the tasks I had given myself to get through the weekend. No one noticed my speed bump. As I worked, I overheard my uncle comment to his wife: "She sure is one organized, energetic gal!"

I patted myself on the back. I had arranged for every conceivable contingency. Except, as it turned out, for one.

Donna and I sat alone in the kitchen, sipping iced tea. I had just relaxed, this being our last day of the reunion. She talked about her part-time job waitressing at a Chinese restaurant where Brenda also worked.

78

Donna asked: "Of course, you know Tom's wife works with us?"

"Who? Whose wife?"

"Tom's. You know, your old boyfriend."

I got up from the table to put distance between her news and me. Leaning against the far wall, my knees weak, I muttered "No, I didn't…know."

Donna turned in her chair to make eye contact. "Oh, I thought maybe Brenda told you. They've worked together for the past year."

"She wouldn't have… told me," I informed her. Brenda knew the subject was taboo. Donna, so young during my pregnancy, had been kept in the dark about it until her own, when my parents offered her the scantest review of mine. Donna didn't have details.

Blithely, Donna continued: "Yes, I even saw Tom. He asked about you. Wanted to know how you are. I guess his wife's been keeping him well-informed. He knew all about Sweden and about this reunion and about David. He even commented that his two girls are about the same ages as Scott and Todd."

She paused, expecting a comment. I could imagine Brenda filling in Tom via his wife, letting him know my life had gone on just fine without him, letting him know he hadn't been able to ruin it. She would see this as being loyal to me and I couldn't disagree. But what had Donna said? Tom had repeated, apparently in a way as conversational as "So, how are you, anyway?" what he knew of my life. And Donna had also mentioned his children?

"Girls?" I repeated in a quiet voice. "No boys?"

"Nope. He did say he had hoped his second would be a boy. But she wasn't." Donna gave a little laugh.

So, God upheld one bargain with me then. He had withheld sons from Tom. Justice lit a tiny corner in me. But it was quickly snuffed.

"Tom asked if you were happy," Donna continued in a merry, guess-what-else-I-can-tell-you way. Straightening in her chair, she added another helping: "You won't believe this. His wife goes to Bible Study once a week—at our old house, no less. Tom told me when he drops her off it's like yesterday for him, driving into our driveway. He's been inside our old house and he said nothing much has changed." She leaned forward, suddenly inspired, "Lee, you know what? You really ought to call him sometime, say hello."

Speechless, I inched along the back wall, working my way to the seat of the chair at my desk. On the way down, I held onto the carriage of my typewriter. I turned the typewriter knob absently. It ratcheted. The clacking was background to what I would now tell Donna, what I would now tell myself. I had not said it aloud since it happened. The words stuck in my throat, so I whispered: "You don't understand, Donna."

I swallowed hard, then pushed it out: "He…he denied paternity."

Donna's large dark eyes bugged, "He what?" Then: "I didn't… know, Lee. How could he do… *that*, after all your years together? I thought, you both agreed to…you know." As if to herself, she added, "That explains what he meant. Lee, he told me that when he married his wife, she was pregnant. His mother tried to interfere but, as Tom told me, he wouldn't let her do that to him, not again."

I wanted to fold over and over into myself. But before I could reduce myself further, I had to ask: "He said it like that, Donna? He said 'not again'?"

Donna thought, remembering. She was sure he had described it that way: "not again."

A vestige of a memory slipped in place: his mother, Ellen, saying Tom had denied he was the father. But could it be? Could it be that it wasn't…Tom…who denied? That it was his mother who did it for him? Had *she* called those shots? But, if so, he had…gone along? Why?

Immediately, I steeled the door in my mind. But even then I knew that no barrier would be substantial enough to bar the memories now. I could feel them flex their muscles. They would come out and there was nothing I could do to stop them.

* * *

The next day I restored our suddenly quiet house to order. Meanwhile, memories began to trickle through the gaps around the door I had slammed, as if water from an open faucet in a distant room had finally reached an outlet. I knew I was giving up any ghost of a chance I had left to keep my memories away. I was no match for the force of those memories, not any more. Not only were my reserves shot, the memories were stronger than ever. It was as if, instead of waning, they had been fed by my denials and protests.

In a class exercise, I was once told to imagine an elephant in my living room; then I was told to wipe out the image. The more I tried, the more vivid the image became. Trying not to think about the memories had worked like that. But knowing the memories were coming and there was nothing I could do to stop them did not help me cope.

Two things did help. I was alone in the house because Dave was at work and the boys were on a play date. And the memories were not just abstract images impossible to express; instead, these images were accompanied by words. The words were mine; they were original. They weren't others' lyrics broadcasted over the radio, nor were they others' words arranged in orderly columns of a newspaper I could clip and contain. There was good and bad in that.

As memories swamped my new life, I felt as helpless as a hurricane victim. But, thanks to the memories being accompanied by words, I told myself there was hope. I could expunge all those words and put them somewhere else. I would be like a water extraction company that disaster victims call to sop up an in-house flood. After the memories were extracted, they could be driven away in a commercial tank. Once the tank left my driveway, I could restore my life.

My typing business, one of my friends who was an author, and my ghost-writing episode in Sweden had shown me what to do next. I sat at my desk, turned on my Smith-Corona typewriter, rolled a sheet of paper behind its platen, and my hands began to take dictation. Like a bloodletting, small clotted words and larger words I didn't even know I knew pumped from my brain, flew through my veins, and made headway for my wrists. As they bumped into the pads of my finger tips, they arced like electricity to tap messages from hidden places in my heart. On and on, the words flew. Pages filled. A stack grew on the left side of my desk.

Knowing I would work at the boys' elementary school in the Fall, I had turned over my business to my friend, Marie, at the beginning of the summer. My plan at that time was to make the most of the care-free days that remained. Instead, I now divided my time. In the morning, the boys continued to hear the furious pecking of my typewriter, as they had when I was in the typing business. In the afternoon, my day was theirs.

From secret-keeping and the script I had been given to forget, I learned some tricks I now only had to refine. I had learned how to act as if nothing was wrong. A difference was, I couldn't draw an inference from my pretense to convince myself the happy role was real. When I pasted a smile on my face or I laughed, I knew it was phony. But I learned if I kept the smiles and laughs going, they often took hold. [6]

I started the writing at a safe place. In the same way I order up dreams, command an overnight solution for a practical problem, and tell myself to wake at a certain time, I made a deal with my memories. Channeling the stories would be limited to the summer and they would arrive in chronological order. With the easy stuff first, I began writing about my younger years.

1958

Age: 13

Rhode Island

I remember what it was like at 13, facing life with skinned knees and scabby elbows. I remember greeting each day hungrily, immediately full of happy plans.

Maybe I would call for Brucie, Paul and Susie with at least one of my three younger sisters, or maybe my younger brother, tagging along like ducklings behind their mother. Then perhaps we would go into the woods to feed the puppies we had found. I remember how the puppies looked: all pink-eared and nosed, snuggling together in the base of that hollow tree, pathetically mewing like kittens.

Or maybe I would have called on Katie and we would go to the dried out river bed to swing on a Tarzan rope we had found tied to a huge tree that protruded from the hillside like a masthead. I remember the sensation of gritting my teeth, swallowing my fear, clinging fiercely to the rope and, after taking a running leap, swinging widely out, out and up, the wind rushing past me and blowing through my hair.

I remember that I organized a Talent Show starring The Kids (as I called my sisters and brother) and our friends. Neighborhood parents baked cakes and cookies to be auctioned and that money, together with a small admission fee, raised $21.00 for Muscular Dystrophy. Later, the local newspaper printed a picture of me presenting that grand sum to the local foundation director. I still have the yellow, dog-eared clipping in my scrapbook.

If it were raining, there would be different things to do. I probably would take The Kids down into the basement where we would play my parents' stack of 78 rpm records. Perry Como's "Linda" is one that comes to mind ("When I go to sleep, I never count sheep. Instead I count all the charms about Linda… Because miracles do happen…."). To the lyrics of these records, I would choreograph little skits for The Kids to put on for our proud parents. I remember always reserving the starring role for me.

Most days back then ended with a huge game of Kick the Can. After supper, the children in the neighborhood—all ages, no discrimination then—emptied out of their homes. We'd appoint one luckless kid "It." It had to run to a can placed upside down in the middle of our quiet street. It would kick the can hard, sending it sailing. The sound of the can clanking while skipping to a new location signaled to the rest of us standing nearby to skedaggle in different directions. Laughing, we ran to our hiding places, peeking around corners. Then, while It was away from the can-post trying to find someone else to tag, one of us hiding in the opposite direction would sneak to the can and send the can flying again, releasing anyone who had had the misfortune of being captured. Then It would have to start over. Into the early evening under the streetlights, we endlessly repeated this routine, getting giddier with each round.

At 13, I would wake up and know that whatever I did, I would be happy. And I would know it was time to get up when I heard "Heyyyy Richard-a-ard." That would have been Marky, calling for my brother at the back door. If I went to the window, I would have seen them both dart down the street, after still another friend, Marky's dark head bobbing alongside Richard's blonde. I would affectionately watch them and then I would dress.

I most vividly remember, though, the day Mom and Dad called me into the living room. Dad casually sat there in "his chair," his long legs stretched out on the light green plastic hassock in front of him. Mom perched on the arm of the chair, her hand resting on Dad's arm. A familiar pose. But they looked, because of their penetrating gaze, as though in a Victorian portrait. I stood facing them, wondering.

"We're leaving Rhode Island," Dad announced. As a smoke ring rose upward from his cigarette, he explained "We're moving back to Manchester." The cloudy ring screened Dad's soft, full mouth and, soon, his finely chiseled nose. It spread before his arresting blue eyes and his high forehead. I watched it finally disappear above his receding, silvering hair. I hadn't had to look at my mother to confirm he was serious. But a second later, I did. And I saw what I needed to know: her hazel eyes registered worry.

I wailed "Not again!" Then I put on a drama show worthy of an academy award. I noted with satisfaction I had made an impression. Mom looked distressed and a flicker of something disturbed Dad's determined eyes. I knew they were thinking of the example I would set for The Kids.

I stomped out. I flew down the driveway, wondering how Mom and Dad could ruin my life like that—taking me away from all my friends! I flashbacked on our former houses located on streets in cities here and there, where I always left friends behind. "Not again," I repeated. "Not now."

I was pivoting at the end of the driveway to search for The Kids and incite them to riot when Dad called "Lee! Come back here!"

The instant his tone registered, all resolve swept away. Whimpering inside like an independent puppy spanked by an adored master, I retreated from my rebellion.

"We are moving, Lee," Dad said calmly after we re-entered the living room, "and that is that."

"But Dad," I began, wondering if I dared to pout. He stubbed out his cigarette in the floor ashtray beside his chair and left me alone with Mom.

"Don't give Dad a hard time, Lee," Mom implored. She was always beseeching me for something or other and, in my present mood, I would have ignored this request if she hadn't mentioned Dad's name. And something told me this was no ordinary request for cooperation. "Dad's firm has had to file for bankruptcy and he's been offered a job with an old friend. Now don't go telling Dad I told you this. No sense making him feel worse."

"But I don't want to move," I finally said, a little ashamed.

Mom and I studied each other. I noticed the set of her thin lips, the downcast of her sleepy hazel eyes. I couldn't overlook the pug nose we had all inherited, the gene in me more exaggerated than in the other Kids. Choosing to read my silence as agreement, Mom concluded, "Come help me fix supper."

I sighed loudly, trailing Mom as she walked barefoot ahead of me to the kitchen. I can see her now, her chubby body on short, sturdy legs. I focused on Mom's cap of recently dyed hair. When she first arrived home with it, Dad had uncharacteristically offered a disgusted look, although he otherwise stayed in character: silent on criticism.

By the time Mom and I reached the kitchen, sparkling with white appliances, I had charged a battery of persuasive arguments for remaining in Rhode Island. But, as if Mom sensed this, she erupted in a coughing fit, ending with the usual crossing of her legs to prevent wetting her pants. I tensed with resignation. There was little competing with her, as she probably knew, when she pulled out this ace. Over the years, her many illnesses had honed protective responses in all of us. In me, it signaled: get ready to take care of The Kids.

There were many such signals. In third grade, for one, Mom got tuberculosis and had to be sent to a sanatorium. We had moved from Portland Maine by then and were settled in Manchester, the other side of the city Dad now wanted to return to. Donna, only months old, was placed in one orphanage equipped to handle babies. The four oldest of us were placed in a Catholic orphanage. They wore long, flowing brown habits topped with white-tipped bonnets. Brenda and I were placed in "Big Girls," Sissy in "Little Girls," and Richard in "Little Boys." During outdoor playtime, Sissy, Brenda and I would meet at the chain link fence separating the Boys' Yard from the Girls'. There, we would talk to Richard who inserted his fingers between the links so we could hold them. While Mom recuperated, Dad traveled weekdays as a salesman, returning home on weekends to collect Donna and the rest of us. Mom's mother, MaMere, and I teamed up with him to care for The Kids.

Unlike my siblings, I have happy memories about life in the orphanage. To me, it was like being in the dorm of a summer camp. In the school on the site, I especially loved the learning the nuns nudged in me. I picked up French so fast and did so strongly in my other subjects that, if my terror of Mother Superior hadn't painted a blank in my mind during my oral test with her, I would have skipped a grade. Had I been skipped, it might have changed my life, my reason for writing this.

But now in Rhode Island, poised to move yet another time, I stood listening to Mom's racking coughs. Then, considering Dad's recent troubles, I set the table and helped her with supper.

At the dining room table that night, between passing the peas and the mashed potatoes, Dad introduced the move. "Oh, by the way…" he began.

The Kids as one turned to me. Brenda with her long blonde hair, curling softly around her sweet fair face; Sissy, my Birthday present, born on my birthday when I was three years old, with her short, brown hair showing off a widow's peak and an oval face dotted with sunny freckles; Richard with his tousled blonde hair and light blue eyes; and even my seven year old "twinnie," Donna, so-named because our baby pictures looked alike, with dark brown hair and eyes and a round face. I debated what to say but a quick look at Dad silenced me. I continued to shovel in my supper.

With the deal sealed, I began to hope Mom and Dad would find a new house soon so we could get the waiting over with. From past experiences, I knew I could invent myself all over again. Maybe this time, I would be more sophisticated. It was time to stop looking like Annette Funicello. Maybe I could try to look more like Natalie

Wood. For that, I'd have to grow out my hair. At least I had some control over that.

1974

Age: 29

Cape Cod

The words had flown as if their container was uncorked under pressure. Now I made myself stop typing. The pitcher of icy lemonade I had put on the back step had been slurped dry by two thirsty boys, and they reminded me I had promised to take them to the beach to play with Marie's children. When we got back from the beach, I had to make dinner. I needed to get cracking.

We gathered our usual beach things: plastic buckets, towels, blankets, and saltwater-rusted Matchbox cars. As the boys and I moved these things from house to car, I reflected on my latest round of writing. It hadn't been so bad, I decided. In fact, it had been kind of fun.

It was good to realize that, despite our frequent moves, our family was the one constant we took everywhere. We were like a familiar banged-up metal trunk that would hold up, no matter how it was thrown around. I thought about the word "familiar," wondering if it stemmed from the word "family." I liked wondering where words came from. It seemed to me I had looked at roots of words in high school English. What did my teacher—what was her name? —Mrs. Fearon! What did Mrs. Fearon call the study of where words came from? "Etymology?" Something like that. The cells in my brain danced with delight.

My heart was involved too. The memories reminded me how much my father adored my mother. When she walked by him, he teased her with a "pat-pat on her poh-poh," wherever that term came from. In return, Mom's eyes lit up whenever Dad came into a room. She reached up to his waist to wrap her arms around him and he stooped over to nuzzle her hair. Their affection was a feedback loop. It overflowed from them to us Kids, between us Kids, then back upstream to our parents, like the herring runs at Brewster's Grist Mill. I had overlooked—no, forgotten—how much love I had grown up with.

That is . . . until Mom and Dad stopped loving me.

I jammed a brake on that train of thought. When its caboose crashed, I forgot for a second where I was going with that idea. I had been thinking about my family with its Disney Technicolor love and then the color suddenly turned sepia-muddy. As I waited for inklings to return, I mused on people who blamed the hot topic--the "epidemic of teen pregnancy"—on the teens' parents; "dysfunctional" parents they were called in the newspapers where I found my clippings. I kept that thought on track: it seemed to me my parents were the opposite of cold and unloving. They loved the stuffing out of us. But that was then.

Which sentiment was more real: my parents' love for me in my childhood or the love they aborted in my teens? How could I cobble together these two types of parental love? It was as if I walked with one foot on a city sidewalk and another on a much lower road below. The terrain was grossly uneven. My thoughts limped as I tried to reconcile those love warps in time.

I thought more about time. Had I blindly tried to follow my parents' lead on love with my own love? Had I been over-eager? Did I want to one-up my parents' brand of loving? To love the way they did with each other but on my own terms? Would that have been a way to gain permanence I could control, to not move again?[7]

If I had waited just one more year, I would have been in sync with the timeline ordained for middle-class Catholic girls like me, a doctrine that called for me to marry soon after high school, have babies, and stay home to care for them. My family hadn't moved for four years. Given past history, we were due. Was I trying to bend time to my need for security? Or, did I simply have sex because it was…time? And Tom was in that time?

As I prepared supper that night, I wondered why I had so many tiring questions. And why were possible answers in the form of still more questions?

Before my first round of memories, I had storms of questions that still hung off-shore without resolution. How had I forgotten in the first place? Where had my memories been hiding? Why did I suddenly begin to remember? Why now? Why didn't I notice "golden oldies" on the radio before, and news about adoptees' searching? Why was I compelled to respond to these intrusions by blasting the radio and clipping and hiding articles?

Now more questions were popping. Why was I enslaved by memories? Where was the line between past and present? How could I keep my past and present separate?

The only way to iron out questions, it seemed to me, was to stop having questions. Questions and I didn't get along . . . before. And we weren't getting along now. Anyway, my deal with the memories was to purge, not analyze. I didn't have the will to play "Twenty Questions." I had made summer-y promises to my boys and, if there was going to be any play, it would be with them. I also didn't have time to spare. I had to dispense with my memories before school–and my new job—began. To make that deadline, I needed to write full steam ahead; no distractions.

1958 – 1959

Age: 13-14

New Hampshire

Before we moved from Rhode Island to New Hampshire, I sat in a bubble bath with a phone in my hand, asking my neighbor to play "Bonie Moroni" for me. Since the lyrics described Bonie "as skinny as a stick of macaroni," the song was perfect backup for my scrawny limbs that poked above the froth like a couple of scraggly twin pines on an island.

Then Dad burst through the door. He had noticed the long phone cord snaking under the bathroom door. He yanked the phone out my hand to save me, he said, from electrocution.

As I typed this scene, I smiled to recall my hero.

1974

Age: 29

Cape Cod

My smile quickly faded when I remembered that my sentiments about a heroic Dad no longer fit the Dad who had put my needs last in line. I had to amend Dad-as-hero to Dad-as-once-upon-a-time-hero. I was back to trying to reconcile the shifts in my parents' love for me.

I thought more about Mom. But the situation with her wasn't any better. She had been my confidante, a friend of sorts. When she wasn't ill, she was stellar. When Dad arose in the morning, he was known to say: "I wonder what fun Mom has in store for us today." Except for retreating when I needed her to come forward for Michael, she gave us memories that could have shone for a lifetime.

Take her idea for our "Night Before the Fourth." On the eve of July 4th, we piled pillows and blankets in the "back-back" of Dad's station wagon. In the trunk of Mom's sedan we piled coolers of food and snacks. Then the seven of us drove to Pine Island Park, a large amusement complex on the outskirts of Manchester, where the airport is now. We gorged ourselves on the rollercoaster, the fun house, and all the other attractions. As twilight drew near, we returned to the cars to move them to the drive-in section of the park.

We began to unpack the picnic we had prepared and settled down to be terrorized by the usual Grade B movies. That's where we saw all the scary shit Hollywood had to offer back then: *King Kong*, *The Body Snatchers*, *Godzilla*. Munching on snacks, we rotated between cars until, one-by-one, each of us kids sprawled on pillows and blankets in the back of the wagon for on-again and off-again naps.

When we got home, Dad lit a fire in the pit in the back yard and we had a cool, misty-dawn breakfast of hot dogs and hamburgers. Then we went to bed until noon when the July fourth parade began downtown, which Dad would never miss.

It would be simpler if Dad and Mom were either wonderful parents or awful parents. After Michael, I had decided they were awful and, since they were a package deal, I kissed off the whole family in my mind as much as I could. But with the memories, the bigger picture was being pieced together like a jigsaw puzzle. Now I didn't know how to assess my parents, which only triggered another round of questions.

But I had thought of an experiment and decided to test it out. I would treat any question-provoking Journal entries like the Sunday newspaper. I would enjoy the comics and take the sections with hard news to the dump. I would enjoy the good memories and set aside for now anything that provoked deep thought.

1959

Age: 14

New Hampshire

Not long after we began our new school, Brenda confided to me that her new classmates were teasing her about her "big things." I looked down and to my alarm saw she did indeed have "big things." I was curious why they were bigger than mine. Even so, I would have dismissed the comparison, except it apparently mattered—a lot— to the girls in our new world.

In other moves we'd made through the years, I had slipped into my new groups of friends without a major problem. I only had to invent a new hairdo or show another part of me. But in Manchester I needed, like Lulu, to get from "crayons to perfume." Although I already had in mind to transform my Musketeer Annette Funicello into Natalie Wood, it was trickier than any other change I had invented.

Instead of absorbing me into their circle, my new friends circled around me, checking me out like a novelty, referring to me as the "New Girl." They were judging to see if I fit in. Did I share their interest in boys? Was I cool—just the right shade of casual—enough?

I wasn't ready for boys or cool. It was as if being able to enjoy kid stuff had been thrown under the wheels when my family car crossed the state line. I couldn't know before we left Rhode Island I would never again enjoy a game of Kick the Can with kids in the neighborhood, or be only-friends with boys who wanted to help me feed abandoned puppies or share the thrill of swinging on ropes over dried out river beds. If I had known, I would have appreciated it more. I would have memorialized the details in a Hallmark card to store in a be-ribboned part of my mind.

Instead, all I could see was that my new friends and I had different interests. I still wanted to play hopscotch on the girls' side of the paved school yard, while they wanted to cluster in circles near the boys' side and look nonchalant. To me, it didn't even make sense. As winter approached, younger girls jumped rope ("A" my name is 'Alice,' my husband's name is 'Al,' we live in 'Alabama,' and he sells 'Apples'", and so on, either through the alphabet or until the jumper tripped, whichever came first). Jumping around like that, those younger girls got warmed up. That's what I wanted to do.

But my older crowd stood in circles, looking all la-la-la as they discreetly shuffled from one foot to the other. The cold air barreled up our full, gathered skirts, the only barrier between the cold and our undies being several gauzy petticoats that were starched heavily enough to stand on their own. Our coats weren't much help either. We had to leave them open since a closed zipper couldn't contain all our petticoats without us looking like a bunch of Humpty Dumpties. Even though pleated skirts were

98

becoming a fad, and these allowed zippering, pleated skirters couldn't close up their coats either because then they wouldn't match full-skirted friends who had to keep their coats open. I had never had a rule book for stuff like this.

By the time the first bell signaled us to leave the pavement, we were in full shiver. There would be a second bell to say we should be in our seats but the time between bells was generous. Since we couldn't be excused after class had begun, we were supposed to spend the interval between bells in the industrial-green bathroom in the basement getting everything out of the way.

Part of the "everything" included a warm up. Now beyond the boys' once-over, some girls did Jack LaLanne's Jumping Jacks. Others marched in a long single file toward the only small mirror in the room. Along the way, they untangled their own and each other's wind-blown hair. They reapplied red lipstick, a generous amount since it had to last.

When my new best friend, Diane, expertly applied her lipstick without a mirror I gasped as if she had pulled a bunny out of a hat on "The Ed Sullivan Show." I didn't know the first thing about lipstick. Mom didn't think I needed to worry about that yet. I had agreed but now Diane demonstrated how far behind I was.

Then there were the dance moves. Girls also used the basement bathroom to practice something they called the Jitterbug. My parents' old 78 RPM records were a far cry from the 45 RPM rock and roll that blared from the new portable radios the other girls proudly carried to school. Knowing a little about Frankie Avalon and a few other popular singers made the rock beat something I could pick up on. And although the dances I had choreographed with the Kids to entertain our parents weren't anything like the Jitterbug, they served like a primer for the hip-swaying, push-pull-turns Diane began to teach me. It was a relief to find something in my new world that came naturally.

When I described the steps later to Mom, who was always interested in knowing the latest hip thing, she got a faraway look on her face. It occurred to me she might have danced at my age. "I did," she assured me. "I was as tiny as you are and the boys could do flips with me. But our crowd didn't call it a Jitterbug; we called it The Swing."

It turned out that "flips" were acrobatics of a sort. As Mom told me what flips looked like, I realized they were part of the Jitterbug too. Diane had already described them to me. Boys grabbed girls around their waist and threw them off to one side, the girls pointing up their toes, after which they were bounced across the boys' waists and thrown skyward from the boys' other hip. "Sometimes, too," Mom said, "they would put me over their head and I would pose up there like a ballerina."

It was hard to imagine. For one thing, Mom was chubby. I asked "Did Dad dance?"

"No, dear," Mom answered with affectionate tolerance. "He has two left feet."

"How could you stand it? Obviously you loved dancing the way I do. If I had a boyfriend who didn't dance I would have to do it anyway, and he'd just have to understand."

Dancing was my only salvation in this strange new world. For the most part, I bluffed with the girls, trying to make it look as if I knew what was coming next, and trying not to look surprised when it came.

* * *

Diane had taken to the habit of stopping by my house so we could walk the seven blocks to school together. Neither of us wanted to be seen walking alone, so it was a good deal for each of us. I could also use the time to inexpertly pump her for information about what was cool without alerting her and everyone else to the fact I didn't have the foggiest idea.

But Diane tested me one day when she asked, "Who do you like?"

At first, I couldn't imagine what she meant. Did I like our eighth grade teacher who taught those of us assigned to her classroom because the administration thought we were smart? Or did I like the eighth grade teacher who taught in the other classroom? Or maybe she meant "What do you like?" as in the outfits others were wearing? Could be, too, I realized, she was asking who my favorite singer was. But none of these seemed to fit the intensity of her stare. At a loss, I raised my eyebrows.

"Boys," she said. Swallowing some exasperation, she explained: "Which boy do you like?"

I knew the boy-question would come eventually but I didn't think it would happen this soon. I tried to delay. "I don't like anyone," I answered, trying for the truth. But when her eyes popped as if she had a hard time believing it, I knew the truth would never do. I hedged: "At least not yet."

"But don't you think Tommy is cute?"

I hadn't noticed him, hadn't noticed any of the boys. As if to make things more clear, Diane described him as "the boy who sat in the first row, third seat."

Suddenly I matched up two widely-spaced thoughts, as if I had just won a round on the new TV game show, "Concentration." "Wait a minute, Diane. Didn't you say you liked a Tommy in our class? Is he the one you are talking about?"

She admitted I had guessed right. But then she thrust up her chin. "But I can't have him, so you might as well." Though she laughed, her lower lip trembled. I wondered which was real: her laugh or her lip.

As we entered the school, Diane confided, "I think Tom likes you. He's always looking at you anyway. Lucky stiff." Again there was the laugh with the bouncing lip. To keep things safe with Diane, I decided I would definitely not choose Tom if I had to choose someone, which I hoped I would not.

Back in the classroom I gave some consideration to the boys, trying to decide *who*, just in case. It had to be someone up to the girls' standards or my good taste would be in question. That narrowed the field. Then there were the boys who were already taken by one of the girls or in the process of being taken, which was pretty much the same thing. I didn't want to be known as a boyfriend stealer. And because I had decided to not choose Tom, I looked his way.

Tom sat at his desk thumping absently but rhythmically with his fingers. He had one leg drawn to the desk riser, exposing gray argyle socks. He was slouched down in his chair. I was surprised to like what I saw. Instantly, though, I thought of Diane and began a debate with myself.

On second look, he wasn't so cute after all. His skin was too dark, the opposite of the males in my life; my father and my brother were both blonde and blue-eyed. Then I argued against the dark-skin complaint, since I had to admit my Portuguese ancestry was alive and well in me. But he didn't have pimples, which earned him a lot of points. Then I assessed his height. He seemed awfully short. I quickly owned up that I was short too.

The contest went on. He sure is neat, I observed. And now the credits rolled: those chinos have the sharpest crease and you can even see the white of his head in the carved part of his Vitalis-hard hair. He was up on the fads too. I could tell that by the way he rolled up his long sleeves and unbuttoned his two top buttons to show a lot of undershirt. I concluded: he certainly has a nice straight nose …much better than my pug.

Tom's desk-thumping grew louder. As he became more absorbed in what he was doing, those around his desk egged him on. Later, Diane explained, "He plays the drums, too. You should have seen him in last year's talent show!"With that, I decided I would change my mind and accept the casual laugh, not the trembling lip, as my guideline. And —**IF**— if I was forced to choose someone, it would be Tom.

Even so, I froze the next day when Diane asked my impression of him. I stalled. "Oh, he's okay."

She looked wounded. It occurred to me she may have wanted to fix me up with Tom so she could have an excuse to talk with him, and in talking with him, she may have thought she could win him over. I really liked that idea. I had come to see that liking someone who didn't like you back was just as good a ticket to being accepted, maybe even better, than a real boyfriend. Since I wasn't ready for a boyfriend, I had a way out. I told Diane she could try to fix us up.

I had hardly been seated when I saw Diane whisper to Tom, both of them ignoring the group that had lingered around his desk when they overheard she "had a secret." To my surprise, Tom immediately bolted from his desk, slipped into the supply closet nearby and dragged a comb through his dark hair until he had an even neater, higher front wave, like Ed Byrnes' on "Seventy-Seven Sunset Strip." It had all happened so fast— and was so uncool—I knew he couldn't possibly have thought about it beforehand. When he turned from the mirror, he was greeted with laughter and backslaps, and Diane's crestfallen face. Even with his dark skin, I could see his blush. He avoided looking in my direction like the plague. Later, though, as class was in session, I caught him looking at me. "Oooh boy," I thought. "What now?"

Slowly, though, I got used to the idea. I could see the benefits. He more than fit the girls' standards. And he was even shyer about the whole thing than I was. Tom was safe.

MORE

There is empirical evidence that the unconscious mind, as popularized by Sigmund Freud, consists of many hidden attributes, including repressed feelings and forgotten memories, which may be accessed by consciousness at some later time.—Wikipedia. Web.

*

There is scientific evidence that the relief that comes from writing things down is more than just psychological. Dr. James Pennebaker, a researcher in Texas, has conducted studies that show that when people write about emotionally difficult events …their immune system functioning increases. — Kathleen Adams. *Journal Writing.* Center for Journal Therapy. Reprinted from The Illustrated Encyclopedia of Mind-Body Medicine, The Rosen Group. Web.

*

Journal Therapy, often referred to as "writing therapy," is an effective way to treat many medical, social, developmental, and psychological issues. This extremely beneficial therapy has been shown to help a person manage their behavior and inner and outer conflicts. Many people who struggle with deep emotional conflicts or traumas are unable to express their feelings in a verbal or physical way. By putting emotionally challenging situations on paper, a person has the ability to view them from a different perspective and gain insight into otherwise hidden facets of their behavior and actions. — Author Unknown. Good Therapy.org. *Journal Therapy.* Web.

*

Horticultural therapy is an emerging field of clinical practice. When a client manifests a change on their environment…the psyche is positively affected. Their self-belief grows as they realize they can impact their own destiny and find personal growth and restoration.— Fiann Ó Nualláin. *Horticultural Therapy.* bordia.ie/about gardening. Web.

*

"I am always searching for ways to make myself simpler. Gardening does that better than anything I know. It reduces me to who I am. It casts off the superficial and the artificial. It leaves me with the essential… me."— Richard Goodman. *French Dirt: The Story of a Garden in the South of France.* **Web.**

CHAPTER SIX

1 9 7 4

AGE: 29

CAPE COD

- AND –

1 9 6 1

AGE: 16

NEW HAMPSHIRE

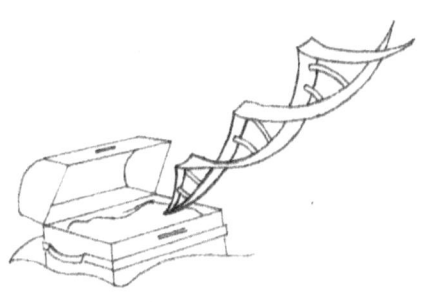

1974

Age: 29

Cape Cod

I turned over my palms. They were cupped so tightly they could have held water for an hour. I thought Tom was safe? Along with everything else, I had forgotten my early impressions of him. Asking myself about Tom was by now a familiar sign that more perplexing questions were on the way.

Like: How could I have been so naïve? Tom, alongside my parents, who had also proven unsafe, made me ask if my ability to know someone's real character was seriously out of whack. When I didn't have memories, I didn't consciously mistrust anyone. It was easy for me to take people at face value. I saw myself as optimistic, even Pollyanna-ish; for me, the glass was always half-full. It would be a sea change for me to be pessimistic. I didn't want any part of doom-and-gloom. The very thought of changing my overall view of the world and the people in it made me deeply sad and more than a little scared. How much of me would these memories eat up?

Comic strip characters couldn't ease these questions. I gave up on that idea. The only way to lighten the load, it seemed, was to arrest the questions in the first place. But I hadn't had much luck with that. What I needed was more self-discipline. Where it was going to come from, I didn't know.

Although I couldn't avoid more memories forever, I could hit the "Pause" button on channeling for now. Like a wind-up doll with a rusty key in my back, my fingers unfurled, I pushed back my chair, and I cranked upward. But I remained stooped, as if I were still bent over my typewriter.

My anatomy successfully asserted itself for the last upward ratchet. But now I felt like an old lady who had seen many changes in her lifetime.

Before they died, each of my grandmothers had made many adjustments. They had seen horses give way to cars, cars to planes, and planes to rocket ships to the moon. But my changes were more social. I saw freedoms and choices where there hadn't been any before. I only had to look at my original family for proof. Time had created very different outcomes for Donna's and my pregnancies.

Things were also changing in others' lives, too, which threatened, annoyed, or confused me no end.

Some news carried downwind in the air and drifted like autumn leaves to my back yard. Everyone knew, for example, about a big Supreme Court decision the year before. Women with pregnancies could now control their situations through a medical procedure called abortion. When I first heard about this "reproductive right," I had a flashback: mom taking me to a doctor to confirm my pregnancy; the doctor taking me aside to say "You don't have to go through with this;" me answering from an adamant place I hadn't visited for a while: "Yes, I do."

I now wondered if the doctor had been speaking in code. Was he offering me an abortion? "Abortion" was a word I had heard even less than "adoption," and I had only heard the word "adoption" once before. If I had known what the doctor was talking about, would I have taken him up on his offer?

By then I knew Tom had denied paternity and I was devastated. But I was already attached to my baby. I had been attached to my baby before he was even conceived. He would be a living extension of Tom's and my relationship. He was our dream that, even if Tom didn't live up to his end, I felt bound by some assembly-line destiny to follow through on mine. Maybe my emotional investment was even stronger because Tom turned his back on our deal; I had to do his part too. And, I so didn't understand Tom's denial. I still thought it was some horrid misunderstanding. I clung to the hope he would charge back into my life on his white horse at full gallop, scoop me up, and spirit me to Mississippi, as we had planned.

Another piece of news I had recently noticed was that girls who were pregnant in high school were not being kicked out of school any more, the way I had been. I went to the library to find out how that had happened.[8] I learned the option for pregnant girls to stay in school arose out of "equal opportunity," a legislative Act called Title IX. The law seemed to say that if boys who impregnated girls could stay in school, then it wasn't fair for girls to be expelled. I was crushed between the fairness to others now and the unfairness to me then. I thought again about the caption under Tom's high school yearbook picture: "Boys will be boys." I had inhaled sharply when I first saw that slogan. And I still did, just picturing it.

Other news items had found their way to me when I clipped articles on adoption. The adoption articles weren't the only news on the page, of course; they were surrounded by other news.

I had read that some women thought television was a hotbed of problems for them. Some women at NBC filed what they called a "sex discrimination suit." A woman's organization—known as the National Organization for Women (NOW)—was often referred to in the papers, too. NOW was making trouble for a couple of television stations, filing petitions with the FTC to deny the renewal of the stations' licenses.[9] A new publication—*Ms. Magazine*—seemed to be another troublemaker. As an arm of NOW, *Ms. Magazine* included articles about how women were portrayed in ads. This complaint seemed nitpicky to me. I didn't understand their concern about women being "sex objects." What was so bad about pretty girls posing with cars?

I had learned more about *Ms. Magazine* and other things in issues of Dave's *Newsweek,* which were around the house. Sometimes I read a few pages when I picked up *Newsweek* to straighten the clutter on an end table or to dust.

Once, I had noticed a special report on family issues. Wondering if there was anything in there about adoption, I read every word. But the report discussed stepfamilies, family therapy and how the family was shown on TV. It didn't relate to me. I wasn't aware of anyone in a stepfamily among my friends, of anyone who went to family therapy, whatever that was, and I didn't see anything wrong with the way the family was shown on TV. No sooner had I thought that, though, then I remembered Tom's multi-step-family. I also remembered I didn't like it any more when Archie told Edith to "stifle."

Over time, I had read more in *Newsweek*. I had begun to notice women's names were listed as writers and reporters. The face of a woman named Barbara Walters, a television news reporter, was plastered on one of *Newsweek*'s covers. I learned she had an adopted daughter. I wondered why these women weren't home with their children and what the real mother of Barbara Walters' daughter thought about her child's adoptive mother bypassing her own living room so she could beam through others' television sets into their living rooms. It seemed every time I opened a new copy of *Newsweek* someone was whining about "women's issues."

I didn't like any of it. I wished the "feminists" — especially an upstart named "Gloria Steinem"—and their organizations would stop trying to change what I knew. Why would I want a career like they harped on? The only career I ever wanted was motherhood.

I didn't let Dave see me read his *Newsweek*s. I didn't want him to wonder if my interests were expanding. They weren't changing; he was safe on that front. If anything, my devotion to him and our family was being reinforced by the news of the day. While I knew he was joking when he talked about dividing our responsibilities—saying I was in charge of the family; he, in charge of the world—I rather liked the idea and believed he did too. Still, if he misperceived why I read *Newsweek*, would he change toward me? How much could I *really* trust my faith in him?

Having circled back to questions, I heard evidence of my career achievement in the TV room. As if on cue, Todd came into the kitchen, asking hopefully: "Time to go, mom?"

1961

Age: 16

New Hampshire

Tom and I were now in our second year together. Since Diane fixed us up, we'd only been apart a few months. When our eighth grade drew to a close, Tom went as usual to his family's cottage at Hampton Beach for the summer. When he returned, he expected us to resume our relationship. But Mom sidetracked me.

Though she took me to Hampton to see Tom a few times, she spent the return trip home telling me how important it was for me to "play the field," which she assured me was how she had spent high school. I could see what she meant. Since many elementary schools fed into our high school, many new friends—boyfriends?—awaited. Didn't I owe it to myself to see if I liked any as much as I liked Tom?

Even before I made the freshman cheerleader squad, several boys let it be known they wanted to be fixed up with me. So I sampled a few to see if Mom was right. But those boys only irritated me, proving they were stand-ins for the boy I really wanted. In the end, I put out my own word: I wanted to go back out with Tom.

Now we were sophomores, a couple known to spend all their spare time together, a couple who even looked alike. That's why I was one of the first to know about the spring fashion show. If I hadn't sabotaged a position on the varsity cheerleading squad by lighting up a cigarette in public, I might have known even sooner. But Tom had learned about it, and that was good enough.

The cheerleader captain had gone into band practice, Tom said, and asked for volunteers to stage entertainment during the breaks in the fashion show. He and a senior, Don, who was also a drummer in the band, had had a good natured feud going all year about which one was the better drummer. Tom argued for Gene Krupa's style; his friend, for Buddy Rich's. They had toyed with the idea of staging a drum battle to settle the dispute once and for all. Tom wanted to know what I thought of it. When I got excited, his enthusiasm uncorked. His eyes, bright with plans, lit me up. "I can't wait to tell Don you think it's a good idea!"

The day of the fashion show was delightful. I remember walking over to the high school hangout, Costa's, for lunch. My jacket hung over my arm instead of me huddling inside it as I had for months. I couldn't wait until after school when Tom and I would walk home together. Then we could inhale the

114

same fragrant spring air and talk about the exciting night that lay ahead for him.

But at the coat racks, Tom apologized. He had forgotten, he explained, about an audition out of town. He couldn't walk me home.

"How far out of town?"

"Not too far," he answered. He seemed evasive. He countered: "Why?"

"Oh, I was just worried about you getting back in time for the drum battle."

A little smile crossed his face. I wondered what he was thinking behind those twinkling gold-brown almonds.

"Oh, I'll be back in plenty of time."

"Will I see you before the show?"

"No. I'll meet you after." He seemed to think about this. "I may be pulling in at the last minute."

Although I had more questions, he quickly grabbed his jacket from the coat hook. As he ran down the school stairs, he called over his shoulder: "See you later, alligator!"

Later, Diane, Candy and I met Sandi outside the high school doors. I was electrified. My Tom would be up there on that stage wowing everybody with his talent! When we arrived I looked all around for him. But Tom was nowhere to be seen.

"Lee, come on," Sandi insisted. "We've got to get seats before it's too late. He'll show up. Don't worry."

We were handed programs as we entered the bustling auditorium. I was relieved to find the drum battle was scheduled last. The overhead lights dimmed and the spotlight illuminated the stage. The cheerleader coach stood tall and slim behind a podium. She had discarded her favorite uniform of pleated skirt, cardigan sweater and blouse for a smartly tailored one-piece dress with a heavy circlet of pearls around her neck.

Candy leaned over. "I'll bet they're pop beads from Woolworth's!" She was not a fan of the coach.

A student from the drama club gave a reading during the break between Casual Dresses and At-Home Slacks. Bored with her, I had time to admit I regretted that a Varsity cheerleader had caught me lighting up the forbidden cigarette in public, which disqualified me to advance from the JV squad to the squad that tonight pranced in new fashions. I had been an enthusiastic cheerleader and would have been a bouncy model. Becoming captain of the Catholic Youth Organization's cheerleading squad had been a decent substitute, but it was a substitute.

During intermission I intensified the search for Tom. I enlisted everyone I could find, but no one had seen him. As if to myself I muttered: "That's really queer."

"Queer? Tom's not queer" quipped Candy.

"Candy," I scolded impatiently, "for God's sake, be serious. Where could he be?" His funny attitude of that afternoon and his conspicuous absence gnawed at me.

Candy sucked in her cheeks to show how hard she was trying to be serious. She looked to each of us, her dark eyes dancing. Finally, Sandi and Diane erupted in laughter. I followed.

Sandi suggested "Maybe Tom's back stage."

"But all the other performers are out here. It's not like Tom to avoid me." Suddenly, I saw Don, the other drummer, in the crowd. I waved and caught his eye. But by the time I got over to where he was standing he had disappeared.

The fashion show continued through the Evening Gowns and Bathing Suits. Now it was time for the last act: Don's and Tom's drum battle.

Unlike the other acts, the heavy, navy blue velvet drapes scooted dramatically across the stage, shielding everything behind them. There was a lot of shuffling, and I imagined new props were being set up, probably the drum sets. It took a while. The audience stirred. There was mystery in the air.

"What's going on?" Candy asked.

"How should I know?" I answered hotly.

"Well, you don't have to get nasty about it, you know."

I turned to her apologetically. "I'm sorry. Just nervous, I guess."

"God! You'd think it was you up there."

I realized that was exactly what I thought. Tom and I were a part of each other. He was like my right arm and I didn't know what my right arm was doing, or even where it was.

The sound of drum beats thumped softly, then more loudly. The audience riveted its attention to the drapes, which slowly drew back. Half of a drum set became obvious and then the other half, with Don behind it. The curtain continued on its way. Another drum set. Empty! A soft murmur spread. Those in the row in front of us turned to me. "Where's Tom?"

I could only shrug helplessly. Now I was getting worried. Had he gotten into an accident? "I *told* you something was wrong," I complained to Diane.

The other drummer began to hammer on his drums.

"Hold it! Hold it!" a loud voice commanded from the back of the auditorium. The heavy doors had noisily swung open, slapping against the seats in the back rows. I cocked my head to see who had disrupted the show. But others had risen from their chairs to do the same and my view was blocked.

"It's Tom!" Candy was standing on her chair to peer over the crowd.

"Tom?" And then I saw him take long strides down the center aisle, sport jacket unbuttoned and flapping behind him, narrow tie askew. One arm was raised like a cop halting traffic.

"Tom?" I could only repeat. *What is he doing?*

He bounded the stairs to the stage, planting himself there, hands on his hips, sport jacket flung behind them. "You think you can start without me?" he yelled.

I slithered down on my spine, covering my face with my hands.

"Look, Lee, look." Diane elbowed me. She shifted in her seat and leaned forward. I noticed everyone around us aped Diane's posture.

I continued my slouch, but I did spread my fingers to peek.

Tom was saying "Why you don't even know how to hold those sticks, never mind play those drums!"

The audience stilled. Then the other drummer began to smile. He tried to cover it quickly by sucking in his cheeks, as Candy had done earlier. But it was too late. Now everyone knew the whole thing had been staged. The audience clapped and cheered at the joke on them.

Tom somehow kept a serious face. I was tremendously impressed.

His voice cut through the noise. "I'll show you how to play the drums properly. Sit there and take a lesson!"

The other drummer now laughed openly. But the audience kept silent, not wanting to miss anything.

"Oh, yeah," Tom finally managed to say. "I think *you* ought to take a lesson from *me.*"

At last I could see Tom's jaw muscle work. This told me -- and only me who knew him so well – that he was suppressing a smile. Then he turned to the audience "We'll let *you* decide."

Tom slid into his seat, picked up the drum sticks and, holding them high, turned them like a majorette with a baton. Then he lowered his head as if to make sure his first beats would be just-so. Soon he began to wail on his drums. After a few seconds, Don yelled "That's nothing." And he tried to one-up Tom. Tom interrupted with several sharp clangs on his cymbals.

I bolted upright. Gnawing on my knuckles, I followed each of them with my eyes, like a ball at a tennis match. They took turns flailing their drum sticks in intricate, loudly thumping patterns. Without missing a beat, Tom slid to the floor and banged against it, then the metal fronts of his set, working his way around to the opposite side of the drum set, where he again took his seat.

Don did the same with his drum set.

They continued to alternate their performance. The time for each performance increased, as did the intricate movements. The tempo built. Then abruptly they stopped and the silence was deafening. The audience burst as one into riotous applause. "More! Morel" they cried.

I could see Tom was tickled and my heart burst with pride. I joined in the chorus insisting on an encore.

The drummers nodded to each other. They began a duo. Thanks to the spotlights, I could see beads of perspiration bubble on their foreheads. The din they created was incredibly moving -- a wild African mood. The audience caught the fever. Like an orchestrated Broadway musical, it seemed everyone moved in their seats in unison: shoulders gyrated, feet tapped. No one was inhibited; by itself, this was a feat in the early '60s where everyone sought others' permission before taking a step and no one marched to their own drummer.

Finally the battle was over. The audience stood to offer the performers their enthusiastic applause and cat whistles.

The overhead lights glared, startling us back to reality. In a trance, I accepted the congratulations of those around me. "Tom was terrific!" "Aren't you proud of him!" I could hear people addressing each other, *"That* was something!" "OUT-standing."

To Diane, Sandi and Candy, I kept saying in wonder "I didn't know…I didn't know."

I stood against a wall in the lobby waiting for him. I saw him walking, craning his neck to look for me, surrounded by his new fans. When he saw me, he smiled broadly. I smiled back, shaking my head. When he reached me, the crowd parted. Diane, Candy and Sandi moved several paces away. Tom and I stood there, grinning at each other. He, sheepishly.

I opened my mouth to speak. It took a second for words to form: "Tom…you skunk…you didn't tell me!"

He threw back his head and roared. I could see others around us laugh too. That he had managed to trick his girlfriend of more than two years the same way he had tricked them seemed to make the whole performance twice as much fun.

As he ushered me to the car where his older brother sat waiting to bring Tom's drum set to their house and to chauffeur us to mine, Tom added: "I knew if I walked home with you after school I'd spill the beans."

"You mean you didn't really have an audition?"

"Nope."

"Tom! You lied to me!"

"That," he emphasized, "was the hardest part of the whole thing. And when I got home from school, I nearly called you. I had to practically sit on my hands."

"But *why* didn't you tell me?"

"Don said if I told you he'd kill me!" he answered, laughing. He opened the car door and I slid in the back seat with him.

"Hi" I called gaily to Tom's brother, my excitement still on overdrive.

He grunted. Tom's expression changed completely. A dark mood descended like a sudden storm.

Confused, I looked between them. I elbowed Tom. After he turned, I cocked my head, knitting my eyebrows together in a question mark. But he didn't offer any comments or body language. Instead, he turned again to stare out the window.

After we were dropped off at my house, Tom and I stealthily made our way into the attached barn, our special place to be alone when it was warm enough. After we pushed the heavy barn door open a little, we shuffled sideways into the barn. As the barn door creaked shut behind us I asked "What's with you and your brother?" Apprehension began to cloud my starry night.

"Nothing much," he answered. He searched in the blackness for our blanket to spread on the floor.

I grabbed his arm. As my heart beat wildly, I demanded: "Tell me!"

He turned to face me. "They're giving me a hard time at home." He sat down and lit a cigarette. I could see him above the match flame, and he looked serious.

I thought how unfair it was that on this night of nights he should be so troubled. Why couldn't everyone at his house leave us alone!

"Your mother?" I asked. "Is she still on our side?"

"I...I don't know. I know my grandmother keeps harping on the subject with her." He looked at me. "I didn't want to worry you."

"Oh, Tom, I love you." I flung my arms around his neck and clutched him as fiercely as if his family was lined up behind him, ready to drag him away by the nape of his neck. He certainly had a strange family situation. I had never heard of anything like it, except maybe Elizabeth Taylor who, now that I thought about it, his mother resembled. Like Liz, Tom's mother had also been married several times. For many years, Tom and his older brother had lived on weekdays with their grandmother and uncle on Manchester's west side. Meanwhile, Tom's other five siblings lived on Manchester's east side with his mother and step-father. Tom lived with his mother only on weekends.

He held me with one arm and ground out his cigarette with his free hand. When he kissed me we clung together as if to make up for a whole winter of postponed making-out. We allowed ourselves to tumble far from the perplexing outside world.

"I love you...I love you...I love you," he murmured urgently, as if he wanted to make sure I understood.

"I know, Tom. I know," I assured him.

We rode together in tandem as if attached to the bridle of a parachute. With abandon, we allowed our strong currents to take us to a faraway place. Along the way, we clung, pressed, and tried to merge through layers of clothing.

As if warring messages shot through his neck, reason angled his head in one direction and the thrust of his body in another. He cried out: Please, baby …please …God …got to…got to."

I was his Siamese twin, sharing the same confusion of pain and pleasure. Desire pulsed through my veins while, lower down, a new hunger gnawed wide, and wider still, until a craving to complete what we started took over.

I could feel his hand jump decisively to his zipper, then hesitate.

I groaned. "No, Tom, no."

"Oh, baby," he sighed loudly. Several moments of mounting agony passed. "Just let me take off my trousers. I'm so hot!"

I passed my lips over his forehead wet with perspiration. "Okay" I agreed. While he slipped them off, I took time to try to compose myself. He laid beside me, breathing heavily.

"Let's take a minute," he said. "I've got to cool off."

Side by side, we tried to stop panting. The knowledge that his jockey shorts were exposed tantalized me. Although our eyes had by now adjusted to the dark and I could have seen them, I didn't dare. Instead, I wondered what he looked like in them, what he felt like in them. These thoughts excited me and I leaned over to kiss him. We were off again.

I could feel him better. I was trying to envision how his body connected together when he whispered "I'm going to take it out."

I waited in anticipation.

He misread me. "I won't do anything. I promise… just take it out."

I nodded. And then I could feel the whole of him, as nature had made him. It was thrilling.

My woolen skirt lay in tangles about my sweating waist. I felt his hard, swollen penis as it ground against the front of my cotton pants and then it flipped between my legs, pushing relentlessly at the barrier of my panty's crotch, thrusting the cotton into my vagina. My canal behind the opening expanded into a moist, throbbing cavern, needing his plug to fill it, to thrust through to my brain, to send signals of appeasement that would override the tension in my body. I wanted him to tear aside the crotch of my panties, take me, fulfill me, love me on the inside to balance the love that poured from me to the outside. I writhed, twisted and ground with him, agonizing at the delay.

He groaned pathetically and loudly, and started to manipulate it with a swift motion back inside his shorts, saying "Sh… shouldn't have d… done that …." But it remained out, throbbing against me.

I knew we were nearing a decision. I acted without realizing it. I pulled up my knees between us and flung him off me. I pushed him to the side. I suffered with him.

Later I said, "I'm sorry. I had to do that. Do you understand?"

He knelt beside me. He took my face between his palms.

His eyes looked as mushy as mine felt. *"I'm* the one who is sorry, baby." He dropped his hands and leaned his back against the wall. He exhaled so deeply, the old barn sighed n return. "I let it go too far. You did absolutely the right thing. I didn't want to do anything to you. Oh, I mean, I did." He looked at me, gesturing emphatically with his hands for me to understand.

I nodded.

"But I couldn't hurt you. I never want to hurt you." He raised his eyes to the rafters lining the ceiling.

"I'm going to try to never lose control like that again." He turned to me, "But if I do…promise me you'll always say no. Promise?"

"Yes, Tom. I will. I'll always say no."

There would be no more making out in the barn. We had gone there several times since the drum battle. Each time we became aroused beyond pleasure, to the point of pain. Tom had tried setting little rules for us. No lying down, stopping before we got too hot, and so on. Nothing worked. We learned history would repeat itself and we'd look at each other, feeling frustrated and raw. "No more" Tom had said in a maddeningly responsible voice, and he meant it.

I was realistic enough to know our relationship was ideal. I, too, didn't want to introduce a new element, especially one that would likely be continued. We had two more years to go before we could fulfill our commitment to marry. We already felt guilty about taking things as far as we did. If going All The Way produced even more guilt in Tom and me, could our relationship remain good? It wasn't worth the risk.

Yet, I loved becoming aroused and the emotions it sparked. I loved hovering with Tom on the brink of the tantalizing unknown called sex. Each time was different, challenging in a new way. Would we stop? Could we stop? I knew I would miss it. But now we limited ourselves to time with my family, as we always had; to double-dates we fixed up with his friends and mine; and, for our only alone-time, we spent days cuddled in the crevice of "our" boulder by the Merrimack River.

1974

Age: 29

Cape Cod

I could only thank God my high school pal, Sandi, was coming for a visit. She had stuck with me through all the awfulness, even visiting me in the home for unwed mothers despite her mother thinking it was a bad idea. Now married and a mother— roles that arrived for her in the right order—Sandi and her family planned to spend a weekend with us. She and I still had things in common. We loved our husbands, kids, clothes, and home decorating.

Most important to me now, though, Sandi, more than anyone, might understand what I was putting myself through. There was even some hope she would understand why I had to do it. If she figured it out, I would ask her to explain it to me. Since I apparently couldn't sort out my own thoughts, Sandi seemed the next-best bet.

I began by confessing to her I had been upset because I wasn't invited to our class' tenth reunion. She looked into my soul with her familiar crystal blue eyes and said she wasn't surprised I was remembering. She thought I had "put it away too fast." When I told her forgetting was the professional advice I had been given, she said she had always known the advice was "bull-pucky." Then she offered a little gallows humor: "You should have asked me."

A possible answer to one of my "why" questions was in my ear space: I had put it away "too fast." Then I remembered why I hadn't wanted such answers in the first place. Answers only gave rise to more questions.

Sandi said she had expected me to "feel it" someday. Why hadn't she warned me? But on the heels of wishing she had warned me I now knew if Sandi had waved a flag in my face, I would have cracked the flagpole over my knee or over her head. I would have denied, denied, denied and not known I was denying.

Did this mean Sandi knew me better than I knew myself? What does it say about a person when others see places inside her she can't?

Maybe that's true of all of us? Maybe it takes someone on the outside to see others objectively on the inside? I still had so many defenses in play that windows to my mind were effectively shuttered. It was different for Sandi. She had wanted—still wanted—me to be happy, so her sensitivities were activated but not her personal defense system.

Over the weekend we did the usual: clamming, cooking, and taking our kids here and there. On their last night, we plunked her son in the bathtub with Scott and Todd. We casually moved the water around them in lazy circles. While the water was still tepid, we cupped some in our palms, upending them to gently rain on the boys' shoulders. We talked. We mused like old friends will do.

When Sandi and her family left, she invited me to let her know what I was writing. Joking, she said she wanted to read the parts I wrote about her. That was sweet, but I didn't know if I could tap support 180 miles away. Charges for long distance calls were too great for regular updates. Since I wasn't fluent in self-explanatory words, and wasn't motivated enough to become fluent, much of what I might say to Sandi would likely be gibberish anyway.

Still, it was good to know she knew what little I did. I stoppered her strong caring like it was a decorative bottle of Avon perfume. I imagined a place for it on my desktop. In my memory-writing, I knew I was about to turn a corner. If I needed smelling salts, hers just might help me come around.

1961

Age: 16

New Hampshire

As Tom and I walked home from school with spring finally warming our winter-chapped cheeks, he suggested we play hooky the next day. He thought we should spend some time at our place by the river. I threw my head back in surprise. I had played hooky a few times, after getting Mom's permission. She knew I was good for a day off. The next afternoon I'd stay after school to make up the work I missed, Mom would sign my absence note and nothing would be lost. But Tom had never played hooky. My surprise grew when I discovered he had given this adventure some thought. He had it all worked out. "I'll get excused after first period," he said. "But I think it would be better if you waited until second period. Okay?"

The next morning I packed a lunch big enough for an Army. I remember looking out the jalousie kitchen windows as I wrapped sandwiches in waxed paper. Even the morning felt warm. Knowing I would meet Tom by the river for a day of snuggling and talking made the day the most perfect, ever.

After second period I went into the Ladies Room and removed my lipstick. I practiced several sick-looking faces in the mirror and decided on one particularly convincing one. I positioned it and went to the principal's office.

Mr. Boland looked at me after I made my request, silently playing with the pencil on his desk. "Are you sure you can't stay in school?"

I faked a groan. "I'd rather go home."

"Then you won't mind if I call your mother to come and get you?"

I hadn't expected that. I kept my expression fixed. "No … no … I don't mind." I wondered how I was going to pull this off now.

After he told my mother I was not well and asked her to come and get me, I asked hesitatingly "May I talk with her, please?" The principal handed me the phone. "Mom? Listen. I really think the walk will do me good. I'll see you in 15 minutes, okay?"

I had satisfied Mr. Boland. He knew my mother was aware I would not be in school. I could still sneak down to the river to tell Tom the deal was off. Then I'd go home. But on the way I passed a phone booth and got inspired. I searched in my pocketbook for a dime and finally found a lint-covered one. I blew on it and dialed my home number. "Mom, I'm really feeling much better. I think I'll stay in school after all."

"You sure?" She sounded worried.

"Oh, yes. It was a bad headache but it's going, I think." Although I didn't like lying to Mom, I couldn't help but feel triumphant when I emerged from the phone booth. I reasoned I'd tell Mom about it sooner or later. In the meantime, I could have my day with Tom.

Giggling with my success in outmaneuvering Mr. Boland, I ran to the river. Tom was standing on the boulders looking for me. I waved a wide sweeping hello and he enthusiastically waved back.

"Hi!" I called as I got closer.

He grinned widely as if to say, wasn't this a great idea? "How did it go?"

I told him and he shook his head. "That was quick thinking!"

I was proud he thought so. "How did it go with you? Did the old man give *you* any trouble?"

"No" he said, taking my books and setting them on the boulder beside his. "Not a bit. I just went in there and tried to look sick …and he let me go."

I laughed, remembering my own face. "Let me see it."

"See what?"

"Your sick face!"

He lowered his eyes half-shut, exaggerated a downturn of the corners of his mouth, while tilting his head lopsided. He looked wonderfully ridiculous.

We sat down on the warm boulders. Aiming my face into a sunbeam, I mused, "I wonder why he gave *me* so much trouble."

Tom cocked his head, looking at my face from all angles. "Maybe because you're the healthiest looking sick kid he's seen all day!"

"He's only seen two probably. You and me." I snapped my fingers. "Hey! Do you suppose he knows we are going out. That would make sense."

Tom thought. "No. How can they keep track of who goes out with who. West is a big school." He considered the possibility further. "Well, we have been going out for a long time."

"More than two years," I reminded him, a smile splitting my face.

"And two more to go," he said, adding, "Let's sit in our chair."

We descended to our craggy nest, a crevice in a large boulder. Part of a bank of other boulders, "our chair" had a niche that fit our backs if we cuddled close; it even had a fairly smooth seat upon which we could plunk our butts. We began to make out. Later, I sat nestled in his arms, allowing the swooshing sound of the river to sweep around us like a velvet cape. Above, two birds on a branch sat side-by-side like lovers on a bench, caroling as though it was Christmas. On the riverbank beyond, a flock of their extended family darted among the trees. As they swooped, they draped their airy streams in scalloping. It reminded me of the scene in Walt

Disney's *Cinderella* when birds wound long strips of organza over Cinderella's bell-shaped dress. I remembered her dress was pale blue, just like the heavens that was backdrop to all the nature I was seeing as if for the first time.

Tom nuzzled his face in my hair. He kissed my neck, sending shivers to my big toes. As I turned to receive another kiss, I looked into and through his eyes. Wondrous things echoed there. I was as intoxicated as the taste of champagne I'd had last New Year's.

"I love you, Lee," he said.

I never tired of hearing him tell me. Not that long ago, Mr. Cool had choked on those words. When he first admitted it, I felt as if I had brought a colt to halter.

While I had had to wait until he told me first, those "three little words" easily left my own tongue. All members of my family wore "love" like their favorite bathrobes.

Tom looked at me, one eyebrow cocked.

"Oh," I said, realizing I had hesitated with my answer. "Tom? How do you make one eyebrow shoot up like that?

He offered his shy smile. "I don't know. It's not anything special. My eyebrows just go where I tell them to."

"Wow." I experimented with my own commands. "Am I doing it now?" I felt blindly above my eyes to find both eyebrows had sprung to my hairline. "No? Am I hopeless?" Then I brightened, "Maybe I need to train them." I admitted to Tom I was still trying to straighten my pug nose. "See" I described, pointing to parts of my nose, "before I go to bed, I take a strip of scotch tape, stick it to the top of my nose, bring it over the tip, and then down under my chin."

"I hope you give up on all that before we get married." He laughed. "I don't want to sleep with you if you have tape all over your nose. Besides, I like your nose just the way it is."

I was quiet for a few seconds, imagining sleeping with him. Then I imagined how his straight nose and my pug nose would combine in our children. "Our kids will be beautiful," I decided out loud. "And, back to the eyebrows, do you think it would help if I also taped one eyebrow up while I slept?"

Obviously imagining the taped eyebrows alongside the taped nose, Tom laughed. He placed a hand on each of my brows, pushed one down, and pulled the other up. "There you go! I think it would be easier if I just followed you around like this."

Settling back, he told me, "You know, Jackie wants to meet you."

"Jackie? Your brother?" He had so many siblings from his mother's several marriages that it was hard to keep track of their names. It would have helped if his family had invited me to spend time with them the way mine did with Tom. But that wasn't how they did things, apparently.

"Yes. I told him all about you."

"You did? Really? What did you tell him?"

"I told him you were pretty and that I loved you. I also told him we were going to get married after graduation and have three kids."

I mouthed a stunned "Wow."

"What will we name them? Our kids, I mean?" he asked.

We decided our first born, a son, would be named after him. Then we threw out many girls' names. Finally, we decided on Barbara Ellen, the Ellen after his mother to keep her on our side, and Deborah Lee.

I sighed."I can hardly wait."

"It'll go by fast," he assured me. "Look how fast these past years have gone."

"Well, all these decisions have made me hungry" I declared. I stood and pulled him by the arm. "Upsy-daisy."

We retrieved our lunch bags, found the warmest boulder on the block, and relished our time together—outdoors, in public—not in the barn and not chaperoned by my family as we usually were.

Afterward we returned to our chair and cuddled together. We closed our eyes, enjoying our peaceful place. Later he said "God, I nearly fell asleep."

Drowsily I answered, burrowing further into his arms, "That would have been soooo nice."

Then I looked at him, and was overwhelmed. [10] A promise shone brighter in his almond eyes than the mid-day sun on our shoulders. I was reminded of an old song by Gene Autry: "You are my sunshine, my only sunshine. You make me happy when skies are grey. You'll never know dear, how much I love you. Please don't take my sunshine away." The last line dragged a cloud over my head. I mentally swatted at it, as if it was a pesky fly. I would not allow any bad notions to settle nearby.

As time grew close to when we usually arrived home, Tom scooped up my books along with his own and, as usual, filed the stack under his arm. With his free hand, he held one of mine. In happy silence, we walked along the dirt path toward the street. Tree branches in light flower arched overhead, screening the sky. At the end of the path, we pivoted onto the busy city street that led to my house. He turned toward his own to practice forging an absence note and I went home to share my day with Mom.

For dinner, Mom made my favorite meal: baked ham with pineapple, scalloped potatoes, cauliflower *au gratin*, and cinnamon rolls. We girls rotated after-dinner clean up and my job that night was to clear the table, package the leftovers, and put them in the refrigerator. There were a lot of leftovers. As I parceled these into small bowls with saucered lids, I realized I would have to open and close the refrigerator a few times before all the leftovers were put away. The door was on a tight hinge and always annoyingly shut itself before we were through shoving stuff inside.

As I went about my mindless task, I recalled Gene Autry's soft croon about losing his sunshine. I suddenly got the idea to have my own "Beat the Clock" show. I would challenge the clock of love. I lined the leftovers on the countertop; there were about six bowls. I took a couple more items—Miracle Whip and Heinz ketchup—out of the refrigerator to add to the counter line-up. I didn't want to make things too easy. I wouldn't fix my game like the quiz show "Twenty-One." No scandals for me, not even in private. With items in place for my race with time, I reminded myself of the rules I'd made for my game: "If I can get all these things into the refrigerator before the door closes, I'll know Tom will love me forever." I almost made it. Only the blood-red bottle of ketchup remained on the counter.

A few days later, Tom and I watched "American Bandstand" while we waited, as always, for The Kids to come home. Donna and Richard would soon charge in the door, looking for another drum lesson. Ever patient with them, Tom would pull drumsticks from the binder of the three-ring notebook he carried to school. Then he and the kids would pound MaMa-PaPa on a variety of surfaces—books, pans, whatever—as Tom tried to instill in them the right drum beat. Meanwhile, I noticed that The Shirelles were guests on the show to sing their record "Will You Still Love Me Tomorrow?"

As the camera panned the teenage dancers on the show, Tom pointed to a couple on the floor. "There's your favorite. You know, people think you and I are Manchester's Kenny and Arlene. A cute couple, they call

139

us." He tilted his head and dimpled his cheeks with his fingers in a sure-fire way to make me laugh.

Absently, I answered "But you don't dance. If I am going to dance, which you know I love to do, I have to go to Club 96 on Friday nights while you practice with your band or go on a gig."

The light in his eyes briefly shuttered, as if he held something back.

Suddenly concerned about secrets between us, I admitted being defeated by my game to beat the clock. Pointing to the television screen where the Shirelles were taking a bow, I pouted, on the verge of tears: "You aren't going to love me tomorrow!"

Tom looked at me with surprise. Then he burst out laughing, throwing his head back. This was not his usual laugh. His more normal laugh was a wide, closed-mouth grin, as if he was too shy to fully open up. To me his grin was sweet, reminding me of Elvis Presley's "Teddy Bear." But now, with every guffaw he folded over, lower and lower, looking up at me between folds to confirm I was for real. Soon he was in full roar, falling from the couch to the floor on his knees.

From his place on the floor, he offered, "Lee, you are such a nut!" Seeing my serious face, he added: "Look, you've got to believe me. I'm going to love you forever. In fact, I'll bet you are going to stop loving me first."

I protested. "No way, Jose."

"Ok," he said, "here's the bet. If you stop loving me first, you owe me $10. If I stop loving you first, I'll give you $10."

Between Tom's reassurance, and the Kids who now tromped in with their innocent energy, I was back on my happy track.

1974

Age: 29

Cape Cod

After I channeled the river scene onto paper, I sat like a statue as I usually did, trying to find room inside to store yet another layer of memories, readying myself to deflect yet another round of questions. But this time, when my ring finger pressed a period after the last sentence, the punctuation mark ricocheted off the page and splattered into my third eye. The splatter was too abrupt to repel, too messy to quickly mop up, and too terrible to ignore. My 29-year-old heart had been in flight—high and low, but mostly high—throughout the scenes. Sitting at the desk, my hands in my lap, I could feel my eyes soften.

Not with tears. With...Oh, God...could it be? *Was I still in love with Tom? No, **NO!***

What damage had my social worker done? She never tried to explore with me my feelings for Tom. Thinking now about my sessions with her, I remembered one of my fantasies back then. In this fantasy, Carole intuited—

finally, correctly—that my bristling about Tom was a clue to how I really felt: despite calling him a rat, I really still loved him, missed him, agonized every minute over the loss of him.

It would not have been impossible for her to figure that out. Surely she had learned in social work school that hate and love are opposite sides of the same coin. Even I had read that somewhere, and what did I know? In my fantasy, she would see my truth. She would call in his family and try to mediate our situation. That failing, she would advise him to run away with me. I now exhaled a full-bodied sigh, punctuating it with **Damn it all to hell**.

I mentally shook myself by the shoulders. That was then. But what damage was I—without help from anyone— doing to myself now? There was no reason for me to continue to love Tom, not after…everything. Then Donna's replay of her conversation with Tom abruptly interrupted: "My wife was pregnant when we got married," Tom had told her. "My mother tried to break us up but I wouldn't let her do that to me again."

What did that mean? Why did Tom tell Donna that? Was he trying to send me a message? Surely he knew Donna would tell me, just as my sisters had told him things about me. Was Tom also having a hard time putting our situation behind him?

I firmly insisted none of that mattered any more. I loved my husband; he was a fine man and he was exceptionally good to me. And my precious kids? They were, well, my very life. I wished I could find a comfortable place—a safe space—where I could protect my feelings for my family from the onslaught of my past.

I wanted a hippie handbook. I wanted to memorize the page where hippies talked about living in the moment. In a commune with other hippies I might have been able to practice hanging out in the now. It sounded like something specially ordered for me.

I wanted to learn how to hold onto present-time. Sometimes, I could grab the tail of a moment but it always slipped away like a kite on a sudden gust, leaving me mired in yesterday or, to remedy that, fixated on tomorrow. [11] I needed an everlasting present-moment right about … now. Thanks to my memories, time was a quandary.

While I typed a scene, I was in a blissful void where words just flew through me. In the next moment, with the words on a page, I was drawn into the past, where the memories were first made. No sooner was I back there than an uprise of confusion thrust me onto an uncertain horizon of tomorrows. That blissful void, that specific scene's present moment when I was betwixt and between, where did it go? How could I hold onto it?

Time wasn't the only quandary. I could not predict my emotional or physical reaction to a scene. My reaction to the river scene was different than my reaction to other scenes. After other scenes, I was in a stupor and had to usually make myself move. Now, though, not only was I aghast at being still in love with Tom—IF I was—but I was jittery. I needed to get rid of some excesses: excess love, excess questions, excess confusion. I had to get away from the house. Take the kids and go. I needed to tell someone. It would have cost a fortune to call Sandi. I needed someone local. I needed another confidante. Which of my friends would be safe enough for me to blow my cover? Pictures of my current friends paraded across my mind. I blew a traffic whistle on the first.

Smiling at me was my pal, Marie, she with gentle blue eyes in a Mary Worth face and a thick blonde confection of a hair bun. I remembered affectionately I hadn't been in Brewster two days before she arrived on my doorstep. Like the Welcome Lady, she carried gifts and goodies, which she had made herself. Afterward, she called frequently to ask how I was doing, and soon we were fast friends. We shared typing jobs, recipes, went to the beach together, coffee-klatched together, and I trusted and valued her enough to reveal everyday complaints about my husband as she did hers. Time and again, she had proven her quest to be kind. I committed, with a pronounced gulp, to brave a talk with Marie.

When I told her I had something important to tell her, she asked if I wanted to come over. I did indeed want to go over. Her full-Cape was the perfect setting, if there was such a thing. I had loved Marie's house since she and her husband bought it through an estate sale. It was a wreck when they took it over, but it was built in 1777 and a perfect fit for their interests. They named it "Old Glory," painted the name on a quarter-board to hang out front, and

144

then they proceeded to return their old Cape to its former glory.

As the rehab got underway, Marie decorated in warm-and-friendly, becoming by example my mentor in all things antique. From the "keeping room's" exposed beams and fireplace, she suspended ironware interspersed with sea grasses, which she collected from the beach and dried upside down in the "borning room." She then divided her assortment into small bouquets, wrapping the stems together with strips of rawhide.

Cozily crowded upon the wide, yellow-pine floorboards throughout "Old Glory" were pieces of pine furniture in a deep patina coaxed by her husband, who liked to track yard sales for finds he could refinish. Meanwhile, Marie liked to pick out reproduction wallpaper and wall paint in colors that were authentically colonial. She also stenciled old milk jugs and metal trays, probably giving away more as gifts, including to me, than she kept.

After we settled the boys with Marie's kids in a front parlor, Marie and I worked in her kitchen. We made tuna sandwiches mixed with chopped dill pickles. The goal was to forestall our children's inevitable check on the food situation, which would put them in earshot. But I was scared to reveal my story and couldn't eat. That alone got her attention, as she knew me to eat…a lot. I was glad our usual cups of tea were already poured into her antique china cups so I could sip from mine and appear more normal. I inhaled some steam to talk.

Some will to follow-through wafted toward me from the area behind my chair. I was comfortable in that space. To me, Marie's house embodied the passage of time in a peaceful way I could only hope to have in my own life. On some earlier visits with Marie, I had given a little nod to any spirit who may have lived in or visited Old Glory over the centuries. I now felt a return nod. For the feeling—even if it was just wishful thinking—I was grateful.

Marie wasted no time. "What's up, sweetie?"

With Marie I would need more words than I needed with Sandi. I would have to start at the beginning, which Sandi already knew. But words came in a whoosh, as if from the bellows that decorated the hearth of Marie's fireplace. To my ear, telling my tale to Marie seemed a little less discombobulated than it had with Sandi. Maybe it was a little easier with Marie because telling Sandi had given me some experience? Or maybe it was harder with Sandi because the pipeline to our shared history was pre-primed with raw emotion closer to the surface? Though easier with Marie, the telling was still intense, and soon she was fetching me tissues and looking as miserable as I felt.

As it turned out, some of her misery wasn't for me. Her first comments were about David. She wondered if I had told David about Michael before we married. Learning I had, Marie explained her concern, saying it would be hard for me to tell David after-the-fact since "he always seemed to like things nice and proper."

I didn't know what to expect from Marie, but her response missed the mark. I was no longer good and proper? Quickly I realized she wasn't the one judging me; I was the one judging me. I knew Marie was Compassion Personified, capital C.P. I knew I could keep talking and she would keep listening. But would I first have to understand what I was talking about?

I wondered how necessary that really was. Maybe I had expected too much of myself? Maybe in fumbling to explain things to Marie I would be more able to explain things to myself? On the other hand, maybe I would just confuse myself further and lose Marie's support? I was back to arm-wrestling with my various selves.

What did I really want to do? Did I want to type and think, to type and tell, or to just type, shut down, and shut the hell up? I admitted that telling Sandi and Marie ironed more wrinkles in my brain than did arguing back and forth with myself.

What I did with Sandi and Marie was to hand over some of my brain work. In the end, it hadn't turned out quite as strange as I thought it would. It wasn't so different from passing-on other things. After all, I knew how to hand things up, down, over, and off. As the oldest of five, I handed things down. As an adult, I handed over recipes and offered childcare to friends. I handed off my typing business. As a mother and a wife, I shared love. With that thought, I realized handing-over was a kind of sharing. I always got something back, too. Stronger relationships, more fun, more love.

147

Isn't that what women do? Share? I thought of my tea time with Marie, and the ritual that sharing had been for women across time. Instead of shutting out sharing, I should try to get more of it. But I sensed I had wheelbarrows of unfinished work to share.

Sandi, living far away, wasn't easily available to me. And I didn't want to wear out Marie. It would be lopsided to lean on her too much, and I hadn't detected any need she could share with me that would even things out. But, with a third friend, maybe I could spread out my brain work a little more.

I decided to tell my friend, Deb. A couple of years before, Deb had brought over her two young boys to play with Scott and Todd. There was nothing unusual about that. This time, though, she had a dilemma. Collapsing her long, lean body on the back step, she told me she had recently acquired a lot of letters, papers and journals that had been handed down through her husband's family, a family whose 18th century ancestors had helped to settle Brewster.

"What am I supposed to do with all this?" she asked with a little laugh. "I mean, it seems to me I should do *something*."

It was clear to me what she needed to do. "You must write a book, Deb. You might have to fictionalize it, if you don't have enough day-to-day info in your materials. But put your degree in creative writing to work. People are already talking about the bicentennial; the timing is perfect."

She looked thoughtfully at me. "I think I knew that. I just needed someone else to say out loud what I didn't realize I'd been thinking." She trilled a little laugh in her throat. "If you know what I mean."

I did. And as she began to put her book together, she ferried drafts over to me. If she got discouraged, I encouraged. Often, I also freed more time for her to write by taking her boys for a play date. Since then she had received a book contract with a major publisher for a nice chunk of change. She told me sharing her thoughts about her book with me had been helpful.

Yes, Deb was a good one to talk with. I knew she would reciprocate what I had offered her, and she was a good listener. I also knew she could keep a confidence, which suggested to me she may have learned to guard secrets the way I had, the hard way. I felt there was a lot to Deb under that relaxed and easy-going way of hers.

I was right. Deb was a find. She told me she had taken college courses in psychology. Then she paused, as if to gauge whether she should say more. Probably because I had taken such a risk with her, she took one with me. She revealed she had taken herself to a counselor once, when she was younger. I could tell that was hard for her to admit, and I could understand why. Counseling was considered the last resort, and she thought if people knew that about her, she'd be ostracized. But she wanted me to know I wasn't crazy. Using her experience, she offered her perspective of what was happening.

"In each of us," she began, "there is a part of the psyche...."

"Psyche?" I interrupted. I wanted to make sure I understood every strand that went into this lifeline she wiggled my way.

"It's part of the brain you can't see in an X-ray. It's one way the mind works." Seeing I understood, she continued. "In this psyche—this hidden part of the brain—is something Freud calls an...." She paused as if to underscore "*unconscious*. Have you ever heard of Freud?"

I nodded. Heard of him, yes. Did I know details of his work? No. But I knew she was about to tell me about it, and I was all ears. "How does the unconscious work in the mind?" I asked. "What does it do?"

"For one thing, it stores memories and the everyday things you see but don't think are important. Dreams are made there, too. If the unconscious becomes... uncomfortable...with what it knows and thinks it's something you should learn, it finds some way to display it to you."

"Like, as part of a dream?"

"Yes, or like throwing all those memories at you. Your unconscious must think this is stuff you should know about. Maybe it got tired of being your warehouse," she joked.

"It should raise its fees, then," I joked back. "I would pay more rent if it would keep warehousing my memories. But seriously, it's costing me, well, everything, to be at the mercy of these memories. I don't get why they are important. There's nothing I can do about them."

"Once the unconscious makes a decision to unfurl itself, there's nothing you can do to stop it. Maybe hypnosis, but I wouldn't recommend that."

"Oh, I don't know. Hypnosis sounds good to me. I think I've been trying to hypnotize myself to get control of the memories. But they are stronger than anything I can do. I would undergo hypnosis, as long as I didn't come away," I laughed, "clucking like a chicken."

Deb's chuckles tapered to a point. "I don't know why the memories are back, Lee. I just know you have to listen to them, hear them out. They are trying to teach you something. It's quite amazing, isn't it?"

"That's one word for it," I admitted, now feeling stuffed with even more words that I couldn't apply, at least not yet. But Deb was alive and well and functional after her ordeal, and that was promising to me.

Deb was willing to explore with me the psychology of what I was going through. Marie continued to exercise her empathy muscle. And, when I could afford it, Sandi was a phone call away.

I could focus more on typing. It was now the end of July; I had been memory-channeling for five weeks and in three more weeks I would have to report for duty at the school. I knew I was about to crash into troubling parts of my story. To get through it and to meet my deadline, I vowed to type even faster. No perfectionism for me. When I had a typo, I would use it for momentum. I would back-space to the errors, xxxx over them, and rocket forward as mindlessly as my unconscious would let me.

MORE

From my unpublished dissertation:
Women and Mentoring: The Tradition, the Process, the Vision.
The Union Institute. 1993.

During the Inquisition, women were tortured until they framed other women as witches. To avoid that, some ran into the ocean in group suicides.

*

After these "Burning Times," Lillian Faderman (1981) says women in the 18th and 19th century recuperated as a collective by forming "sentimental friendships." As she examined the correspondence of 19th century women, Lillian said it was virtually impossible to find any that did not reflect "a passionate commitment to another woman."

*

After World War I, the common view of women as asexual collided with the new Freudian view of sexualized women. This raised questions of lesbianism between affectionate women.

*

As a result, women restrained themselves. They re-centered their discussions on men, such as suitable candidates for husbands and proper marital behavior. Also meeting with social approval were interactions between women that were purposeful and domestic.

Women provided a wide range of helping to each other such as tending children, offering transportation, and shopping for fashions. They mentored each other in traditions like spiritual rituals, pottery, chanting, dancing, weaving, quilting, embroidery, sewing, and mending clothes. Their mentoring also included decorum, décor, furniture placement and personal and family grooming.

*

Women sought each other at church services, quilting bees, genteel teas, and coffee klatches. In some circles, they also met in meetings of abolitionists, suffragettes, prohibitionists and feminists

*

As society shifted what it meant to be a successful woman, women's mentoring also shifted its contents. Mentoring could adapt because mentoring between women is not a separate, definable entity; it was, and is, an energy—a process characterized by encouragement, support, mutuality, friendship, a "caring family of traits," and informal teaching.

CHAPTER SEVEN

1974

AGE: 29

CAPE COD

- AND –

1961 – 1962

AGE: 16-17

NEW HAMPSHIRE

1961

Age 16

New Hampshire

The presence of Tom's mysterious mother—Ellen—filled our kitchen. Perfume alone, she took over the house. We were overdue for a visit; rather, I was overdue for a visit at her house. Her son had been a member of our family for years but she apparently had never understood the etiquette of returning that favor to me. Problem was, this wasn't a social call. This was a call to arms: to remove me from Tom's.

Tom had arrived late at his grandmother's house, where his mother was scheduled as usual to pick him up and take him back to her house for the weekend. But when he opened his grandmother's back door, Ellen said he promptly "threw up all over the place." He was drunk.

Unfortunately, I had been in his company earlier in the day and hadn't been successful in monitoring the line between a slug of Chianti and too much Chianti. I didn't have experience with alcohol. He hadn't had enough experience either, or so he proved. As he grabbed for his turn at the bottle, I reminded him that the Chianti wasn't a good idea, that his mother was waiting. Ellen was furious I hadn't done more.

She looked from my mother to me in stony silence. She clenched her mouth firmly, making faint parenthetical marks on either side of her ruby lips. She flew at me in a rage, shaking her finger not two inches from my face. I threw my head back to suppress an urge to bite her finger. Then she sprang for my mother, who backed away the way I had.

"Do you know what…what that daughter of yours did?" She continued to shake her finger at me, while she glared at Mom.

Mom was struck dumb for a second; then she recovered. "Now, let's calm down. Let's go into the TV room where we can sit down and discuss this. I just got home and Lee was about to tell me something. It was probably about this. My daughter tells me everything. You know," Mom added as she led the way, "I don't think you should be saying these things about Lee. You don't even know her. Have *you* ever made an effort to get to know her?"

Tom's mother was suddenly at a loss for words. She silently followed my mother down the hall. I took up the rear, not knowing what to say either.

Before I sat on the loveseat in the TV room, I looked out the window behind it. Through the window, I saw Tom sitting with a man in his mother's black Ford. His uncle? His step-father? I expected Tom to come in the house. I needed that to happen for, surely, he would know how to deal with her. I was worried I'd say the wrong thing.

Ellen launched into a more controlled tirade. "I want you to tell me who gave Tom that stuff he drank." It was an imperial command.

My thoughts raced. Tattle-tale. Stool pigeon. I was certain she would tell the authorities if she knew names. But I didn't know names either. We had climbed into a car owned by someone Tom called "Gerry." It was Gerry's friend who had offered the Chianti; I didn't know Gerry's friend's name. What would Tom want me to do? I confessed I wasn't any help.

She replied evenly:"You're lying." Her eyes glinted like rusty nails, which she threw my way as if she hoped they were spiked with tetanus. I gave her a little more, all I had to give really. "Well, his first name's Gerry but I don't know his last name." My eyes kept returning to the window. Why didn't Tom come in here and help me out?

Ellen sat down and lit a cigarette. I remember Ellen wore black slacks, which zippered in the back. She also had on a blue print long-sleeved blouse in a soft fabric. The bracelets on her wrist jangled as she shook out the match. She was incredibly glamorous, looking for all the world like Joan Collins. Finally up close to her, though, I could now see that she wore too much make-up and her hair appeared to be dyed its harsh blue-black color.

I looked out the window again and saw Tom leave the car. He ran by the window. "Oh, good," I thought. "He's coming in the house."

"…college only one year. I guess I was impressed by his uniform…much too young…" Tom's mother was talking but I hardly heard her. My ears were trained on the back door where I expected to hear Tom's arrival.

157

"Leona!" Ellen barked. "Are you listening to me?" Almost no one knew my legal name. How had she learned *that*? It made her seem even more powerful.

"Yessss. Tom…I thought he was…Is he alright?"

After she told me he was "disgustingly drunk," I looked out the window again. I saw Tom get back in the car. That was confusing. I wondered why he hadn't continued into the house.

"…have been seeing too much of each other." Ellen had resumed talking and her words shot me back to reality. "I think you and Tom should separate. See other people."

I sat suspended. "We've tried that," I said, remembering a self-imposed time-out we had tried the previous fall. With body language that read "helpless," I tried to make her understand. What she was asking was impossible. I stared at her for so long without blinking, my eyes felt dry.

Mom spoke up. "I agree they've been seeing too much of each other."

Now Mom was the shocker. I would have expected Dad to say that. He quietly reasoned everything out inside himself and then hit you by surprise. But Mom always spoke from her heart, never sheltering her thoughts. Whatever she thought, she said. And, she had never so much as hinted Tom and I were seeing too much of each other.

Mom explained: "I don't think we ought to force them to break up, however. They'll just sneak out behind our backs and I won't have Lee sneak around."

Ellen exhaled a long stream of cigarette smoke and ground the butt forcefully in the floor ashtray beside her chair. She stood up. Up. And up. Even though she wasn't much taller than my mother and me, she was like the giant in "Jack and the Beanstalk" after he was disturbed by the "smell of an Englishman." She boomed, "Tommy will do as I say." She slowly enunciated each word: "Tommy. Will. Do. As. *I*. Say."

In a trance I politely walked Ellen back to the kitchen door. When she left, I didn't try to emerge from the trance. It was a more comfortable place to be.

Diane, Candy and I were climbing the stairs to the high school the next morning when, out of the corner of my eye, I saw the black Ford drive up to the curb. Something told me not to turn around but to continue into the building. Once inside, I burrowed into a sheltered corner, away from the windowed doors. I waited. Diane and Candy went ahead, up the wide, dusty stairs.

Tom came through the door. Out of the corner of his mouth, he said "Wait until I've gone up the stairs and then meet me at the coat rack." He never broke his stride.

At the coat rack, we faced each other. There was no thought yet to take off our coats, or to get to our homerooms. "Boy," he said, "I really messed things up, getting so bombed. I could give myself a good swift kick in the you-know-where. My mother told me about her conversation with you." He extended his palm imploringly. "Why did you keep looking out the window?"

I was stunned. "The window?" I shrugged, trying to remember. "I saw you in the car. I saw you get out. I thought you were coming in the house but then I saw you climb back in the car. I was worried about you."

"Oh, that. I had to take a leak and I was told not to go in your house. So I had to go in the backyard."

I found myself wondering where he had gone so I could picture it better.

"But my mother said," Tom continued, "that you kept looking out the window and didn't pay any attention to her when she was talking about us breaking up. She thinks you don't really care." He kept moving his palm up and down for emphasis.

"Lee," he continued in a rush, as though he'd lose his nerve if he waited any longer. "They think you're playing me for a sucker."

It was such an incredible thing to say, I had no response. I took off my coat and tried to think. He dropped his books on the floor and hung his own coat on the next hook. I reached over and casually, but deliberately, entwined our coat sleeves.

When I turned back to him I was startled. I saw unmasked hurt. They must have planted doubts.

I squeaked "Why do they think I'm playing you for a sucker?"

He looked down, shielding his eyes from scrutiny. "We're going steady. But you still go dancing with your friends on

Friday nights. You dance with other guys there. My brother hears stories. You also went to the Junior Prom with…with… that other guy."

"Alan," I supplied absentmindedly. Then: "Tom, you never told me. I mean about the Friday night dances. You never said you minded."

"I didn't think I'd have to tell you. If you…really loved me, you wouldn't go."

I felt awful. Friday night dancing was innocent. It was my night to be with the girls; his, to be with the guys or to practice with his band. It seemed to me one night apart each week should have eased his family's concerns we spent too much time together. "I…don't know what stories you've heard," I stammered, "but I can assure you I've never done anything except dance. The Prom? You're right. I never should have gone. But I made that date during the week we tried to go out with other people. You know, what your mother and grandmother want us to do! You never said anything about the Prom either."

He was quiet for a long time. Finally, he spoke. "They've given me an ultimatum."

"An ultimatum?" Dread pooled in my stomach. "What's that supposed to mean?"

"They've given me a choice. I either give up my drums…or you."

My face reacted. Jaw dropped. Eyes widened. Tears sprang to the surface. "Tom, no," I whispered hoarsely.

161

He looked me over thoroughly. Then a smile began slowly on his face, spreading into a cocky grin. "I told her I was giving up," he paused for effect, "my drums!"

When my muscles relaxed, I realized how tense I had been. Still, the tears hovered. How could they do that to him?

There was love on his face. And something more...relief. He had bottled up inside him all the insinuations of his family and then his own doubts. He had finally spilled his guts. Because he kept that stuff from me, our relationship had been suffering and I didn't even know it. That scared me most of all.

"I'll handle them," Tom finally said. "It's going to take a little time. She'll come around. We've got to play it cool. I'll call you whenever I can. When the phone rings once at your house, it'll be me. Then call me back at my grandmother's. That way I won't have to ask for you by name."

To be clear about the rules of the new intrigue, I asked, "Am I going to see you at lunch?"

He thought. "Yes, I guess that's okay. If anyone should see us and tell my mother, I'll cremate them. After-school is out for now, though."

A long week of once-ringing phone calls and listening to him whisper over the line came and went. Tom told me he kept telling his mother good things about me and he said she was softening.

As we whispered on the phone one evening, he said, "My mother just came in."

"Sh...should I hang up?" I stammered.

"No," he said, his voice suddenly determined.

I heard her say to him, "Who's that you're talking to?"

"Lee!" he answered firmly.

I prepared to hang up. I was sure she would grab his receiver and start yelling at me. There was a long silence. Then Tom said triumphantly, "She's gone in the other room."

"That's all?" I gasped with relief.

"Yes. I did it!"

"Tom! My hero! Can you meet me? Out in my backyard? Go for a short walk?"

He thought. "Yes. I'll *tell* her what I'm going to do."

I was relieved the conversation had taken place at his grandmother's, while his mother was there to pick him up but before she had spirited him away to her house on the other side of the city where he spent most weekends. If he had been at his mother's house, he would not have been able to just pop over. Under his mother's own roof, he may even have been reluctant to "tell her" what he was going to do. Once again, I tried to fathom his complicated family situation: grandmother's during the week; mom's on weekends.

Staring at the black phone now returned to its large, dial-fronted cradle, I shrugged off the confusion. I raised my arms over my head and pivoted in place, stamping my feet and screaming, as if I had just made a date with Sal Mineo.

My brother Richard came running. "What's wrong? What's wrong?"

"Nothing, you little dumpling, you." Laughing, I pinched his cheek and ran into the dining room where Dad sat pouring over his account books at the table. I hugged and squeezed him. "Hey, what's that for, big girl?"

"Tom and I are back together again!"

I skipped around the table. Brenda and Sissy came into the room. "Come join me," I chirped. They got in back of me and skipped, too.

"What are we skipping for?" Sissy finally asked. I told them.

"Oh, *good,*" Sissy declared. Brenda agreed. Dad shook his head, smiling.

I threw on a sweater. Dashing out the door, I yelled: "I'll be back in a half an hour." I ran out to the driveway in time to see Tom cross the next-door neighbor's back yard. When he reached my garage, I threw my arms around him. I rested my cheek against his. He felt like a cool spot on my pillow.

* * *

164

My parents went away for a weekend, taking my brother on a special outing, as they had earlier taken each of the rest of us. They told me I was old enough to be left in charge of the kids. I looked forward to being in command. But Tom and I had made plans to double date Friday night. We had fixed up my friend, Arlene, with his brother's friend, Frenchy. With my new babysitting job, everyone would gather at my house.

Playing grown-up started productively enough. After Mom and Dad left with Richard, I fixed supper. I supervised the girls doing the dishes and then "allowed" them to go outside for a while. When Arlene and Frenchy arrived, they pointed at my face, and I explained I had caught poison ivy. They laughed at all the pink clumps of Calamine lotion on my face. Then I showed them around the house. When we got to my bedroom, they were impressed by all the pillows.

I grabbed a pillow and flung it, no special target intended. Tom caught it and threw it at Frenchy. Then more pillows were thrown every which-way. Still giggling, we went down to the breakfast bar in the kitchen. If it had just been Tom and me, we would have been content to simply be with my siblings, as we usually were. But the other couple wanted to "do something."

I remember noticing a cabinet door was ajar. As is my compulsion in such matters, I got up to shut it. I noticed Mom's car key hanging seductively on a cup hook. As a joke, I slipped it off and swung it in my hand. "Here's what we could do," I said, swaying it back and forth like a hypnotist with a watch.

Everyone's eyes followed the movement. "Yeeeeeah," Tom drawled. I looked to the other couple. They were both transfixed, looking hungrily at the key as if it was a T-bone steak.

"I…I guess I'd better put it back," I said. But I didn't. Instead, I heard myself continue "…even if we could just go around the block."

"Yeeeeeah," repeated Frenchy. After some nervous giggling, the decision was made, and then extended when Frenchy suggested, "Let's go out to Baxter's Lake."

I delegated babysitting responsibilities to Brenda. Then, as the only one of us with a driver's license, Frenchy got behind the wheel. Within the hour we were parked in the deserted parking lot of a small, brown sandy beach. Boarded summer homes flanked adjoining streets. We climbed out of the car and stretched. The area seemed ominously lonely. I felt spooked.

"Let's go home now," I suggested, trying to keep a frightened edge from my voice. I wanted to get out of there.

Frenchy threw the keys to Tom. "Hey, you've driven your grandmother's car to the beach, haven't you? You drive back. You can't make out with the poison ivy kid there, so Arlene and I might as well have the back seat." The image of Tom driving and me sitting beside him in the passenger seat appealed to me; it would be a preview of what we would do come summer when he got his license and for the rest of our lives. Even so, the image carried a shadow. This wasn't right, not tonight, not this way. But we had to get home and now I wanted to get there as soon as possible. As Tom backed out of the lot, I turned on the radio. I noticed he maneuvered his way expertly up the bumpy narrow road that led out of the lake settlement to the highway.

I saw a truck lumber toward us and I instantly knew that truck—not the boarded cabins—was connected to my foreboding. "Tom, that truck," I warned loudly. The rest was lost in an explosion of scrunching and scraping. Then the noise ended and we four sat in paralyzed silence.

* * *

As I ran away from home that night, I replayed that scene over and over in my mind. My parents and Richard had come home a day early and, after taking a look at Mom's car, Dad punished the lot of us by sending us to our rooms. Even Richard, who, as he pointed out to Dad, had not been at home with us, was marched up the stairs. As he stomped on the treads, he muttered something about dumb sisters. I knew I had to warn Tom that my father would no doubt insist he tell his mother.

Programming myself to wake up at 3:00 in the morning, I walked in the dark about seven miles from my house on the west side of the city to his mother's on the east. It was now the weekend so that's where Tom would be. Across from her house, I found a tree with a low, broad branch in a vacant lot next to a general store. Reviving my inner tomboy, I climbed the tree and waited for the rest of the world to wake up.

I must have fallen asleep in the tree. Next thing I knew, cars were zooming by. An occasional person went into the general store. By the third person, I got an idea. If Tom would go to the store, I could talk to him! But how could he know to do that? With a "what the heck" attitude, I put my fingertips to my temples. Concentrating fiercely, I repeated: "Tom. You will go to the store. Tom...."

When Tom came out of his back door, I nearly fell out of the tree. He crossed the street. I looked skeptically at my fingertips. When Tom mounted the sidewalk in front of the store, I called to him. He looked around, surprised. Not seeing me, he took another step toward the store.

"Tom," I called again. I waved my arms so I didn't blend with the branches.

"Wha'? What are you doing up there?" He looked quickly over his shoulder and finding it safe, he took a few steps closer to the wooded lot.

"My parents came home last night," I whispered loudly.

"Oh God!"

"I'm running away. Or, at least so they think."

"Running away? You can't run away."

"Course I can," I assured him.

He shook his head and laughed. "Look, I've got to go in the store. Sit tight. I'll be right back."

"Ok, but hurry. This branch is killing me."

I saw his shoulders shake as he went into the store. A few seconds later, he emerged with a pack of cigarettes. He scanned his parents' house. Then, slowly he unraveled the string that released the cellophane from the pack. "You've got to go home," he insisted.

"I can't go home. They'll kill me."

"What did they say last night?"

"It's a long story."

"Listen," he said, looking around. "I can't stand here…talking to…a tree! What will people think?"

I laughed.

He looked down at the sidewalk and I could tell by his shoulders he was laughing again. "Go home, Lee," he finally managed to say.

"No. I'm going to stay right here. There's plenty of room for you." I patted the area next to me on the branch. "I'm lonesome up here by myself. Try to come out later and join me."

"You're hopeless," he concluded, but he smiled while he said it.

I watched him go into his house. Several minutes went by during which I missed him. Then I must have dozed off again. When I woke, I saw Dad's station wagon pull up to the curb. Tom must have busted me; I couldn't understand why.

"What the hell do you think you are doing," Dad asked, as he held open the car door and told me to get in.

Although I felt punchy from lack of sleep, I noted with relief Dad didn't seem as angry as before.

"We're going to Tom's grandmother's," Dad informed me.

"Will Tom be there?"

"You won't be seeing Tom again," Dad answered evenly. "His mother made that very clear on the phone."

That didn't surprise me. I would have been more surprised if Dad said she was taking it well. As we drove to Tom's grandmother's, I remembered the one and only time I had been there. Tom and I were on a committee to help plan our eighth grade graduation dance. Tom had given me my first kiss in that house. Ironic, I thought, that years had passed since then and I had never been invited to get to know their family. Now, under the worst of circumstances, I was going.

I wondered if *she* would be there. Would Ellen rave and rant, wagging her finger in front of my face? I realized how I must look after spending half the night walking across the city and sleeping in a tree. The Calamine lotion must have dried in thick blotches on my face. My hair must be a mess. And surely I must have bad breath, since I hadn't yet brushed my teeth. I wished Dad would stop home first so I could at least take care of that. I wasn't taking the situation lightly. Rather, I was looking ahead, wanting to even the odds so this wouldn't permanently scar my relationship with Tom or his family.

I didn't realize how nervous I was until Tom's grandmother opened the door and I found myself trying to hide behind Dad's tall frame. When he took a step into the small foyer, I took the same step, crushing myself between him and the wall. I peeked around him and saw Tom sitting on a hassock in front of a stuffed chair. He was staring at hands folded on his knees. He seemed scared and small. I wanted to go to him, to talk about everything. I squeezed out from behind Dad and sat down on the couch, never taking my eyes from Tom. Keeping his head low, he raised his eyes to look at me. I read despair and defeat in them.

It was then I noticed Ellen. She stood near him, her back straight, her arms folded in front of her. She instantly reminded me of Snow White's stepmother, the wicked Queen, as she plotted Snow White's death with a poisoned apple. When her eyes met mine, I quickly looked away. But not before I saw her fury stiffen the straight of her back.

Still, I wasn't too worried. I had every confidence in Tom. He would find a way. He'd call me later. We'd work things out. Someday, after we married, we'd enjoy a good laugh about this; maybe his mother would even join in. All I needed was a signal from Tom as to "when," when we'd talk. I stared hard at him, willing him, as I had earlier, to give me some indication. But just as I saw his eyelids raise, Arlene and Frenchy stepped in front of us to take places on the couch beside me. I had to start my willing over. As though Ellen sensed my new power, however, she exploded. In a tone meant to say she had taken all she was going to take, she issued an imperial order: "Tommy, get in the kitchen and wait. I won't have you even in the same room as her!"

To my surprise, Tom rose meekly. Without a word, he left the room. Now I began to really worry.

Dad faced Ellen. It was clear it would be their confrontation. I knew she would win.

Dad looked like Dwight Eisenhower, but he was no general. He was too reasonable to be a fighter. He saw every situation from all viewpoints. Having made that apparent, he would then humbly, but clearly, offer his own. I took a glimpse of Ellen and decided to rack an inner point by twisting her last name in my mind to something insulting, like "Snot-Ass." I knew that once Snot-Ass saw that Dad understood her side, it would be all over but the shouting. Her shouting. She wouldn't even hear his point of view over the sound of her own voice. My only hope was Dad's attractiveness. Even as his daughter, I knew he was very handsome. Could his looks soften that much-married woman? I doubted it.

I could see Tom and Dad were proxy voodoo dolls. Snot-Ass would stick in her pins and I would receive the pain. There was no way to protect myself. Although the hidden issue was my close relationship with her son, the issue on the table was the car accident. I grudgingly admitted Snot-Ass was justified in being angry about that. I wasn't inclined to defend myself against something that seemed to me obviously indefensible. Still, for Tom's and my sake, I was willing to try. I realized, though, that even if I did get in a word edgewise, whatever I said might interfere with Tom's work to later bring her around. I decided my first impulse to bite my tongue was the right one.

"…truck never reported the accident," Dad updated Ellen. I perked up when Dad asked if Tom could come back into the room to relate his side of the accident. To not accept responsibility for a wrongdoing was worse to Dad than the crime itself. But Snot-Ass noticed my perk. I was a beat behind her in finessing my behavior.

Ellen refused. "You can find out anything you need to know by asking these other three." Then she proceeded to walk over to me. Wagging that finger, she accused, "I know *all* your little tricks." It seemed to me she knew some I hadn't yet discovered. She turned her attention to Arlene. Like flipping a switch, she changed her tone. Now motherly, she cooed, "You seem like a nice girl. What are you doing hanging around with *her?* And, you" she clucked at Frenchy. "I know you. You sometimes hang around with my other son. I'm surprised at you."

Arlene looked at me. I could tell she had seen through Snot-Ass' monologue and was suppressing a laugh. She emboldened me. Good, I thought, let her laugh. Let her explode into a house-shaking laugh. It would be a delicious climax to this sorry situation. I threw a smile at her. On cue, she spurt a giggle. Hearing this, Snot-Ass rescinded with her eyes her nice-girl comment.

But now I was tired and wanted to go home. I didn't want any more games. Especially since I was losing so grandly. I tuned out the cast of characters and kept my head a blissful void. As we left to go, I rallied enough to be chummy with Arlene, my parting shot at Snot-Ass.

As Dad started the car, he said, "I'm going to drop you off first. Your sisters, especially Brenda, were crying all over the place this morning, for God's sake, when we discovered you were gone. At least you can set their minds at rest."

Later, I was ready to get my life squared away, to accept my punishment. But Dad only said, with a tinge of sympathy, "Your worst punishment will be losing Tom." I didn't believe him.

I realized Tom was probably grounded. I figured it would take a week before he could call me. By the middle of the second week, I was frantic. I had to talk with him.

Then I remembered Ricky, the leader of Tom's band. Surely Snot-Ass let Tom go to rehearsals. Gigs were scheduled. The previous winter Ricky had had a party so band members and their wives and girlfriends could meet each other. Ricky and I had hit it off. When they later played at the Veteran's Hospital, he had even insisted that Tom bring me along. I called Ricky.

He said, first thing: "What happened between you and Tom? He says you and he are broken up."

Tom said that? "Surely he didn't use those words, Ricky," I probed. "He must have described it some other way."

Ricky was silent. "You mean you don't know?"

Now it was my turn to be silent.

"Tom won't talk about it. I've asked him why. I've told him I think he's a dummy to let you go. He's staying mum. What happened?"

Just then I needed the big brother his tone promised. I told him about the accident.

"Is *that* all?" Ricky was surprised. "I've gone on joy rides myself before I got my license." He composed himself. I can have him call you. We have a rehearsal in a few days."

Suddenly I couldn't wait another minute. I had to know, now. On an impulse I asked Ricky if he could take me over to Tom's. In the plan Ricky and I developed, Ricky would park a few blocks away, get Tom, and bring him back to the car.

I raced around, changing clothes, combing my hair, putting on lipstick. Ricky honked his car horn and I sped to the car. I fidgeted during the drive. He parked several blocks from Tom's mother's. As he left the car, I called him back. "Ricky, wait!" I unclasped the chain that held Tom's ring around my neck and slid the ring from it. I held it tightly in my hand, willing magic power into it.

175

"Give this to Tom for me," I pleaded. I was betting that once Tom saw the ring, he would come to me and beg me to keep it.

The minutes passed like lifetimes. Eventually, Ricky came back, folding his tall frame inside the car. He was alone, and angry.

When he held the ring out to me, I recoiled. "What happened," I asked. My heart thumped wildly.

"Tom said he couldn't get out of the house. He wants you to keep the ring."

I looked dubiously at the ring. Taking it suggested we were still going out. "Does that mean we aren't broken up?"

"No. Tom says it's over—at least for now—but he wants you to keep the ring."

But it couldn't be over. "D…Did he tell you to tell m…me that?" Though I pleaded with Ricky to help me understand, he looked as helpless as I felt.

"Tom should talk to you himself."

"Y…yes, he should," I agreed, still staring at the ring. I wanted to keep the ring. I wanted to make it a permanent fixture in my heart. But I couldn't accept it if we weren't going steady. Where was the category to put this in? Either I was going steady or I wasn't. I needed Tom to explain.

Ricky understood this need. It seemed to me Ricky would make Tom talk to me if Ricky had to dial my number himself. It felt wonderful to have him help me. With my Tom-limb missing, I needed a crutch.

I held onto the ring during the ride home. When we reached my driveway, I gave it to Ricky. "I can't keep it, not knowing" I explained. "If we really are broken up, and he tells me this on the phone, please give it to him for me?"

Ricky promised he would.

* * *

When I heard Tom's voice on the phone, I crumpled with relief. He had the same voice. Surely he must have the same feelings. I would know if things had changed. I could tell they had not. I took the long cord from the mirror post and brought the phone into the TV room where I sat on a chair and prepared to talk for a long time. Just as we always had.

"I'm so glad you called," I breathed. "Are you doing alright?"

There was a long silence. Then he said, "It's over."

I couldn't believe my ears. "Wh…what did you say?" I bent my head lower as though his voice came up from the floor.

"It's over, Lee. Th…there's nothing I can do. It's got to …to be this way."

I clutched the phone in both hands. The metal impressed my palm like a notary seal. "No, Tom, no." I could feel my voice waver as his words turned over in my heart. "You can't mean that. You can't." I started to cry.

There was silence. Then pleading: "Baby…baby… please don't cry."

"Tom…Oh, Tom." I sniffed, trying to stop crying. I needed to make the most of these moments. I needed to keep talking to him. Hadn't we always talked and straightened things out?" Are you trying to tell me… you don't love me anymore."

"I…I didn't say that."

Hope surged. "But, if you still…love me…"

"I can't, baby. It's impossible. Maybe…later. Sometime later."

It didn't make sense. Either he loved me or he didn't. If he loved me, he wanted me. Then, now. "Wh…when later?" I asked, trying to consider an alternative. If "later," then I needed a date.

"I…I don't know. Not next week. Maybe not for a long while. I just don't know."

It was beyond me. Love was not something you postponed. You couldn't say "maybe later" to someone whose only model for loving had been two huggy, kissy, fanny-patting parents.

"Do you mean that, Tom? That…it's really over?" Saying it triggered more tears. I kept wiping them away.

"For now, baby."

"For God's sake...don't call me 'baby.' Do you know what that does to me? Don't call me *baby*." I thought: he's trying to break up with me. He tells me he loves me and he calls me baby. He's going to drive me nuts. "Tell me you don't love me," I insisted. To myself, I thought: now that would at least make sense.

"I can't...Don't make me say that, ba...I don't want to say that, Lee."

Desperate sobs choked my throat. "Please, Tom," I pleaded. "How...how do you expect me...me to...go on. Tell me please. Tell me you don't love me."

There was another long silence. "I...I...don't...love you."

I waited expectantly for his words to register and for some ripples to smooth out. In surprise, I cried "It...didn't help."

I heard him chuckle. More hope. I'd always been able to make him laugh. Laughter had been an important part of our relationship. Laugh, Tom, I silently urged. Want me back so I can make you laugh and be happy. And you can make me happy.

Instead he said "You made me say it. I didn't want to. I don't mean it."

I could tell he was trying to end the conversation, that there was no more he felt he could say.

"Don't go, Tom. Don't go! Let's talk!"

"I've got to hang up now, Lee. Really."

"Tom," I whispered, stroking the phone as if it were he. Tears tumbled onto my fingers. "Tell me you love me, Tom."

Softly, he complied. "I do, baby. I love you." The dial tone was his goodbye.

I found myself at the river. The hot surface of the boulders seared my bare legs. It seemed appropriate to suffer on the outside like I was suffering on the inside. The river below rolled along merrily, disrespecting my pain. I was amazed at the hurt. I was surprised by the physical side of it. I had had no idea that emotional pain could ache in...my legs, my arms, my head, my insides, within my very bones.

I looked down at the boulder that was our chair. All our shared confidences, our dreams, our hopes, our laughter came back to me. One scene tumbled on another, like a silent movie reel. I raised my eyes to the mockingly bright sky and pleaded "Dear God. Help me get over him."

I climbed back to the path, touching as many bushes and trees as I could, as though strength from their tap roots could tunnel through their branches and fly into me. I pivoted on the corner as I turned onto my street, remembering all the pivoting Tom and I had done, our steps synchronized like marchers. I passed my Victorian house, standing tall and sun-kissed and loaded with memories I couldn't face. I went past the general store. There, Tom and I had waited while Mom worked at her part-time job over Christmas, waited for her to come home so we wouldn't be alone in the house and suffer with temptation.

I continued to Diane's house. We sat on her back steps. She pulled out tissues from a box of Kleenex and handed them to me one by one. Serving as a friend to my heart, Diane gathered its pieces and gave them back to me in the right order. I turned my face into the hot sun as though to fuse the ducts to my tears.

Suddenly, crying became old, tiresome. I laughed instead: "I'm going to find someone who has never been out with a girl, who won't kiss and hug me and stuff."

"There you go!" Diane congratulated. "If that's the kind of guy you want, you'll get him. You'll get over Tom…that mama's boy."

"Yes, I will," I answered firmly. "I will work so hard and keep so busy and have so much fun this summer that in September you'll have to cart me off to school in an A&P shopping basket. Just you wait and see."

* * *

That summer I carhopped at A&W. After waiting on an attractive woman, I noticed she kept watching me. As I did when I knew I was being watched, I sat on the outdoor bar stool, my back as straight as if I had a book on my head. Mom promised good posture would make me look like a lady. Still, I was baffled. Why would a woman watch me?

181

As I retrieved her tray, she asked "Have you ever done any modeling?" When I told her I hadn't, she introduced herself and asked if she could talk to my parents about me doing some runway modeling for some shows she was putting together. At my house, she had me turn and walk. Then she confirmed I was a size 5. She hired me. I had been discovered. Sandra Dee, look out! On the heels of that thought came another: Wait until Tom hears about this…from someone else!"

* * *

The fall and winter went as planned. I finagled a date with the best looking guy in school and kept him on the hook for school events. I modeled periodically. I tightened my friendship with Diane, Candy, and Sandi and other girls. My relationship with Tom had taken first place for so long, I didn't realize how much I missed girl talk.

I also ignored Tom, which was tricky. Although we hadn't shared a classroom since the eighth grade, we now had several classes together.

Meanwhile, even though Tom found a girlfriend, it didn't stop him from fixing attention on me. I could feel his eyes drill through me on a regular basis. And, at the lunch spot across from the school, he fed the jukebox every day in a way, I soon learned, involved me.

Diane finally revealed what he was up to. "Everyone— except you, dummy—has noticed that when he plays the song *Walk on By*, he mouths the lyrics to you. Everyone watches his performance. I don't know how you missed it.

You know the words, right? 'Wait on the corner. I still love you but we're strangers when we meet.'"

I didn't believe her. Not until I caught him in the act. And then I was stunned, and hopeful. Maybe it was getting close to the "someday" he promised, the time when we would be together again. In the next second, I shrugged away optimism. If he still loved me, he wouldn't pantomime a song. He'd call me. He'd tell his mother to fry an egg. I began to unravel until I realized unraveling would only take me backwards, to the terrible sadness I needed to leave behind.

* * *

When I answered the phone on New Year's Day, my knees buckled. Tom was on the other end.

As if time hadn't passed, I unwound the long cord from the mirror post of the telephone table and took the phone up the stairs. At the top step, I leaned against the wall, as I had a thousand calls with him before. My heart repositioned itself higher in my chest, where it belonged.

"I...I remembered last year," Tom said.

I barely breathed. "I remembered too." The year before Mom had secured his grandmother's permission for Tom to stay overnight on New Year's Eve, always a big deal at our house. Every year, we girls spent days making a feast that ranged from hors d'oeuvres to bonbons. We would set the dining room table with the best china. Dad and Richard would put on the sport coats they wore every year. And as we always did, we girls wore tiaras and long bouffant gowns, often made by my mother.

With Tom there last year, though, we weren't all gussied up. Otherwise, the ritual went on as usual and his place in it strengthened him as part of our family.

Now Tom wanted me to know he had remembered. After reminiscing, a silence stretched. Did he want to say anything else? Were we getting close to "someday soon?" But he only begged off, wishing me a "Happy New Year." It seemed he left a lot unsaid. Which was why I wasn't surprised when he called again the next day. This time he just wanted to know if he could use his former one-ring signal to call me once in a while. When he hung up, I was more confused than ever.

I turned 17 in February. Many girls my age talked a lot about sex; having it, what it was like, not having it. I wondered if Tom and I had had sex if he would have capitulated so easily to his mother. We had been afraid sex would add an element to our relationship we couldn't retract. Once we crossed the line, could we enjoy each other in the innocent way we loved? Yet, *not* having sex hadn't helped us either.

Turning this over in my mind during study hall, I looked diagonally across the large room to Tom. He was slouched down on his spine, doodling over and over on a piece of paper. I could see his eyes move, watching the results. As though Tom felt me looking at him, he raised his eyes to return my gaze. He sat straighter, staring at me in an unusually purposeful way. He dropped his eyes to look at his paper, and then raised them back to me. After a couple rounds of this, I wondered: is he trying to tell me something? About his paper?

Just then a hall monitor came into the room with some notices. I volunteered to pass them out. I could go to Tom's desk and give him the opportunity to show me…whatever. I went up and down the aisles to deliver the notices. As I approached Tom's desk from behind. I saw him move the paper to the side I would pass by. Did he want me to take the paper? I quickly looked at the teacher, who was watching me. As I placed the notice in the center of the desk, I looked down and quickly scanned his doodles:

Tom Loves Lee.

Tom and Lee

Later, I wondered if my eyes had played tricks on me. Even when we were a couple, he wouldn't have written anything so sentimental. It wouldn't have been cool.

But that afternoon the phone rang once. I looked skeptically at it. Was it Tom? After one ring, the sound stopped. Soon it rang once again. I dialed his number, worried I was making a mistake. It wouldn't be right to chase him. In our iffy circumstances, it was better to play hard to get. But it was impossible for me to play hard to get with Tom.

When Tom answered, I asked anxiously "Did you call me?"

"Who? Me?"

I had been wrong. Embarrassed, I apologized: "Oh, I'm sorry then. Goodbye."

"No! Wait!" He chuckled. "Yes, I called. Umm… something happened this morning and I just had to tell you about it." His chuckle grew a laugh. "Guess what I found in the car this morning?"

"I'll play your silly little game," I teased. "What did you find in the car this morning?"

"A skin. A used one."

My heart fell. His? Then I replayed his words. He wouldn't have said it like that. I sighed with relief. He was still a virgin. "Whose?"

"My brother's!"

Tom told me he found it between the backseat cushions of the car. He dangled it in front of his brother, threatening to tell their mother. I groaned, imagining Ellen's response. Then Tom and I both laughed, thinking the same thing. Together, Tom and his brother tried to flush the "skin" down the toilet but it kept "bobbing up."

"Finally he just grabbed it out of the bowl," Tom said. "I guess he buried it or something."

Just then I heard voices in the background. Tom whispered, "My mother just came in."

"Oh, God. I'm hanging up."

"No. It'll be okay. She's a little suspicious but…."

What was she was suspicious about? Was Tom mentioning my name to her, trying to feel her out?

Then I heard her voice demand angrily: "Who's that you are taking to?"

He shot back, equally angry, "Who do ya think?" There was silence. Then: "Guess I'd better hang up."

I was encouraged that, in some things, I was apparently still his favorite confidante.

* * *

In late March, Tom's girlfriend of the previous few months—Carol—called me. I was getting ready to go on a modeling assignment. In rehearsal, I had been asked to try on a bikini, the newest thing in bathing suits. But I couldn't pull it off; I was still getting used to the idea of two-piece suits. Thinking about the moves I would make on the runway, it took a second to register what Carol had said.

"Tom and I are broken up, you know. I'm calling because I was talking with one of his friends the other day. It seems Tom told him the only girl he will ever go out with again is," she sighed, "you."

The tip of every split hair on my head was excited. I expected Tom to make a move soon. He stared at me almost constantly. When I looked at him, he didn't avert his eyes. He was building up to something, I could tell.

Diane had noticed too. "What's with you and Tom? During English, he only has goo-goo eyes for you. Mrs. Fearon is getting ex-asp-er-ated. Spill the beans!"

Diane was right about Mrs. Fearon. The next day she glanced over granny glasses to Tom. "Ahem," she said, nailing him with her steely blue eyes. "Do you think you could make arrangements to stare at Lee on your own time?"

I pulsed with empathy for Tom's embarrassment. He shifted noisily in his seat and stammered an apology.

At home that afternoon with a silent telephone, I decided I couldn't wait any longer. My patience had worn paper-thin. I reasoned that since I was still going steady with the guy I caught the previous fall, Tom was afraid of being rejected.

As if modeling, I paced. I went from one side of the house to another, trying on this and that approach to find a good fit.

I decided I needed a new way to move him along. I liked to write notes. Whenever I tried to describe something to one of my girlfriends and the right words wouldn't come, I wrote them a note. It felt clearer to me to see my thoughts in black and white. I could see if the note reflected what I really meant. I could edit it as I needed to. I would write Tom a note. Nothing fancy:

Dear Tom,

Many months have gone by and I'm wondering if you are ready to cough up that $10 bet we made.

Do you remember how the rules of the bet
went? I don't owe it to you. If you want to
talk about this, please call me.

Lee

I wrote the final draft of the note in my best penmanship,
folded it in half, and then once again for good luck, making
sure all the corners were even. I placed it on the center of
my bureau, the exact center. The note had to be perfect. I
climbed into my bed and faced the bureau. I opened my
eyes every once in a while to make sure the note was still
there, that nothing had disturbed it. Then I snuggled deeply into
my pillow and draped the blankets around my neck. I didn't
say my usual prayers; I was afraid even that would jinx
things.

* * *

I knew the note was passed to Tom before English.
Oblivious to Mrs. Fearon's pointed sighs, he stared and
stared. I knew he was trying to decide.

After school, I gaped at the phone, willing it to ring. It
rang, once.

"Lee? I, uh, got your note." His voice dropped low. "I
don't owe you any money, Lee."

He wanted to talk.

I vowed this rendezvous would end with a punctuation
mark, an exclamation point to tower over the question

189

marks that had marred the previous months. Like countless women before me —in gardens, castles and hovels—I plotted a seduction.

Intuitively, I knew Tom would play his role. He would play it for the same reason that men, going back to Adam, always have. Although on a subterranean level Tom would know it was my conquest, not his, he would gain a victory anyway. He would satisfy his biological imperative to get laid.

I half-reasoned that, even if the worst happened and Snot-Ass broke us up again, at least I would have become his First. It had always been in Tom's and my best-laid plan for us to share this First together. For me, that hadn't changed. There was also symmetry in losing my virginity to him: he had been my first kiss, my first love.

I didn't think it through. It never occurred to me I would join a long line of women in my village's version of the Inquisition. I couldn't imagine my village would rip-off my flesh and blood. It did not enter my scheme that parts of me would become caged in stocks for decades to come.

The backseat of a borrowed car was my Garden of Eden. Rain pelted our windows, its streaming curtain and noisy paradiddles a welcoming touch of privacy that made our love nest cozy, even homey.

The date was Friday, April 13, 1962. The time: 7:00 p.m. Before we even built a full steam of passion, I broke the promise I made to him long before. I didn't say "No." Penetration hurt, just as other girls told me it would. But I followed their advice to bend my knees and I got through it. Afterward, we sat in our separate and silent disappointments. There wasn't any towering exclamation point, just a new even bigger question: what had I done?

A very worried and ashen Tom had his own question. When would I get my period? Two weeks later, I got our answer. I told Tom minute-one. He was over the moon with relief. So was I. The anxiety about a pregnancy had landed both of us on the opposite corner of where we had hoped to be. My plan, I now realized, had been stupid, stupid, stupid. What we really needed was to relax and re-discover our former comfort with each other.

But my period wasn't business as usual. It was scant and lasted less than a day. That told me more than any visit to the doctor. My period never arrived the same way twice. Sometimes it came in 28 days and sometimes it arrived as late as 40. Whenever it came, though, it was copious, crampy and lasted at least four full days. With a period that only lasted a few hours, I knew I was in trouble.

Tom was a wreck. One of us had to take charge, and it obviously couldn't be him. I borrowed a book from a friend that had all the states and the legal ages for drinking, for signing contracts, and for marrying without parental permission. I put the book between the pages of a magazine and Tom and I looked through all the states. We hoped to find a nearby state that would allow two 17-year-olds to marry without permission. Tom saw it first: "Mississippi." Mississippi would have allowed our marriage at age 14. He placed his index finger under the information. We looked at each other and turned up our New England noses. But our Yankee snobbery was short-lived. We had to face the practical. How could we get there? He could "borrow" his mother's car. But we immediately recoiled from that idea, remembering how things had turned out the last time we borrowed a car.

No, we would have to save our money and take a bus or something. I had returned to the A&W, so I had a head start over Tom, since he wasn't working. Tom wanted me to quit the A&W. He didn't like "all those guys flirting" with me. His ego gave way when I pointed out quitting wouldn't be helpful. He promised: "I will go in and out every store on Elm Street. I will find a job." It was the most resolute and decisive I had seen him in almost a year.

But days, and then a week, went by and he hadn't made a move except to find a new mask for his face. His eyebrows were a rubbery furrow; his twinkly eyes, sludge pots; and, the lines of his mouth, a downward cast. I knew we needed help…from someone else.

Tom had made me promise not to tell my parents. If I did, he said, "They will tell mine. And that will mean disaster." I thought, though, that my parents could be reasoned with. They now knew from experience what Snot-Ass was like. I thought there was a chance they would help us without involving her. Maybe one of them could even take us to Mississippi.

I had to take the risk. I didn't want to tell them both. Only Mom. As a woman and a mother, she would understand. As if she sensed things were changing, Mom revived her old ritual of tucking me in. I took it as a sign. I told her.

She was taken aback but without the hysterics I had thought was a possibility. I implored her not to tell Dad until she and I could talk the next day. But the news was too big for her to handle. Within minutes, my father was in the mix.

As Tom predicted, Dad wanted to involve Snot-Ass. All the parents should discuss this, thought my father. It then seemed to me, since he had had a run-in with Ellen before and knew what we would be up against, that Dad believed he could handle her. Knowing his reasonable style, and knowing hers, I thought he must know something I didn't. Maybe he had fighting muscle I had never seen. He did agree to talk first with Tom.

Tom was furious for a couple of seconds. Then he slumped. His dejection was total and absolute. After Dad and Tom went for their talk, Dad summarized for me—as Tom stood beside him looking as stooped as an old man— that Tom would tell his mother the next day. I looked at Tom to check his reaction. His face was as gray as an unglazed ceramic bowl at the back of a dusty shelf.

Then my father said: "You may find that the best thing to do is to put your baby up for adoption."

Adoption was a word I had only heard once in my life; a new girl in town was rumored to be adopted. Now Dad had given it a life that applied to my own. I didn't know where to put that word. Surely, this statement would jolt Tom. Surely, he would look as aghast as I felt. But Dad must have mentioned it to him during their talk because Tom's expression didn't change. He continued to look as if he had emptied out. As he turned to go, I didn't know he was walking out of my life.

The next day, Dad told me Ellen had called him. He had told her he would talk further when I was in the room. I imagine Ellen did not like being put off. Later, as he and I sat around the dining room table, Dad lit one of his Kool's and dialed her number. As every puff of smoke disappeared in the air above us, I felt more and more of me go with it.

As though through an ear horn, I heard Dad repeat some of Ellen's part of the conversation. Obviously incredulous, he stressed her word "promiscuous." I didn't know what it meant.

Then he used the worst words of all: "Are you telling me, Ellen, that Tom has denied paternity?"

1974

Age: 29

Cape Cod

Having typed Tom's denial, I remembered how it had made me feel. Or rather…not feel. His denial had been so surreal, there was no knowing what steps to take next. With Ellen's words, all parts of me had turned numb. Over the years, I had somehow banked warm flesh around that iceberg.

Now the icy core of me was thawing. With the melt-down I felt more abandoned and afraid than I had ever allowed myself to feel. Although I sat in the security of my Cape Cod home—an adult woman, a loved wife, a treasured mother—I didn't know who would care about me. Maybe that security even worked against me. If I couldn't feel safe now, then when could I?

I suddenly remembered Deb telling me that, as she wrote her books about her ancestors, she felt each character's plight. She said it was sometimes rough moving herself through the pages. I wanted to talk with Deb about what she coined "character-transference." But my main character wasn't an invention. I wasn't fictional. I had lived the events I wrote about. What difference did Deb think that made? And what did Deb think about the psychology of feelings that were so raw they felt like they just happened, when in fact they had occurred more than a decade before?

But, as compelling as my need was, I didn't have time to talk with Deb, not that day. The irony wasn't lost on me…I would have to postpone understanding my postponed feelings. Just as I had to keep moving on back then, so did I today.

A Swedish couple was coming for dinner. When we went to Sweden, we were the first part of a banker's exchange program. *Stockholm Sparbanken* had just sent over the second half of the exchange: Ingrid and Sven.

When Dave first told me the Swedish banker was a woman, I was surprised. "Well, how does that work?" I wanted to know. "Her husband is coming over with her? What does he do? They have kids but their kids didn't come with them? I don't understand that kind of arrangement."

I paused, wondering if I wanted to pose my next question to Dave: "Can I ask them about their relationship, like how they handle childcare and Sven's career?" From our trip to Sweden, I knew their government gave new parents a generous stipend so one or both of them—they could switch off —stayed home with a new child during what Sweden saw as the all-important first two years. Sweden also had government-funded day care and health care for the whole family. These were alien programs to me. Like everything I didn't at first understand, I wasn't sure I wanted to know anything that might spell change. Yet I admitted I was becoming more curious about things and I was interested to know how those programs worked in real families.

Dave told me to be careful with my questions. "You don't want to offend them, you know."

As it turned out, Ingrid and Sven arrived for dinner at our house the evening Richard Nixon resigned as President of the United States. I couldn't track—and didn't want to track—all the ins and outs of the whole Watergate scandal. The simplest event to follow was when Nixon's secretary, Rose Mary Woods, admitted to a jury that she was responsible for inadvertently erasing some of a tape recording. Working with tapes when I typed others' books,

I could see how that could happen but no one else wanted to give her the benefit of a doubt, so I just shut up. I would be glad when the focus was off Nixon and Watergate.

Ingrid was surprised when I said I didn't plan to watch the resignation speech. "But this is important part of your American history," she said in stilted English. She added firmly: "I would like to see it."

They were our guests who had traveled half-way around the world to get here, so turning on the TV was the least I could do to be hospitable. After all, her bank had showed us an amazing time when we visited them. I chalked up her interest to cultural difference.

Ingrid gave me more to think about when she complained about the television commercials. "Those ads demean importance of your history. In Sweden, we would never allow capitalism to share," she paused, hunting for a common expression, "the stage…with such event."

"You don't value capitalism?" I asked incredulously.

"Yes, we value, but not that much," she explained patiently. "Sweden is more socialist."

When I looked as if I didn't understand the distinction— which I didn't— she continued: "In socialism, we know to take care of each other. Maybe someone is fine now but maybe they not so fine later. We happy to chip in for rainy days."

Later, Ingrid's philosophy drifted lower and lower on the inner currents of my mind. At bottom, one of my favorite childhood storybook characters took form. In a fairy tale told by the Scandinavian Hans Christian Anderson, Thumbelina was tiny, small enough to sleep in a walnut shell cradle, but when she was encouraged to "dance and sing," she "was nine feet tall." I wondered what would have happened to me if I had been a small and needy Swedish citizen who became pregnant. Could I have emerged from my experience dancing and singing and feeling nine feet tall, the way I did with my other sons' births? Did Sweden's shelter for rainy days apply to unwed mothers? I wanted to ask Ingrid, but I didn't dare.

The next day I knew I had to face my own personal storm, probably the worst yet. It was time to write about Michael's birth. Like all my memories, I had only the barest outline of what was coming next. From writing the more recent memories, though, I suspected that after I fleshed out the birth I would feel as if I had a zipper caught in my skin. If I tugged the zipper in one direction, my skin would tear that way and if I tugged in the other direction, I would rip apart there. Yet I couldn't go through life with half-zippered flesh. It was something I had to get through.

I put Deb and Marie on notice that I hoped we could talk later. I would need both of them. Then I corrected myself. I would need all three supporters. I told myself: money be damned, I would also call Sandi.

1962

Age: 17

Boston

The doctors were all coming to Flo-Crit on December 17th to examine girls due around Christmas. They would assess how ready we were to deliver and, if we "passed," they would induce our labors. Getting home for Christmas could make or break our secrets. You would have to invent a pretty good story to explain to the relatives why you weren't there. I knew my mother was worried. My MaMere usually came for the holidays, and I didn't have a good excuse for not being home. But something more also stretched my nerves.

I had entered Flo Crit earlier than most girls did in their pregnancies. I had been desperate to get away from the rumors. As ostracized as I was, I left home months before I even "popped," which wasn't until October. This late blossoming of my belly worried me. While I knew the exact date—and minute of conception, the medical intake didn't ask me that question. It asked when my last period was. I knew that too, so I put mid-March on the form and they gave me a December 20th due date.

Alone in my room later, I wondered about my dates. I asked around and learned the average pregnancy was about 266 days from conception to birth. I did the math. If I went by the date of conception, my due date would be early January, almost three weeks after the date Flo-Crit gave me. I also compared myself to late December and early January mothers. When I sidled up to other girls to discretely check how far each of us stuck out, my protrusion was more like the January mothers. I wanted to believe the way Flo-Crit calculated, so I did. I told myself Flo-Crit must know more about the countdown to delivery than I did.

The exams to identify who could be induced were on everyone's mind. Those whose due dates made them eligible for an exam—and my December due date was— couldn't talk about anything else and those who weren't eligible—which I wouldn't be with a January date—were subdued and sad. After the exams, the doctors posted the list of those they would induce. I wasn't on it, and I cracked up.

I'd been splitting the feelings I couldn't suppress into stuffable pieces. I couldn't stuff anymore. My reward for being good and sane and productive was to have gone home for Christmas. I had set my sights on it. Now there would be no reward. I would have to continue to suffer through this interminable pregnancy, this confinement at Flo-Crit. Well, I wouldn't do it. I couldn't do it.

Wildly, I wondered if there was some way I could pass myself off as one of the girls on the list who had declined to be induced. She had wanted to go into labor on her own. Maybe the doctors wouldn't discover I was an imposter until after they gave me the drugs? I played out all the angles but I couldn't see how to pull it off.

Instead, I could feel suppressed rage build and build. I let it. I fanned it. It had been a long time since I had been ruled by feelings. I didn't want to tame any knee-jerk responses. I wanted to jerk away. Kick away.

Then I thought about Tom. Tom, who was probably preparing for his Christmas school vacation, who had freedom, who could come and go as he damn well pleased, whose life hadn't changed one iota and would never be affected, unlike my life, which would forever more be stained and maimed. I wanted to scream out my lungs with the injustice.

But I didn't scream. Instead, I allowed the injustice to leak out physically. Walking down the halls, I pushed against a wall and ricocheted off, and then I did it again. I gave up attacking walls in favor of holding my head in my hands while I walked. I could barely see where I was going. It didn't matter. Wherever I went, I would end up in Flo-Crit. It seemed I would be at Flo-Crit for the rest of my life.

I walked and walked, sobbing uncontrollably. These were tears I had postponed. I needed to get them out. If they led me to an obscure, dark place in my mind—the threshold I'd been skirting for months—at least I wouldn't know I was still at Flo-Crit.

I approached a stairway. I looked down at the treads. I teetered. But as part of me released myself to fall, another part grabbed the banister. I turned away from the stairs. My body heaved down another hallway, through the breezeway. I stumbled into the foyer. There, a figure clothed in white—one of the doctors—drew me to him. I allowed myself to collapse against his chest.

After I sputtered enough for him to put together what upset me, he paused, holding me. It felt wonderful. I wanted to stay in those capable arms. Then he offered an equally great gift. "Come to the hospital tomorrow," he said. "I'll see what I can do."

* * *

I blinked beneath the fluorescent lights. I turned to the side, where I saw intravenous flowing in my arm. Vaguely, I remembered I had earlier tried to pull out the tube. I noticed a nurse standing over a table against the wall, looking at a report. Seeing I was awake, she walked toward me, her starched white uniform crackling with each step.

I couldn't believe how different I felt; I had gone from night to day. My body was mine again. I could reclaim my life. And I had a baby! It felt great to have a life, a body and a baby. It was the holiest of trinities. Interest in my baby surprised me but I realized it had been there all along, hiding under layers of who-knows-what. "What did I have?" I asked.

She told me I had a boy and—was this a reproach? — he was one ounce over incubator weight. I shrank under my sheet. So, the January date had been right. How could I make that up to him? I knew I could, now that my body and my mind were my own again. There must be something I could do. After I confirmed he had all his fingers and toes, I asked to see him. She wheeled my gurney over to the nursery and knocked on the window. The nurse behind the glass walked over to us and my nurse flashed a card with my name on it that had been at the foot of my bed. The nurse in charge of the babies looked at me and, making an "O" with her index finger and thumb, she flashed me an "Okay."

She turned away and I felt panicky. But soon she returned, wheeling a baby to the nursery window. The bassinette looked empty. Then I noticed a thatch of dark hair. "Ooooh," I crooned, excited. "Look at him! Will you look at him?"

At the sound of my voice, other girls from Flo-Crit shuffled from the two four-bed wards that had been set aside for us. We welcomed the sight of each other, as if only we knew how it was to survive our kind of battle. The girls pressed their noses to the nursery glass to look at my baby and then approvingly back at me.

"Hey girls," I called. "Remember me? I can't see him."

I wanted to take him in, and in. Now that I saw him in the flesh, I wanted to put him back inside me so I would have time to figure out the reality that the two of us were to each other.

A chorus of "oops" and "sorry" and laughter punctuated my thoughts and the other new mothers backed away.

My baby lay motionless beneath a pale blue blanket. His hands were encased in the mittens of his white gown. He looked like as perfect and serene as a doll. My heart caught in my throat. Like most new mothers, the only words I could croak were "Gee." And then "Wow."

The window between my baby and me had to go. I pleaded to my nurse: "Can I hold him? Please!" Hearing new mothers were normally given the first night after delivery to recuperate and get a good sleep, I added: "Oh, I'm not the least bit tired." I opened my eyes wider to prove my point.

The nurse told me gently I had to get settled in my room. But as she began to wheel me away, my heart strings stretched tightly, painfully, as though I was still directly connected to my baby.

I loved him completely.

"To bed now, mothers," the nurse admonished with a smile. "You'll want to be wide awake for the six o'clock feeding, won't you?"

I totally understood when the mothers answered, almost in unison. "Yes." "And how!"

After I was transferred from gurney to bed, I asked: "Will I have my baby for the six o'clock feeding, too?"

As she raised the bed rails into their sockets with a clank, she cautioned "There's a problem with his weight. But if he still weighs the same by morning, they'll bring him to you."

* * *

The hustle in the hallway, the squeaking of wheeling baskets, the soft murmurs and click of lights drew me from sleep. With a start, I was fully awake. I wanted to show the nurse I was able to care for my son even though I had recently delivered. I was more aware of stiffness and an ache in my lower body now that the anesthesia had faded. But, though I have a low threshold for pain, I easily pushed it away. I was poised and eager.

"Good morning, Mrs. Tuttle," whispered a nurse rustling into the room with a basket of soft blue blanket and squalling red baby that she delivered to one of my room-mates.

I realized that along with the "Mrs." we were now going to be called by our real last names. Funny, I thought, after all the months of subterfuge, of having our last names reduced to an initial, I would no longer be known as Lee H. It felt better to me, more honest.

As the nurse started to leave the room, I stopped her. "Am I going to get my baby? Please?"

Although she promised to check, baskets wheeled down the hallway and still there was no baby for me. Finally, finally, a basket was wheeled bedside. There was no sound from the still form lying within. It would have seemed like there was no baby there at all, except for the telltale patch of black hair that punctuated the basket floor. Thank goodness, I thought, for dark hair—like Tom's, like mine-- that confirmed his presence.

I stretched out my arms to receive him. The nurse laughed at my lack of inhibition. As she picked him up gently, I carefully studied her movements. I would handle him precisely right.

205

I swooned as he—more blankets than body—settled in the crook of my arm. I closed my eyes, drinking in the sensation that he was. When I opened them again, I studied my child. "Oh, he's so perfect," I whispered reverently, looking to the nurse for affirmation.

"Indeed he is," she agreed. She studied him as I had done. "But he is a small baby. We've got to be sure he eats very well. You may keep him as long as necessary to get him to finish his bottle. Don't rush it."

She didn't have to tell me that. I would stretch each second into a year if I could.

She handed me a four ounce bottle filled with a milky liquid. She eyed it skeptically. "Usually new babies just get a sugar and water solution," she explained, as if to herself. "But we're going to see if he can tolerate a little formula. Let's see if we can get some meat on these little bones." She gave him a little poke, which I resented. Then she showed me how to feed and burp him. I absorbed every word.

I waited till she left us alone before doing anything. This was to be an occasion just for my baby and me. He hadn't stirred a muscle since he had been wheeled into the room. His hands were still by his face, reminding me of a puppy dog begging. I placed the nipple of the bottle by his tiny mouth. Miraculously, he opened and sought it. As he began to suck, I marveled at his reflexes.

I carefully watched the formula as it settled against the side of the bottle. I measured out the remainder, waiting for the right amount to signal I should give him the burping I was told he would need. Assured of his progress, I studied his features. A high smooth forehead lightly glistened with baby oil. His eyelids were closed and translucent. I was relieved to note he did NOT have my pug nose.

If not my nose, then, did he have Tom's? Holding Tom's son in my arms made it impossible to deny Tom's role in making our baby. I also couldn't deny the place I apparently still reserved for him in my mind. Or, to deny his presence, I had to admit, in my heart. I sent Tom a message: "He's so beautiful, Tom. Talk to Sandi. Tell Sandi you want to know how I am. All you have to do is ask. She'll tell you everything!"

Pushing that pipe dream aside, I refocused on my baby. After studying the other mothers' burping strategies and taking more mental notes, I pulled on the bottle, only to have him tug more deeply on the nipple. "Well," I congratulated, "you are a strong little fellow. And I can see," I added proudly, "you have a mind of your own."

I pulled the bottle from his mouth. He continued to suck. Discovering the bottle was gone, he drew his mouth into an angry bud. I wondered in pride and fear if he would cry. But as I shifted his position forward, supporting his chin between the crevice of my thumb and index finger, he burped. I laughed with delight. I hadn't even rubbed his back. He was so smart!

"What a big burp from such a little guy!" noted Helen as she came to in the bed across from me. She had chosen not to either see or feed her little girl. I couldn't understand that. But, after all, I couldn't understand myself either. I had rocketed through my own range of reactions. I had gone from processing everything through a foggy brain to focusing on my baby with crystal clarity. Before, I had distanced from the life within me and now I pulsed with the strongest possible connection and adoration.

Helen had called my baby a little guy. "But you'll put on weight, won't you?" I whispered. Once he and I had sealed our conspiracy in weight-gain, I laid back and re-inserted the bottle in his eager mouth.

Soon it was empty but he looked highly unsatisfied. I anxiously twisted. He had needs I had to fill. When the nurse retrieved one of the other babies in the room, I showed her the bottle and begged for another. She looked amazed and left the room.

Soon she returned, smiling proudly, as though she had played a major role in his good appetite. Presenting me with another bottle, she advised me that "The head nurse said he was to have as much as he could eat." She pressed the nipple against his cheek and he opened his mouth like a bird sensing the presence of breakfast. "I guess he really is hungry, isn't he?" she said.

I wanted to say "Of course he is. Didn't I just say so?" But I only smiled back.

I cradled him closer, telepathing that, although he should eat well, he should eat slowly. We needed to prolong our time together. The nurse returned after a time but I told her he wasn't through. Grinning, she left us alone.

When the bottle was finally empty, I put my pillow between him and the metal rail of the bed, nestled him by my heart so he would be comforted by its familiar sound, and we slept together. I nodded slightly when the rustling of another uniform sounded near my bed. I wanted to protest the removal of my son but sleep enveloped me and I sank into it.

I awoke several hours later, acutely aware of his absence, but baskets were again making their way down the halls. This time I deftly placed the bottle in his mouth, as if I'd been doing it all my life. And he accepted it, as if he'd been waiting with assurance I'd supply it. Later, cuddling together, we drifted off into our separate dream worlds. But this time when I awoke I was delighted to find him still by my side.

The nurse came in to take him but I begged "Oh, he's sleeping so peacefully. Can't he stay here, just a little longer?"

"Well, I have this form for you to fill out."

"Oh, I can do it without disturbing him," I promised.

"Oh, okay," she agreed as if she had known all along she would give in.

She handed me a white card. I gingerly sat up, mindful of the pulling of the tight stitches in my crotch and the unsettling of the bed as I shifted my weight. I swung the bedside table over me and looked at the form. It was information that would go on a birth certificate.

There was a blank line after "Mother's Name." Though I was tempted to use my nickname, I printed my full legal name, wanting to make the form as official and binding as possible. A heavy black line was drawn through "Father's Name," leaving no room for me to insert Tom's name anywhere. I tried to ignore the abrupt twist of my heart. Beneath that line was "Child's Name."

I turned to stare at my baby. "What should I name you?" I asked him. "I can't name you after your father as I always thought I would. Your daddy hasn't asked about you, I'm sorry to say."

I decided to give my baby Dad's first name. Maybe when Dad saw his namesake, he would change his mind and let me bring him home. Now I needed a middle name. I relented and inserted "Thomas."

Swinging aside the bedside table, I settled into position to try my son's new name on for size. I tried: Ron, Ronnie, Ronald. I even tried: Tom, Tommy, Thomas. None were right.

What then? I wondered. It seemed strongly to me there was a right name for him hovering off to his side. I struggled to bring it front and center. He looked like a…suddenly, the name came into focus. Michael. He looked exactly like a Michael, even though I had never before had a Michael in my life and didn't know what a Michael was supposed to look like.

In my heart, he would always be Michael.

1974

Age: 29

Cape Cod

Since the boys were at an all-day play date, I had written all I could. Then I had tapped out still more—more about the hospital and about the surrender. Finally, I was drained of memories. This was supposed to signal the end of the channeling stint I had begun at the beginning of the summer. And it was. But now memories that had once been deeply hidden were just below the surface, were hovering above the surface, and were on the typewritten pages beside me. I was surrounded by memories. I hadn't bargained for that.

Although I had wanted to be done with the memories, I could tell the memories weren't done with me. It made no sense. No good could possibly come from continuing my obsession. There wasn't any point to it. But I couldn't think of that now. Now, I needed to rest every bit as much as if I had just given birth.

The next day I would talk with my supporters. Meanwhile I needed a blank mind. My best distraction was beach time with my precious boys.

Scott and Todd knelt on the sand beside my blanket. Having heard Dave and I talk about the new Boston tunnel underway, they put their two heads together to begin a "Big Dig" of their own. I smiled, admiring their industry.

For my own entertainment, I had packed that day's edition of the *Cape Cod Times*. I now knew newspapers held more than the clippings I still cut out. Our local paper also had information I could talk with Dave about, mostly to cover up other stuff I should talk with him about but wouldn't.

Turning away from the wind, I snapped the newspaper into a manageable fold. My eyes immediately landed on yet another article about adoptees who searched. Such articles wouldn't leave me alone. They kept coming and coming, like they were part of a conspiracy to get me. I checked on the boys and reminded them their tunnel couldn't go too far afield, that if they needed a really long tunnel they should loop it around my blanket and avoid disturbing others nearby. Then, sighing at my inability to call quits on my own deep dig, I began to read. The article mentioned an organization called the "Adoptees Liberty Movement Association" which helped people search adoption records. I assumed ALMA was the real-life version of the group in the television movie I had seen.

Back home, I shook out the sand we had brought home in our clothes and in everything else. I put the boys in the bathtub to finish their de-sanding and, glancing at the clock I saw there was still time before Dave came home. Just as I had to listen to the radio, to clip newspaper articles and to channel memories, so did I know I had to phone ALMA in New York. This was scary in a new way. I was putting myself on the threshold where searchers lived. I told myself it was only a phone call. I could hang up at any time.

A volunteer answered on the third ring, just as I was about to take no-answer as a signal to let go of this newest crazy idea.

But I only had to say I read about ALMA in the newspaper and the volunteer took over.

"Are you an adoptee?"

I was shocked. My first reaction was "Are you kidding? My parents wanted me."

Breaking the back of that thought was a sudden realization. So that's how adoptees feel! They feel unwanted, and I had done that to Michael? In just one second, my memories and my role in Michael's surrender stepped aside, and I felt...FELT...what being adopted would have been like, at least to me.

After I stammered a no, the volunteer followed up: "A natural mother then?"

My own self stepped up, an equally lousy place to be. "Yes," I admitted, swallowing hard. I was saying this to a perfect stranger and I continued to breathe? I was as surprised as I had been the first time I missed a Sunday mass on purpose—a sin—and the flames of hell did not lick at my kneecaps after the start-time for the mass began.

ALMA's volunteer wanted to know if I had read the book their founder, Florence Fisher, wrote, *The Search for*

Florence Fisher. I hadn't heard of it. She promised to send me membership materials that included a list of groups that met nationwide, one in Massachusetts. Hanging up the phone, I felt as if I had crossed over a rickety rope bridge.

I made a mental note to catch the phone bill so Dave wouldn't ask about a call to New York. I also mentally tagged the date, three days away, when ALMA's package might arrive; I wanted to be sure I was the one to pick up the mail. Now that I was keeping fewer secrets from myself, more energy was freed to keep secrets from others.

Now knowing about Florence's book, I squirreled the courage to go to the Brewster's Ladies Library, a regular by-station for the boys and me. Though I had taken them there for story hour ever since they were little, I was apprehensive as I entered the Victorian building. The head librarian was a personal friend and I didn't want her to check out the book for me. Maybe she would ask questions. But Beth wasn't on duty when I arrived, so I sent the boys to their favorite stacks and strode purposefully to the card catalog. On the shelf next to Florence's book I found another that sounded similar, *Orphan Voyage*. The jacket revealed the book was written by one Jean Paton, who was both an adoptee and a social worker. I marveled that both books had apparently been under my nose for a while. As a clerk checked out the books for me, I stopped short of asking her to put them in a brown paper bag. But when I got home, that's what I did.

After I collected vegetables from the garden to start supper, I stole a moment to begin to read. I was sobbing before the end of the first page of the Introduction. I couldn't read further. I knew I needed more help than my three friends could provide. Like an alcoholic bottoming out, I turned to a power higher than myself.

* * *

Our Lady of the Cape was a storybook church: white clapboards, tall steeple, high on a hill—all the trappings of a peaceful place. As I entered the cool, calm nave, I was reminded how glad I had been all my life to grow up Catholic. I loved moving the red ribbon bookmark in my missal from one red-edged page to another while I followed the priest's Latin verses. I was also sentimental about the Sacraments that had been part of my life; that is, except for Confession, which I dreaded because I had to make up some sins to make the priest's time worthwhile.

Thinking about my Sacrament of Confirmation at 12 years old, I saw the irony in choosing Maria Goretti as my personal patron saint. She was born in Italy in the late 1800s and when she was about my Confirmation age, Maria was fatally wounded by a neighbor who attempted to rape her. Named the Patron Saint of Modern Youth, Maria was the saint I had hoped would intercede with God on my behalf, back when I first needed help. I hadn't limited myself to her, though; I also prayed to Jesus, Mary and Joseph. And, even though I was soundly rebuffed by them all, I thought it was to my credit I kept right on praying. Surely that had been noted in some account book. I intended to respectfully bring to their attention what their silence had cost me. I knew they would set things right,

215

once I properly humbled myself. I was a little surprised I hadn't thought of turning to them before.

With my petition uppermost on my mind, I walked down the red carpeted central aisle to the front of the church. There, a bank of votive candles sat idle, except for a few that parishioners could use to light their own flame. Choosing a candle in the row closest to the Cross, I lit the candle, and, with it flickering hopefully, I knelt at the altar rail. I tried not to be sarcastic when I allowed that Jesus and all the saints were probably busy with more important things than helping me keep my secrets at bay. I grew meeker as I listed the ways I tried to redeem my Mortal Sin of Sacrilege by living an exemplary life. I gently reminded them I had done my part. Now, wouldn't they—please, PLEASE—return my past to the blissful void it had once been? I closed my petition by regretting I was unable to manage the pain on my own. Not even the three women who were put in my path could help me get through the library books. I acknowledged I needed their divine help.

I knew with every Catholic fiber in my unholy being that I would soon be set free. I waited at the altar rail for a dose of amnesia that would last. But as I took stock I saw the memories were still there, as alive as ever. I then figured the administration of a full round of anesthesia might take more time. I needed to be patient. So I turned from the rail, chose a seat in a pew near the statue of the Virgin Mary, and, expecting to stay awhile, got as comfortable as I could on the wooden bench. Glancing at Mary's gently carved face, it occurred to me I should have brought my rosary beads. Then I dismissed the need. I knew my faith would be enough. Expectantly, I waited. From time to time, I checked my thoughts but everything stayed the same. Even though the longer I waited, the more anxious I got, I exercised, as Dad had drilled during my childhood, my patience muscle.

Suddenly I felt mocked on a grand scale, one of the grandest of all. In an instant, I turned 180 degrees from my lifetime of faith. Here was a second round of proof I had been sold a bill of goods that couldn't deliver. Walking back to my car, waves of dejection and anger rose from the parking lot to sear me from the bottom-up while the heat on my shoulders seared from the top-down. Consuming my center were the flames of hell I had worried about, but they came, not because I had sinned, but because I was a believer.

* * *

Time was running out. I had to get through the books before school started. My legal first name—Leona—means lioness, so I activated her and began to charge through pages. Within the first chapter I was mewing. I dropped all pretence. Seeing me pathetic, Deb helped me find a therapist. Deb understood my criteria. I needed a counselor who would apply a sliding scale for her fee. I wanted someone out of town, so no one would see me enter that kind of office, especially someone who might be a depositor with Dave's bank. I also wanted a woman, which I didn't understand myself, since professional women like my social worker had fostered my loss in the first place. Deb found a counselor in Wellfleet who met the criteria.

Although it was a long drive during tourist season, I was desperate.

I found her in a small white building that resembled the mess unit of an abandoned camp. I took one look at her warm and friendly face and immediately dissolved in tears. Handing me tissues, she listened patiently. After my 50-minute hour was up, she gave me more time. But she didn't have answers and I finally had to go. Emptied out, I hoped she could give me something I could take home. "Why," I pleaded, "am I remembering all this stuff after all these years? What is the point? There is nothing I can do."

She did have an answer for that. "It's because you now feel safe and secure in your life. You postponed your grief until your support system was in place. Now you can deal with things you couldn't before."

Driving home, I saw truth in what she said. Instead of me serving time, time had been serving me. She had told me my support system was now in place. Yes, I agreed, I had my three friends. David was there, too, still telling me he wanted to help. But, in return, I always made a peachy-keen face to disguise the secrets I put between us. I committed to opening up that very night, before hiding re-asserted its appeal.

It was a Friday, the night Dave and I always reserved for just the two of us. For a change, I snapped a pretty cloth over a small table in the living room in front of the side window. I walked two upholstered chairs over to it. I centered a candle. The dinner was on the stove. When he

218

arrived home, he noticed the intimacy of the setting and smiled. I realized too late he was probably envisioning a very different outcome than the one I had in mind. I debated giving him a hint to keep his expectations in check. But I couldn't say any one thing without it leading to another, and we needed uninterrupted time.

We hung out with our sons, advanced by one hour the hands on every clock they were likely to see, and put them to bed. Later, I saw I underestimated David. He wasn't disappointed we had a different kind of intimacy than what he first thought. He had sensed I was hiding things from him and now he was relieved to know what they were. He vowed to stand by me in whatever way I needed. I was optimistic we would weather this together. My main concern now was, I didn't know where my inner winds would take me, and now him.

MORE

* Kelley (2002): Self-concealment can adversely affect well-being by (a) persistent psychic effort to keep things hidden; (b) in an "ironic rebound," a sensitivity to the avoided event; and, (c) inferences of wrong-doing.
* Uysai, Lin and Knee (2010): Self-concealment might obstruct one's (a) autonomy; (b) competence, (c) relatedness.
* Grommet and Pronin (2009): A reluctance to disclose concerns, anxieties, and doubts interferes with the ability to accurately predict others' responses.
* Singer, Hippler & Schwartz (1992): A promise of confidentiality can curb disclosure because it underscores concerns with privacy.
* Jordan, Monin et al (2011): Being unaware of a friend's issues leads to underestimating frequency and intensity of some issues, thus leading to dismissal of one's own and others' similar experiences.

— Originally from: *Self-Concealment.* Psycholopedia. psych-it.com.au .

*

Meyer(1995): In "social stress theory" conditions in the social environment have a strong impact on stigmatized people.
* Allport (1954): "One's reputation, whether false or true, cannot be hammered, hammered, hammered, into one's head without doing something to one's character."
* Meyer (2003): "Minority stress" is unique, since it is an add-on to stress everyone feels and it requires an adaptation greater than ordinarily made. It is also chronic, since it is linked to subtle social and cultural structures.
* Goffman (1963): An individual may perceive that whatever others profess, they do not really accept him and are not ready to meet him on equal terms.
* Smart and Wegner (2000): The cost of hiding one's stigma is the cognitive burden, both conscious and unconscious, of maintaining secrecy. The inner experience of one who conceals is "a private hell."
* Thoits (1985): "Self-stigmatization" is internal and insidious. Even if one's minority status is successfully concealed, one who conceals may direct negative social values inward.

—-Above from: Ilan H. Meyer (2003). *Prejudice, Social Stress and Mental Health...and Research Evidence.* NIH. Web.

CHAPTER EIGHT

1975

AGE: 30

CAPE COD

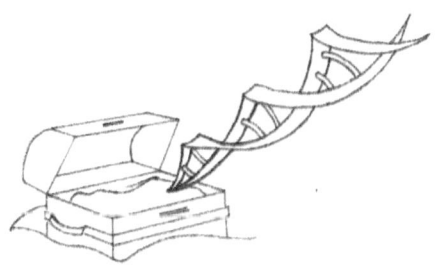

I waited for months for other things the counselor said to make sense to me. I soon concluded she was very wrong on at least one front. She told me that coming clean to David and tapping my friends for support would eventually help me "put things to rest." I did feel more genuine after my confession to Dave, but the release did not take me to a peaceful place. A part of me remained restive, as if I expected another shoe to drop.

It helped that I had been going to my new job every day, and I loved it. Brewster was building a new elementary school and my new boss— the principal hired to oversee both the academics and the construction—was over-busy. We got into a routine where he left things in my in-box and I left them completed in his. When he lighted in his office, he called me in for dictation. I was tickled to test my shorthand with his lickety-split delivery and then to translate the scribbles back to paper for his signature.

I also had to learn to use the intercom system, which differed from the switchboard I had trained on at Flo Crit. During my interview with the principal the previous spring, he had asked if I knew how to run a switchboard. Without thinking, I had told him I did and then I worried he would ask me where. By the time school started, I thought I was off the hook but then I was so clumsy on the intercom, I began to worry again. Each time I fretted, I was reminded of Flo Crit, something I was trying not to do anymore. Soon, though, I figured out the switches and trunk lines and the fear of being found out eased.

As I expected, the best part of the job was being able to see the boys during the day when they lined up for this activity or that, each of us giving the other a discrete little wave. Mid-day, they dashed into my office for lunch money. While I knew I could make their lunches in the morning, they then would have had to keep their metal lunch boxes in their classrooms like the other kids. They wouldn't have been able to feel like big-shots with access to the principal's office and I wouldn't have had an excuse to see them up-close. I took some pride in being able to finagle a job that combined the best of everything I could want in my life.

As my new routine became more familiar, the memories asserted themselves another time, but in a relatively manageable way. The Journal, like a limb with nerve damage, signaled it needed more attention. My typing had about a million typos. It seemed a little dishonoring to leave it in that condition. That, plus I still had many unanswered questions. I thought if I re-typed the Journal, I could fix the typos and get more perspective on some questions.

As I considered my interest in getting more perspective, it occurred to me there were people who could help me on the questions to do with my parents and family: my parents and siblings. Maybe they even wanted to help? I hoped to learn if I had been too hard on them.

I decided to type copies of the re-write for them. With every new page, I stacked two copy-sets—carbon paper attached at one end to onionskin paper—behind the original bond paper. With each new typo, I applied a thin coat of "White-Out" to the error on the top page, and while I waited for it to dry, I carefully pulled back the carbon of each copy-set, erased the error on the paired onion skin with the rubber tip of a special erasing pencil and, with a flick of the tiny brush at the other end of the pen, I dispensed with the miniscule rubber shavings. The evidence of a mistake now gone, I put the papers back together for another go. Re-typing each page took a lot of time, but I wasn't in the same fever I had been when I first typed the Journal.

After I typed ten pages or so, I mailed out the onionskin copies. One set was shipped to Mom and Dad and the other to Brenda. She had promised to read it and pass it along to my siblings. I never heard from Mom and Dad; it was as if their copies had been lost in the mail. Donna had been too young to be directly affected but she was very interested and supportive. Richard confessed he had fought on street corners to defend my name. Sandi reminded me she had visited me at Flo-Crit. Brenda reminded me she had gone with me at least once to see Michael in the foster home. She said she had never forgotten him, and missed him to that day. They all mentioned losing friends—whose parents feared an inherited lack of morality--and they had come to my defense with friends and strangers alike.

Dad had told me my siblings were affected and he felt he had to protect them, but by then I mistrusted everything he told me since he was the one who had raised the specter of adoption in the first place. The Kids themselves hadn't told me at the time about their trials, feeling *they* needed to

224

protect *me*. I had been surrounded by protection of one sort or another. If everyone had dropped their share of protection—if it had been assumed I could handle the truth of what was going on—would it have empowered me or would it have underscored my need to surrender? I couldn't know. One thing I did know: I hadn't remembered Sandi at Flo Crit or Brenda at the foster home. When I lumped my siblings in with Mom and Dad and distanced from them all, I must have buried such memories especially deep.

As if the memories had a to-do checklist, I checked off my 500-page re-write. I felt there were other items on the list but they were in fine print and I didn't know what they were. I didn't feel another wave of compulsion for a while. I wondered if I was finally finding peace.

Eventually, though, I came across the ALMA materials I had received in the mail earlier in the Fall and set aside. Seeing them again, I wasn't sure I wanted to open them up. I had done okay when they were sealed. After I finally decided to slit the envelopes, I had to resist the impulse to read them in the bathroom. But I had promised Dave I would avoid secrets, so I read them at the kitchen table, Dave walking by, glancing worriedly at me, yet trying to look casual. I learned a Massachusetts branch of ALMA met north of Boston once a month, most months. They were now on a holiday break but would resume in January. I told Dave I wanted to go.

Dave balked for a few moments, reminding me it would take four hours round-trip. "What will you get out of this, Lee?" Still, he knew going with me was part of our new deal. We agreed to take the boys and me on a "trip to Boston." Dave deposited me at the front door of the ALMA coordinator's house. Although it was non-descript, it looked like a one-room school house to me. I could even imagine a rainbow over it, like the cover of some '50s grammar school primer.

Betty, the coordinator, swung the door wide for me. Her round young face reminded me of Meredith Baxter's in the television movie I had seen. When I looked around at the others who turned to greet me, I knew I was in the right place. My life with Dave and the boys and my work at the school were my vacation, my resort, my respite. My work—my calling—was here with these strangers. I felt in my bones that this was what my memories had been leading up to. I wanted to unfold a sleeping bag and take a crash course in whatever I was supposed to learn from them.

My new mentors were five adoptees, including Susan, who was both an adoptee and a surrendering mother. Susan seemed to focus on being an adoptee when she told her story. Then, almost as an afterthought, she segued into the surrender of her son when she was 16.[12] "I waited anxiously for his arrival," she explained, because "he would be the first extension of myself." Her adoptive parents were supportive during her pregnancy, she felt, "in the sense they made all the arrangements. But they could not cope with the possibility of my keeping the baby." No one else knew of Susan's pregnancy, a charade she said still continued. She admitted she never even told the baby's father "until after the fact." A large woman with short dark curly hair, she had a way of cocking her chin to one side that seemed to underscore her earnestness. Yet she punctuated her story with soft giggles. It caught me up short. I hadn't found anything funny about anything she said. It made me wonder if I would ever be able to fully restore my sense of humor.

I met Mary Anne then, too. Unlike Susan, Mary Anne's role in adoption was undivided; she was the devoted mother of a missing son. I didn't think I shared her intensity but I identified more with her than with Susan. A woman taller than I (which I was used to), Mary Anne dressed like a hippie (which I wasn't used to). But she had a more tucked-in look than other hippies I had seen on TV. She wore a peasant blouse inserted in the waistband of a long flowing skirt. Her long dark hair was parted in the middle and tied back behind small round ears. Under John Lennon glasses, her pale gray eyes checked me out. She had a habit of sliding those stunning eyes a little off-center when looking at me, as if looking head-on might interfere with some private and deep thought. She also slightly swayed when she stood, the way mothers do who have held babies for years. With the demeanor of a brooding artist, she was Susan's opposite in the giggly department. I appreciated the relief from chuckling but there was something about Mary Anne that suggested she and I might not align our thoughts in the same way. What was different about her, I wondered. What did she have that I didn't? I realized one of the hopes I had for the meeting was to find another woman just like me. Maybe a me-like woman could be the mirror I needed to understand my situation more clearly.

Just as my impression of Mary Anne registered she was "artistic," Betty waved some typewritten pages in my direction. She announced proudly: "Mary Anne is a poet." The pages were Betty's monthly newsletter. She pointed to one page where a long poem began in one column of type and carried into the next. Beside the poem was a black-pen drawing of a woman engulfed in swirls of loops and circles. The drawing was compelling, pulling me like a vortex, round and round, into the woman. It was the kind of art that, if it hung in a museum, you would sit on a facing bench to study. Betty told me Mary Anne had done the drawing, too. In the art department, I was creative in crafts. I had never been classically arty. I admired that in others and my admiration of Mary Anne was no exception.

I must have looked preoccupied as I processed Mary Anne's unique package of gifts. As if to give me something else to think about, Mary Anne added "There's a lot more where those came from." Then she offered a small smile with a short self-effacing laugh that seemed to bubble from one side of her mouth as if she was embarrassed to find herself tooting her own horn.

As I read a few lines of one poem, I lowered myself into a nearby easy chair. This was not a poem I could put off to read later. I had expected her poetry to be Hallmark-sweet, like the cards Dad gave mom and us girls along with boxes of Fanny Farmer chocolates on Valentine's Day. But I could see Mary Anne's poetry held only enough confection to hook me. There wasn't much of a gushy center in there. Instead, some razored bits in some of the lines made me wonder if I dared to sample more. She was unlike anyone I had ever befriended before. I wanted to know more about her story. Would we have a more certain connection there?

When it was Mary Anne's turn to talk,[12] I learned she, now 30, had been 22 when she gave birth to a son, whom she also named Michael. But she did not surrender her Michael for another 14 months, a long time compared to my three months, which my social worker said was really dragging things out. I wondered how Mary Anne held out for so long. Mary Anne also described her relationship with her Michael's father, saying he was "the first man I ever loved." I identified with that, except my "man" had turned out to be a "boy."

"We were both idealistic and naïve," Mary Anne explained, "involved in philosophy and anti-war causes." She described Michael's father as having "overriding concerns" such as completing his pre-med coursework and resolving problems he had had with the Vietnam draft board. Now that I was up-close to a peacenik, I was happy to dismantle my reservations about them. Being as uncomfortable with violence and war as I had always been, I wondered if my reservations had really been my own or had been handed-down to me from David.

Mary Anne worried that news of her pregnancy would be an unwelcome distraction to her Michael's father, so she didn't tell him she was pregnant "until he said he was through with me." Mary Anne's parents weren't any help either. "They reacted with shock, anger and shame," she added, "thinking only about the neighbors and my grandmother."

I could identify with that, too. But when she said her parents had since come around, I wished I could say the same. I could have been jealous of Mary Anne, I suppose, but family was so important to me I could only be glad she and her parents had found a way to bridge their gap. I wanted to talk more with her about that, too.

In another departure from my story, Mary Anne did not spend her pregnancy in a home for unwed mothers. "In my sixth month, I moved in with married friends," she said. "I slept on a couch behind a curtain and helped with babysitting and housework." Her "first step towards losing my child," she believed, "was to choose a Catholic hospital." There, they referred her to their psychological clinic because "I was upset." In an aside, she asked: "Who wouldn't be upset under those circumstances?"

To my horror, I realized my initial reaction was to also blame Mary Anne for being upset. But the part of my brain that controlled nodding knew better than the rest, for I immediately felt my head move up and down. She was right. Any new mother would be upset about an untimely pregnancy with near-zero support. I compared my head's reaction—to blame Mary Anne for not controlling her feelings—to my emotional reaction—to empathize with her. I realized that facing that contradiction in my own self was alone worth the trip to the meeting. Apparently, I wasn't exempt from others' tendency to blame women for their situation. And playing that blame game covered up the real me that had the capacity to understand. I wanted time to figure out for my own life what other contradictions were going on between my mind and my heart. I then thought of feminists' complaints and grew uncomfortable. I had always dismissed what they said. What if they were right about some things?

Mary Anne continued: "When I asked for help to prepare for my child, I was referred to the New Jersey Bureau of Children's Services." With a small shiver she added: "I didn't know they arranged adoptions. They did not tell me one positive thing about keeping my child or one negative result either to me or to my child about giving him up."

Looking into the distance, she described the birth in poetic terms. "I went into labor on an early April evening," she said, "when the earth was just beginning to come alive." Sliding her eyes back to me, she confided, "For years afterward I avoided the warm touch of early spring sun—the memory burned like fire."

That stoked another insight. My own Michael was born near Christmas. I still loved the holidays and all that went into preparing for them with Scott and Todd. My holiday sentiments hadn't changed dramatically. February, though, was a different story. In February, I was usually sick with bizarre things. The year before I'd had symptoms of Rocky Mountain Spotted Fever: rash, high fever, stiff joints, overwhelming fatigue. Although this illness arrives after a tick bite, February was deep winter on the Cape. There was

231

no way to explain that illness, or any of the other mysterious maladies I somehow got in Februaries. I still didn't remember the month I surrendered but after Mary Anne revealed what she called "her anniversary grief," I wondered if I had surrendered in February.

Not being able to fix a surrender date in my mind was strange to me. My 18th birthday was in February. Such a rite of passage should have been a landmark in my memory, a time around which I could say this happened before, or that happened during or after. But a lot of January, February, and March of 1963 was still blurry to me. I then wondered if my surrender wasn't so much a particular date as it was a season, an extended timeframe that reflected a slow deterioration of will, of self, during which advocates of surrender wore me down.

When Mary Anne went into labor, her boyfriend dropped her off at the hospital, wishing her good luck. Afterward, Mary Anne insisted on seeing her child. But instead of being handed her baby so she could count fingers and toes, she was whisked without warning to the psychiatric ward. There, she continued to insist on seeing her baby, prompting one doctor to threaten to transfer her to the state mental hospital.

As Mary Anne divulged this, I suddenly remembered some gossip that was passed around Flo-Crit. A mother who had formerly been at Flo-Crit relayed her experience to another, who was still in Flo Crit when I got there. As I heard it, when the first mother resisted adoption, she was given shock treatments and threatened with a lobotomy. At the time, the story was a lesson to me in how much I could safely ask for. And something else troubled me too: there was a part of me who wished I *could* have a lobotomy so the pain of being pregnant and unwanted would go away.

Along those same lines, Mary Anne revealed that while her son was in foster care, she suffered from post-partum depression "which nobody would attribute to the fact I was separated from my child." She looked steadily at me. "I was treated as a happy person who suddenly became depressed for some unknown reason." After this counseling went on for months, Mary Anne surrendered.

"I immediately became pregnant again," she admitted. It clicked for me that with a new pregnancy she could start over. She could apply the lessons she learned from the first pregnancy and make a new outcome for the second pregnancy, one she could live with. A new outcome would signal she wouldn't be anyone's patsy again. And she could have a baby to hold in her arms that could help to fill the void left by her lost child. I wondered how loaded with similar stuff my own later pregnancies had been. It didn't seem fair to me that Scott and Todd may have arrived on a crowded slate, that they were born to a mother who, unbeknownst even to herself, had a hidden agenda. As if reading my mind, Mary Anne added "I've heard about other mothers who did the same thing."

I looked at Susan and wondered if her teenage pregnancy helped her to compensate for, not her own previous pregnancy, but her birth mother's? When she was told she could not raise her child, did she re-live her mother's own surrender? In that way, had she been able to identify with the mother she otherwise had not known, and, while she was at it, with her baby-self for which there were no memories, no pictures, no stories? However, as I watched Susan look at Mary Anne, it didn't appear to me as if Mary Anne's story had personally resonated with Susan.

I couldn't recall my brain ever firing off thoughts like these before. It was heady to hypothesize why terrible things happened. Since I usually drew blanks for answers to my own questions, I apparently needed to jumpstart my personal speculation by first wondering about others' situations.

Mary Anne closed with a nugget that fit like a rock in my foundation. "In actuality," she said, "one experience can't replace another. There is no new life. Life is a continuum; the past, present and future are interrelated, not separate pieces."

Then adoptees began to tell their stories.

"I feel as if I have a black hole inside," said one. He was a male adoptee ten years older than my Michael. I was spellbound while he tried to explain. "There's the me I can know and that's fine. I've had a good life. But it's as if I have a core I can't know and it's empty and dark, here in the middle of me." He dug two fingers into his shirt above where his belly button would be.

As if to ape his pain, my fingers depressed my own solar plexus. If a doctor were to ask me "where does it hurt?" I would point there—right there.

Others had convinced me my Michael's new life would be perfect. Before the television movie, it had never crossed my mind that prediction was flawed. I had thought some of the angst in the television movie was Hollywood. But now I realized the movie wasn't a dramatization, after all. In fact, the movie underplayed the real thing.

The other adoptees nodded. One woman added: "I was adopted when I was eight months old and I was told about it when I was seven or eight years old. Ever since then, I've felt disconnected on a primal level. I have a thousand questions. I love my adoptive parents very much but I have to get a lot of things straight about my first parents. I would like to know why they gave me up. I would like to know if I have brothers or sisters. To fill this void, I have created mental pictures and learned to love those. I have dreams about the pictures, and then I wake up feeling tortured. It's a strange feeling, loving people you've never met."

I was also struck by something else. Unlike the adoptee who was tortured by missing memories, I was tortured by real ones. Which was worse? To be without memories that could make you real or to have memories that made you painfully real?

Another adoptee interrupted. "I always think about my birth parents on my birthday. It's the one day I know they think about me. I feel connected on that day."

I didn't tell her I considered myself lucky to have passed a decade of Michael's birthdays during which thoughts of him didn't cross my mind, at least not my conscious mind.

Mary Anne assured the adoptee that she thought of her Michael every day since he was "taken."

My eyes opened wider. Hadn't Mary Anne been told to forget and move forward? If so, what made her strong enough to keep her memories alive day after day? I wondered how she moved forward with memories that never took a rest. Were her memories like a wound that became a familiar scar? Yet Mary Anne's pain still seemed fresh, so a scarred-over place was doubtful. There was much to talk to Mary Anne about, but adoptees still had the floor.

A third adoptee cleared her throat, gulping as if to show she was taking a risk. "Sometimes I think I do know her," she confessed. "When I cry at sad movies, maybe she's wiping away a tear somewhere." Her eyes misted, making her point. "When I do something clumsy, like bumping into furniture, as I often do, maybe she is rubbing a bruise and acknowledging she too is less than graceful. When I look in a mirror, maybe she is seeing a face not so different from mine. When my love for animals comes out, maybe she's somewhere hugging a pet." After listening to her, I needed a nap. But there was more.

Another adoptee shared the sentiment: "When I see a beautiful sight, when I'm feeling sad, happy, when special events come along—my wedding, Christmas, the birth of my own children—I wish she was nearby to share these with me."

The male adoptee smiled at this and sheepishly admitted, "I try to concentrate and send her messages."

Another saw things in a different light: "A lifetime of events have gone by since I was with my biological parents. We're two entirely different people now. That's a long time for a mother and a daughter to be separated. Even family feuds don't last that long. But adoption separation is different from other separations. Our lives split apart when I was too young to argue with her. Most children who lose their mothers do it temporarily, in a crowded store or at a fair. I lost mine forever. It's not that I blame her or don't love the parents I have now. In my biological mother's shoes, I probably would have done the same thing; someday I might even adopt."

Betty was a good group facilitator. After encouraging the personal stories, she focused the group on ways to make things better. She said ALMA proposed legislation to open sealed adoption records; it was critical that we all work together on this, she said.

That sounded scary to me. What kind of work? Would that work expose me? I didn't see how I could help with legislation and still protect my life.

But an adoptee emphatically agreed with Betty: "Being told I have to go to court to seek information about myself is unfair. We have enough problems without needing more. It's my right to know about the people who brought me into this world. The agencies and courts which refuse us have never been in our shoes."

Another said she was scared in a different way. "What if the courts deny me the chance and I can't find her until after she's dead."

Like the guttural chant of a tribe around an evening fire, a deep murmur passed among the adoptees.

Looking out the window, I saw Dave pull our car to the curb. I had to pry myself away. I was grateful to each of them. They had taught me a lot and given me much more to think about. But even as I wished I could stay longer, I was also very tired and ready to go. While Betty held the door open, she looked meaningfully at me. I wondered what she saw.

Dave's eyebrows shot up in question before he pulled away. I signalled "Later." But I knew David couldn't later share my thoughts and feelings, which hopped around like tender feet during an initiation to hot coals. To get within a mile of my head and heart, he would have to attend meetings with me, hear what I heard, and feel what I felt. I knew he couldn't do that.

When we arrived back home, I set aside the day at Betty's. The meeting was a learning experience that was bigger than I was. I knew I would continue to digest it, although it felt now as if I had bitten off more than I could chew.

Because I had been in Boston all day, I couldn't fix supper so we went to Laurino's for our favorite meatball pizzas. Later I set up the Scrabble board at one end of the dining room table. We each played the familiar game in our own way. Dave joked. Scott pointed out patterns the tiles took as the board filled. I helped Todd shuffle his tiles and find some words he knew. And meanwhile I saw that finding my own words and putting them on defined little squares on a board symbolized something deeper. I saw Scrabble in a new way. Scrabble was like life. I vowed to never again exchange any tiles, even if my tray was filled with all vowels or all consonants. I would make the most of whatever came out of the bag and not trust the next round to save me.

* * *

I kept thinking about the adoptees I met and the legislation Betty wanted help with. I began to wonder if there was some private way I could ease any questions Michael might have. I didn't want him in pain like the adoptees I met. And, like other adoption agencies I was learning about, my agency would probably deny his questions. They were likely to tell him they had promised me protection, as if they had put me in some kind of Witness Protection Program. It was pointless to argue with my agency, to remind them they hadn't made me any such promises. After all, the terms of the surrender would be their word against mine, and they had the power. I thought about power.

Could I call my agency's bluff? If I took their alleged promise of anonymity as fact, I could write my agency to say I did not want their protection. Thanks to my typing business, I knew how to make a document look official. I could create a "Release of Protection" and submit it to my agency. If Michael searched for me later the agency wouldn't have any reason to deny his petition. This line of thought prompted me to muse about "later."

Michael had recently turned 12. Not all that long ago I believed I could never take him into my new life. Now there was a yawning crack in that belief. I had inserted a toe in there to keep it open, at least until I learned who I was. Until then, how could I tell him who he was?

In addition to learning about me, there was the matter of Tom and his denial of paternity. I would have to figure out what to say to Michael about Tom. For now, I didn't have a clue. But there was time before Michael was likely to search. I could work on the part about Tom "later."

For now, I tried to remember the name of my agency. I couldn't recall it. How ironic, I thought. Here I was with all the memories I didn't ask for and none of the memories I did. I also wasn't sure about Michael's birth date. I knew it was December 20-something. I remembered being in the hospital on Christmas day, so it was before Christmas. Was I released the day after Christmas? That felt right. My parents postponed Christmas for me, no doubt expecting me to open presents with smiles and gratitude. I denied them that, I knew, by sleeping through most of their delayed celebration and for many days after.

I worked the dates backward. Since a typical hospital stay at that time was about five days, his birthday must have been December 21st. But why did the date December 20th ring such a bell? Suddenly, I remembered. The 20th had been my due date. I was elated, which was another irony. Finally, a memory I was happy to uncover.

Oddly, I remembered my social worker's name. My thoughts detoured to my meetings with her. I seethed, another unusual reaction to my memories. My anger was crystal clear and icy hot, unlike my usual confusion. I liked anger better.

If I could reason out the birth date, I told myself, surely I could reason out the name of the agency. Catholic Charities? It seemed to me Catholic Charities figured in the situation somehow. Had my mother taken me there? But they didn't have a home for unwed mothers out-of-state, where I insisted on going, far from Dodge? I chewed on the inside of my lip. Maybe Catholic Charities wouldn't take me as early as I wanted to go, so I could put distance—yesterday—between me and the rumors that had worn me out?

That seemed right, too, as I thought it through: it probably wasn't Catholic Charities. I decided to make sure, so I called and asked if my social worker had ever worked there. A clerk checked their records and confirmed she had not. The clerk seemed sympathetic, so I asked her what other Manchester agencies may have handled a girl in trouble in the early '60s. "It had to be the State of New Hampshire," she said. "We were the only two." She gave me their phone number.

Before I called them, I dug out my 500 page Journal. It still felt hot in my hands. In a margin I quickly scribbled some notes about the due date, the birth date, and the name of the agency. It was important to me that the Journal stay accurate.

I began to massage my idea to Release Protection. Now it didn't seem to go far enough. It was too passive, too dependent on Michael making the move some adoptees were afraid to make because they were terrified they might set themselves up for what they saw as a second rejection. Wanting to make a Release of Protection with more teeth seemed a little gutsy to me. I remembered I was feisty when I was a kid. Maybe I was discovering my liveliness again?

Now what *would* make a Release of Protection more proactive? I told myself to think about it overnight.

The next morning, I awakened with a way to extend a Release of Protection. I had forgotten how exhilarating it was to open my eyes with something dynamic on my mind. It occurred to me Tom's mother probably scared that out of me. The Journal had reminded me how Ellen had wagged her finger at me, accusing me of having a lot of "dirty tricks," and she said she "knew them all." Maybe I didn't want her to know I was able to think while I slept, so I told myself to stop doing it?

My new idea had two steps. First, I would Release Protection for Michael when he came of age; adoptees seemed to think 18 was the magic number. In the second step, I would Release Protection for Michael's adoptive parents while he was still a minor. If they felt it would be good for Michael to get information while he lived in their home, they could get it for him. The adoptees I met did not suddenly feel their loss at 18. It had been a part of them for a long time.

The second step needed some rules, though. I wasn't ready for Michael's parents to call me. I reasoned it might be too scary for them too. Given this fear, I thought the agency should stay in the mix. They could act as an intermediary. The agency could funnel questions from Michael's adoptive parents to me, and relay my answers back. I decided to run my ideas by Betty's group at their next meeting.

* * *

Still worried about where I was "going with all this adoption business," Dave took the boys and me on a second trip to Boston. After they took off to explore a new part of Boston, I entered Betty's group as if it was my second family.

I learned a couple of adoptees in the group had found their mothers' identity since the last meeting. They seemed completely transformed. Their faces were visibly relaxed, as diffused with light as if a switch had been flipped. I had seen that look before but it took me a second to realize it was the look of falling in love. Did a part of them now anticipate meeting their first love, who is—some would claim—our mothers?

They described themselves as feeling re-born, on the one hand, yet feeling finally as adult, on the other hand, as their chronological age said they were. To explain, they added they were now equal to other adults who could get facts about their birth. They now believed they could direct their future, one that was driven by truth.

Hope filled what they had previously described as empty space. It was as if they had been square pegs who could only flop around in their assigned round holes, never quite getting purchase. With their mothers' names, the sharp angles of their pegs had been fleshed out. Now they fit snugly in their space and their faces showed the lack of strain.

I also noticed they didn't volunteer the answer to the question on everyone's mind: how they got information on their mothers. They acted as if they had been sworn to secrecy. That was fine with me. The less I knew about whether or not laws had been broken, the better. I had no intention to go that route myself.

My route would be indisputably legal. After I told Betty's group about my idea to Release Protection, I was told it was brilliant. Mary Anne, though, didn't think the agency would accept a Release. She took some of the wind out of my sails. But as others talked more, I could see the language I could use in a Release become clearer in my mind. I decided I would include a cover letter that brought my agency up to speed on adoptees' needs. "Correction," piped Betty, "Adoptees' *rights*." I liked finding a new way to frame words for this complicated situation.

This time when I turned to leave, Betty took me aside. "You don't really think the agency is going to get involved again, do you? To them, their role is over and done with. They have washed their hands."

I was surprised I had to defend my proposal with Betty. "Of course, I think they are going to get involved. Now that adoptees are publicly saying they deserve equal access to their records, agencies will change their policies. Don't *you* believe that?"

"No, I don't."

"But why introduce legislation to equalize access, then, if it's so hopeless."

"It's an exercise. It may happen someday but not in our lifetime."

"I'm more optimistic than that," I told her with conviction. It seemed to me if I was able to face reality, then *anyone* could. "I'm going to make it happen for Michael." And I meant it.

"Look, Lee," she said, pulling me down to sit next to her on a couch. I perched lightly knowing Dave waited outside. She wanted to make me an offer, she said. "I'm the one who found information for those adoptees," she admitted, gesturing with her pixie chin toward the adoptees. "I know your son is a minor but I think you can handle knowing who and where he is."

I couldn't imagine how I had given her that idea. The thought terrified me. I tried to reason it out loud, "Oh,

Betty. The adoptive parents. If they are half as scared as I am…."

"It's another taboo you would break, Lee. I know. But, listen to me. Just listen. I know I can get your information. If the agency lets you down, let me do that for you. Maybe you could get their priest to act as an intermediary or something."

All the way home I replayed Betty saying: "It's another taboo you would break." Was I really that afraid of breaking a taboo? I realized I was. She had nailed me. When I broke a taboo in the past, I had paid a big price. Tinkering with a sealed record would be huge; I couldn't imagine the cost for doing that. Even so, I was disappointed in myself. I hadn't fully reclaimed my feistiness, after all.

But there was another truth, an even bigger one. I loved being a mother; I had to resist hugging my boys full-time. With Michael's new identity, I would know where to direct my hugs. I would also know I couldn't deliver them and he wouldn't feel them. So, what would I do with all the hugs in me that would have Michael's new name on them? Then a thought hovered like a hesitant finger on a pause button: *where had I been putting Michael's hugs all along?*

I was annoyed with myself. I continued to get more questions without enough right answers. It was like one of those matching tests. A set of questions is in, say, the left column. A set of answers is in the other column. My question column kept increasing and there weren't enough right answers to match up with them.

What I did know for sure is that having Michael's new identity would be too heavy a burden to bear. I was just beginning to rise to my knees after being crushed flat by all the other stuff.

1975

Age: 30

Cape Cod

I was agitated. In June, I finally heard something concrete from Mrs. Fortune, a social worker with the New Hampshire Department of Welfare. Months before, I had chosen her to process my Release of Protection. I liked her name on the staff roster; it had a positive ring to it. But it had taken Mrs. Fortune a month to acknowledge my letter and another two months to reply to my second letter. In her reply she merely said she needed more time. It took her still longer to reply to my third letter, in which I had included a list of possible responses she could check off, along with a self-addressed and stamped envelope.

In her most recent letter, she wrote that she hoped I understood her failure to correspond had not been deliberate. She had to request, she explained, "the closed files from the Archives" to learn "where your son was placed." My heart abruptly ratcheted up two notches: one for her reference to "your son" and the other for her reference to "where" my son went.

Mrs. Fortune had written she wanted to learn the county seat that held Michael's adoption records. It struck me as profoundly unfair that all *she* had to do was ask. For me, the name of the county seat would be critical search information. From Betty's group I now knew the county seat was the area in which Michael first lived and maybe still did. I didn't necessarily want search information—I had already decided I wasn't ready—but the inequality of it smacked anyway.

Then a flashback reminded me that my social worker had told me Michael was placed near the White Mountains. Carole made it seem as if she had slipped up. But, looking back, the way she recovered was as if she had *acted* like she slipped up. I wondered if she had tried to throw me off track. She knew I didn't want to surrender and she may have feared I would try to find him. Or maybe my memory imagined the way she recovered after a genuine slip-up? I would have liked to know if Carole had been devious, but Mrs. Fortune's letter didn't reveal the county seat. Instead she wrote:

> "I was unable to contact his adoptive parents directly and have written a letter to be included in his Probate Court records, which will include your name and present address, and your willingness to meet with him should he request to do so. Since this is the normal course an adopted child would follow in the State of New Hampshire, you may be reassured that when he comes of age, if he

makes the inquiry, he will find your letter
which welcomes his contact with you."

While that letter she promised to write—if she did
indeed write it—would take care of releasing my protection
for Michael—if he searched—it was silent about making
information available to his adoptive parents before then. I
had previewed my Release with Betty before I sent it off,
so I knew I had been clear about wanting that provision.
Betty had also previewed my cover letter in which I
mentioned adoptees' needs during their minority. Had all
that just gone over Mrs. Fortune's head?

Since I sent off my first letter, I had acquired more
mentors. My mind was now like Silly Putty, stretching to
the max in this direction, to the max in another, all the
while maintaining its flexibility and basic substance. I had
befriended three California social workers—Annette Baron,
Reuben Pannor and Arthur Sorosky—who had just
published their book *The Adoption Triangle*. I became pen
pals with each of them, exchanging many-paged typed
letters. They were interested in my perspective, they told
me, because they wanted to better understand surrendering
mothers, to whom they didn't have much access. And they
wanted to follow the progress of my Release of Protection,
which, to their knowledge, hadn't been done before.

I had also begun to post letters in the "Confidential
Chat" section of the *Boston Sunday Globe*. On these pages,
a Globe reader could use a *nom de plume* to submit recipes
and ask others for personal advice on relationships and
such. In a letter the editors posted for me, I queried

adoptive parents. What did they think about the original mothers of their children releasing their agency's protection? If the option was made available to them, would they take advantage of it?

From what I was learning from Betty's group, many adoptive parents positioned themselves in corners opposed to the original mothers.' I didn't understand this. They had all the power. And, anyway, weren't we all supposed to be on the same side? Our kids' side? But I had witnessed that, even the kids, now chronologically adults, were sensitive to any displacement their adoptive parents might feel, so much so that many adoptees kept their searches a secret.

But were adoptees' perceptions real or imagined? While complaining their parents were overprotective of them, were they instead overprotective of their parents? That's what I hoped to learn through the *Chat*. To my surprise, many adoptive parents encouraged me to pursue my Release of Protection.

One wrote: "I have so little to give my children. I wish I had more." From another: "I would love to have the first mother of my adopted child write to the agency and offer to share information as our child matures. I hope such a procedure can be established soon within adoption agencies." The most compelling letter, though, came from an adoptive mother whose letter made me shiver: "My youngest son shot himself. He was severely affected by not having more information about his other mother while he was growing up. No deprivation can be worse than being cast from a void."

When I began to breathe again, I knew nothing would stop me from persevering.

As I told my mentors, if Mrs. Fortune thought I would accept her skirting the issue, she was *very* wrong. With my mentors' encouragement, I flexed my typing fingers and expanded my cover letter to a seven-page proposal. I pulled out all the stops. I excerpted anecdotes from what adoptees and adoptive parents told me. I quoted studies my penpals had provided.

One study from the Baran team, called *Adoptive Parents and the Sealed Record Controversy*,[13] was particularly relevant. Its findings showed that "50% of adoptive parents wanted more information on the birth mother; 75% wanted more on the natural father; and 50% wanted more information on the relationship between the natural parents."

I even secured a copy of New Hampshire adoption law, noting relevant sections on the "best interests of the child."

On July 9th, I sent the entire packet to Concord, the state capital, where I knew I could find whoever directed all the state's Welfare departments.

When I did not receive an acknowledgement of my packet by August 13th, I wrote the Director another letter, this time including a self-addressed, stamped envelope. As it turned out, the Director had passed me along to his Assistant. I could only imagine that conversation. Probably: "Here, you take this fruit cake."

But it was a good hand-over. In time, Arthur Roberge became a special confidante. In fact, when I contacted him in his retirement in the mid-90s, he credited me with helping to change New Hampshire adoption law. Back then, though, he was just a name to whom I directed my growing fury.

In 1975, Arthur said the right things, but, jaded as I was by previous rebuffs, I didn't know if he was placating or sincere. He apologized "for the times you have been in touch with our Manchester office staff with no acknowledgement." He thanked me for my "patience." He found my proposal "very thought-provoking," adding, "A number of suggestions…interest me very much." He demonstrated he knew what I was after:

> "It is my understanding you are clearly asking to share knowledge of your background history you feel might be of interest and help to the couple who adopted your son as well as to try to answer questions all three might have had over the years or are having now in an attempt to answer the 'who am I' experience all children, but especially adopted children, have. At the same time you are neither asking to meet or to learn the identity of the adoptive parents nor to seek a reunion with your birth-son. If I have interpreted your request correctly, it is indeed a most unselfish and heartwarming one."

He did seem to understand.

Arthur also clarified the distinction in the law I had noted, saying: "You are willing to give information, which is a different matter than requesting information." Nevertheless, Arthur said I would have to petition the court of jurisdiction, since, for the agency to do as I asked—to make contact with the adoptive parents—"the records would need to be inspected to learn their identity."

Arthur then gave me the name of the court of jurisdiction so I could petition them directly. And that is how I learned Carole had not "slipped." She had deliberately tried to mislead me about where Michael was being placed. He had not been sent near the White Mountains; he was placed in an opposite area of New Hampshire, one that bordered southeast Vermont. Although I had recently begun to suspect her slip was intentional, I was still stunned. If Carole feared I would search, why didn't she just shut up? Why try to send me on a wild goose chase? She had mapped a cruel hoax that could have sent me up and down blind alleys. I was outraged.

On the other hand, I was surprised how much it meant to me to know, concretely, where Michael originally lived. I felt a glimmer of the same light that shone in those adoptees who had found their mothers.

The Court wrote two weeks after receiving my petition, saying they would review the matter on September 16th. The Court said they wanted to bring in a social worker from their local Welfare department. I notified Arthur. I was sure Arthur would coach his representative what to say.

Meanwhile, I seized the opportunity to add more ammunition to my petition. I thanked the Court for being willing to consider the matter. Among other things, I told the Court that adoptive parents in the school where I worked often apologized for their inability to complete health forms. Michael's adoptive parents didn't need to feel inadequate; I could supply them with whatever they wanted.

I rested my case. The Court couldn't possibly want more. This would soon be over, and I was sure I would prevail. And, that's what I told Betty when she again offered to secure Michael's new name for me.

The Court's decision arrived promptly, as promised. But it wasn't what I expected:

> "The representative of the (NH Department of Welfare) informs me their position is they deem it to be in the best interests of the child not to proceed with any attempt to transmit such information at this time; that should the situation ever require that the adoptive parents receive such information, the Welfare Department would be in touch with this Court and make all the necessary arrangements to see this was accomplished."

Spitting nails, I wondered where Arthur had been. Why hadn't he primed his social worker with the understanding he said he had? Was he just trying to make me mark time like a soldier in boot camp? Was he expecting me to fall out?

Clearly, I couldn't trust any of them. I wrote Arthur to tell him so.

MORE

If we are painstaking about this phase of our development,
We will be amazed before we are half-way through.
We are going to know a new freedom and a new happiness.
We will not regret the past nor wish to shut the door on it.
We will comprehend the word serenity
and we will know peace....
You're only as sick as your secrets,
But the truth shall set you free....
The truth is the truth, so all you can do is live with it.

http://www.cduniverse.com/dream-theater-repentance-eight-regret-nine-restitution-lyrics-8273049.htm

*

- Hobbfoll (1998): Stress has for too long focused on personal rather than social elements.
- Friedman (1999): stigma, prejudice, and discrimination...can lead to mental health problems in people who belong to stigmatized minority groups.
—Above from: Ilan H. Meyer. *Prejudice, Social Stress, and mental health... Issues and Research Evidence*. N.I.H. 2003.

*

- Morris, JF, Waldo, DR & Rothblum, E: (2003): through coming out, people learn to cope with and overcome the adverse effects of stress.
— Drs. Jessica Morris, Craig Waldo, Esther Rothblum. *A model of predictors and outcomes of outness*....Journal of Orthopsychiatry. Wiley Online Publications. Mar. 2010

*

- Meyer, Ilan H. (2003): When group-level resources are absent, even otherwise resourceful individuals have deficient coping. —Ilan H. Meyer. Prejudice, Social Stress, and Mental Health...Conceptual Issues and Research Evidence. NIH. 2003

*

-Through minoritygroup affiliations, stigmatized persons experience social environments in which they are not stigmatized and they get support for others' negative evaluations of them. —E.E. Jones... et al. *Social Stigma: The Psychology of Marked Relationships*. New York: Freeman. 1984

*

In "social evaluation theory," stigmatized persons affiliated with minority groups evaluate themselves in comparison with others who are like them rather than with members of the dominant culture. —T.F. Pettigrew. *Social Evaluation Theory: Convergences and Applications*. In: Levine, D., editor. Nebraska Symposium on Motivation. Lincoln, U of NE Press. 1967.

CHAPTER NINE

1 9 7 5 – 1 9 7 6

AGE: 30 - 31

CAPE COD

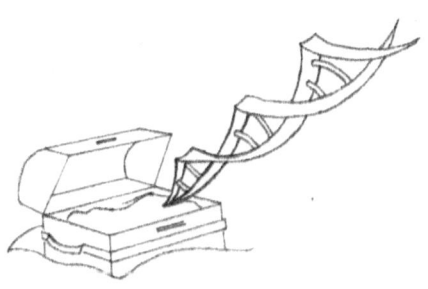

I gave Betty the go-ahead. She would find Michael's new identity for me. She told me she would plow through the records for me by the third week in October. The closer the day came, the more different I felt. I tried to explain these changes in a letter to her:

> My feelings are changing. Since I began three years ago to acknowledge my forgotten past, I thought I didn't want to know his name without the adoptive parents' approval—it wasn't my place, I told myself. But, with the knowledge of his identity close at hand, I realize how very much I really do want to know his name.

> I have been wondering: is it faddish like Kevin? Profound like Elisha? Simple like Mark? Old-fashioned like Harry? Is his last name one syllable or sixteen? Easy to pronounce like Smith or singularly interesting like Ishcabibble? What has he been called all these years when he wasn't considered my son?

> The core of me is anticipating the supreme pleasure of finally Knowing Something. Having something which links, which has form, sides, boundaries--something real, not fantasized, or speculated—something to grasp and something around which to build a perspective.

Although I named him Ronald Thomas after my father and his, he looked like a Michael to me and that's what I called him then. Ten years later, when I began to remember, I called him Michael again, as you know. But soon I will know what the rest of the world calls him and on what title he bases his identity.

Can you digest any of this? I am astounded at the depth of my feelings! It will be absolutely, to use a word normally attributed to lesser things, FANTASTIC.

There aren't words to say how much I look forward to your call. And to say 'thank you,' Betty. Again and again and again."

* * *

October 25, 1975. 4:10 p.m. A flashbulb moment: one of those times you remember where you were, what you wore, and what was said by whom.

Betty phoned from the adoption underground. She began: "I had to invent a whole new way of getting to the records. After a certain year, they began to file things differently. But your letter kept me going."

I barely breathed. "Did you find him?"

259

"Yes," she said simply, grandly. Then she laughed. "Lee, are you psychic?"

"Sometimes I wonder," I answered seriously. "But I don't want to be. Why? What did you learn?"

"His name is Michael."

I pulled out a chair and sat down. "Michael," I exhaled. "Michael." *How had I known this?* I couldn't stop repeating his name. It was on a continuous loop. Finally, the fireworks abated long enough for me to take in more.

Betty told me everything else she had learned. His last name, where they lived when they adopted, where they lived now, and, that as far as she could tell, he was an only child.

How could I possibly thank Betty, my Finder, the one who, in a few short sentences, had taken me through Michael's babyhood to the young teen he now was. I could feel her smile through my stammering. When I finally asked, "How did you learn all this?" she told me I would be better off not knowing some of it.

"As for where they live now, I found out the same way anyone else does. Why should you be any different? You gave them their family! I found them in the phone book."

I was like everyone else? I could find them in the phone book? After years of being stranded on empty margins, I could move onto the lines of the page?

"Do you know how you can really thank me, Lee?" Betty's voice grew serious.

"Yes. What? What can I do?"

"Stay in the movement, Lee. I have a strong feeling you are supposed to help us."

"Oh Betty," I sighed deeply. I would do anything. Except that. That was the *last* thing I wanted to do. It would void all my plans to return to my life with David and the boys, to my life as I once lived it, as I promised David I would do again as soon as I could. Besides," I explained, "I don't have the guts." Betty told me I would get some. I told her they would be too expensive.

Although David had begun to shy away when I advanced updates on my progress in adoption, I couldn't keep my new knowledge about Michael a secret, not even if I wanted to. My face gave me away. I sparkled like a twinkle-toed elf. I was a star in my own fairy tale! Dave later told me my eyes shone, my face shone, my ear lobes shone. After I danced through my revelation, Dave smiled broadly. Cupping my face in his hands, he declared: "I'm so glad to see you happy again." Then saying "I'll be right back," he drove off. He returned shortly with a bottle of wine. I got as physically tipsy as I was emotionally.

I was still on high when the phone rang the next day. When I heard Arthur's voice, I glanced at the clock. It read 4:10, exactly a day to the minute after I learned Michael's identity. It was more than a little eerie, especially when Arthur said why he called.

Arthur said he had told the social worker who had messed things up with the Court to call Michael's adoptive parents into her office. I was astounded to figure out that even as Betty was telling me about Michael's family, his parents were learning I was available to answer any questions they had.

"I didn't think it would really happen," I whispered. "If this had been done before, I wouldn't have…."

Arthur's voice took on a cautious tone. "Wouldn't have what?"

I took a deep breath. "This may shock you," I began, wondering if I should continue. "But yesterday, at this exact time, I learned my son's name and address. I was going to ask their local priest to…I didn't think you'd really do it. I'd been disappointed by your agency," I trailed, "so many times…."

"What name do you have?" he asked, not unkindly.

I told him. His silence told me I had the correct information. Suddenly I knew I could trust Arthur. More than that, I felt we were now on equal footing. I was no longer groveling. In that conversation, I began to call him by his first name.

"What did the adoptive parents say, Arthur? Do they want to know anything?"

"Your son's parents don't have any reason or desire to have additional information at this time," he said plainly.

"They do understand they can go back to the agency if they change their mind."

I was surprised by my disappointment. I had thought from the beginning I would be fine with whatever response they offered. I would do what I needed to do and they would do what they needed to do. Simple as that. Except, I discovered, it wasn't really simple at all.

"Art," I wondered, my mind catching up, "how could your social worker contact Michael's parents when the Court said no?"

"I decided that since no identifying information would be revealed, we could go ahead without the Court's permission."

I didn't ask him why he hadn't done that in the first place. It was now nearly a year and umpteen letters after I sent my first Release. But I quickly forgave the situation. I realized we were all breaking new ground, especially where a minor child was involved.

I also realized if the agency had interpreted the law loosely and acted on that looser interpretation when I first conveyed my Release, I might not know Michael's identity now. I had given Betty the go-ahead in large part due to the frustration of being dismissed (again) as a non-entity, as someone who hadn't done her homework and whose cause had no merit. If the agency had agreed upfront to honor my offer, I may have delayed a search for a long time.

I learned my anger was powerful fuel. Because of repeated delays, I had unfolded in new ways. The whole thing was mysterious, in the divine sense of the word. From Sweden till now, some place deep inside me had become increasingly magnetized. There was an inner pull...urging me...toward what?

It was like a religious epiphany but vaguer. With a religious experience, you know what to do with the impulse. You go to church. You join a ministry. Although I felt a bigger purpose calling me, I couldn't pinpoint what it was, where to go with it, what to do. Then, against my better judgment, I thought of Betty and how she wanted me to repay her. I quickly dismissed it as masochistic.

* * *

With my Release of Protection finally conveyed to Michael's adoptive parents, I should have felt free to take back the life I'd put on hold. That's what I promised David. But now I felt as if I had time on my hands, and there were still some blanks to fill in for Michael. Blanks that might also help me to flesh out my memories or to confirm their accuracy, the way I confirmed my belated sense that Carole had feigned her slip-up about where Michael was placed.

I could now see that during my pregnancy and throughout my meetings with Carole, I had been robotic. Put a foot here, another there. I had apparently made mental notes about others' behaviors that I hadn't been able to absorb for more than a decade. What else had I noted then, that I should acknowledge now? Who was the girl who surrendered Michael? What was she really up against? What else had happened? I was like someone with amnesia whose memories had been supplied to her by someone she once knew, but she still needed to collect more facts to make sure she knew all there was to know, that no critical information was still out there that could blindside her again.

From Betty's group, I learned adoptees were interested in the hospital records of their birth. Having these seemed to anchor them in the reality of being born on planet Earth rather than, as one described it, having fallen out of the sky from Pluto. Okay, then, I decided. I'll do that for Michael, and for me.

The medical information was jargon to me. I could only make sense of two things. I had gained 19 pounds during the pregnancy, going from 92 pounds to 111. And Michael was born with the cord around his neck, which was "divided" so the "infant delivered without difficulty." The report indicated there was initially some "depression of respiration which responded to suction." This info could have been alarming. But I knew Michael survived that early trauma. I knew it because I had spent a lot of time with him in the hospital and insisted on seeing him in the foster home. And now, with his name and Betty's sleuthing, I knew his birth issues hadn't led to something that only showed up later, as some birth complications do. I could rest knowing Michael was alive and well, so I filed the medical report away.

What else? I thought about the time Michael and I were intimately connected, when we were one. I was in Flo Crit for much of that time. What information did Flo Crit have? Would their records reveal any specifics on the stressors I had, stressors which could have pulsed through the blood system Michael and I shared and affected his development? I had only memories to go by. Were my memories accurate, complete? How did others perceive my state of mind?

After Flo Crit received my letter asking for copies of my records, they replied they wanted confirmation of my identity. That meant I needed someone to notarize a statement that I was the author of the request. I typed up a formal request that, for completeness sake, had to include the words "Florence Crittenton Hastings House." The only place where I knew I could find a notary was David's bank. I hoped the notary on their staff wouldn't ask any questions. If he read the statement he would know I was incarcerated for months in a particular residence. Would the notary think it was a drug rehab facility or something like that?

But having lived so long with so many made up stories, I could concoct a cover to casually throw out, if I had to. If pressed, the Florence Crittenton Hasting house would become a dorm in a private school I went to. That sounded good. Still, I got cold feet. Instead, I asked David to present it to the notary at his bank for me and to ask the notary to sign it as a personal favor. Dave took it from me gingerly, as if it was a hot potato. Yet, he did it.

I received a packet of materials from Flo Crit. The first entry detailed my Intake by Mrs. Wallis. I remembered her: dark hair, elegant, as aloof as the white gloves she no doubt wore in public. Although she tried hard not to seem snobbish, I doubted she socialized with girls like me. She was also tall. It seemed to me that everyone who was supposed to help me back then was tall.

Mrs. Wallis' job as my Intake worker was to write impressions of our first interview. The interview took place a couple of weeks before a vacancy was expected.

On July 13, 1962 Mrs. Wallis described me as "a pretty, slightly built and petite girl with a turned up nose and very long eyelashes." The report said I wanted a "wage home," one of a number of homes on the outskirts of Boston that the Crit lined up. I could live in a wage home as an "au pair."

In a wage home, I could help out around a house, babysit and things like that. In return, I could receive free "room and board," maybe even a small stipend. Since I would soon leave my home town to escape rumors and others' pointed stares at my middle, I would need to stretch the money Tom's family had given me to settle the paternity suit. A wage home would help.

The Intake had more to say. Mrs. Wallis saw me as making "an effort to be grown up." But she also said I had a way of "demanding things rather abruptly." My eyes widened; that was a revelation. I thought of Mary Anne being perceived as crazy by the professionals in her life. Maybe I had been more like her than I thought?

My memories of Flo Crit centered on my peers, the wonderful other young women I met during my many months there. But to the professionals there, I was seen as belligerent, at least early on? Well, I thought, good for me—and for Michael—that I let off some steam. He didn't have to share more in-womb space with hostility than he needed to.

Even as I spewed, though, I had also apparently leaked some grief: "As we spoke about the baby," Mrs. Wallis continued, "she wept some and seemed to feel very sad about the predicament she was in." I knew as a female that it was better to cry than not.[14] I had not been able to cry as much as my dire situation called for when I was at home with my family. Three of my siblings didn't know my situation, at least early on, and, for their sake, I had to pretend all was normal—good training I realized for the decade that followed. But at Flo Crit I had apparently been able to release some of what I'd held inside.

I wasn't the only one with an aggressive streak at the time. The report shared an observation Carole, my New Hampshire social worker, had conveyed to Mrs. Wallis about my parents. Carole described my father as "aggressive and dominating," my mother as "submissive." Carole further reported that I "was so conscious of the disgrace, I didn't go out of the house."

The next entry was the date I was admitted: August 2nd.
"L. came with her father, a nice looking man of 45 who had
strained his back and was in pain." Mrs. Wallis felt he was
anxious to get away, saying he told her "he had to get back
to business." Reading this, I remembered my Dad and I
pulling into the large parking lot behind the expansive brick
building at 10 Perthshire Place in Brighton. The concrete
steps to the building seemed as high to me as they would to
a child. My legs were so wobbly, I had a hard time
climbing the stairs. The double back doors seemed the size
of, and as impenetrable as, castle doors at the end of a
moat. Feeling weak, I couldn't open them; my father turned
the knob for me.

From the back door, Dad and I entered a long hallway
that abutted the front reception area. A very pregnant young
woman staffed the switchboard, pulling out cords and
shoving them into holes where lights blinked. I couldn't
blink. I stared at the belly that overshadowed her lap.

Mrs. Wallis led Dad and me into one of the smaller
breakout rooms off the hallway. In there was handsome
furniture, maybe leather, maybe a tabletop desk and a
couple of straight side chairs. Dad took a straight chair,
probably because of his back. I think Mrs. Wallis stood.
Meanwhile, I was directed to a big armchair. When I sat, I
sank into the cushion, feeling like Alice in Wonderland.

Everything about Flo Crit loomed large. Being a lifelong
pipsqueak, I was familiar with looking up at others and
getting lost in overlarge furniture. I had always used that to
my advantage. I was "cute," a junior petite runway model,

the tiniest cheerleader who led the line. But Flo Crit was different. Here, I felt socially and physically like a dwarf in a circus.

Mrs. Wallis noted in her admission report that I "wept uncontrollably." I did, and do, remember crying; I had never cried so hard in my life. It seemed to Mrs. Wallis, I "felt awful to leave (my) family." Apparently, Dad told me to keep my chin up, for Mrs. Wallis wrote "he was sweet and protective with her." But I apparently continued to cry after Dad left until I "caught sight of a baby, was startled, and said in a panicky sort of way 'Are there babies staying here?'"

Mrs. Wallis reported that when the housemother oriented me, and told me about the girl who would introduce me to others, I asked quickly, "How far along is she?" Apparently, Mrs. Wallis believed my "abrupt" and "quick" questions about this strange new world should have been delivered at a more leisurely, conversational pace.

The report continued the next day. Mrs. Wallis wrote, "She throws out questions in a challenging way as in 'You're finding a wage home for me, aren't you?'" She added that she told me I was "putting up barriers to hide behind" and that I replied "These barriers are for men." Mrs. Wallis challenged me: "I am not a man and therefore there is no need for a barrier with me." I didn't know how to say my barriers were for either male or female, for anyone who stepped over my uncertain line of defense. I didn't know how to push back with the right shade of bold.

But I short-circuited contact with Mrs. Wallis by persisting with hope for a wage home. When Mrs. Wallis asked what I would do with my stipend, I told her I would save it for later, that I would use it to set myself up somewhere other than my own family's home.

As I read this on Cape Cod, I realized I had blurted out a plan I didn't know I had at the time. I had thought the decision to leave my family home came later, after the surrender. I now reasoned I must have tucked my spontaneous answer to Mrs. Wallis in the back of my mind, getting myself used to the idea.

I complained to Mrs. Wallis I had a "headache" and I "rushed off to find a nurse with an aspirin." She later wrote I "was arrogant with the doctor." I may have also been more arrogant than I was genuinely interested in finding a wage home, too. When I was finally offered a placement, I was apparently ambivalent, saying things weren't as bad at Flo Crit as I thought they would be.

I looked up from reading about my time at Flo Crit and studied the pictures on my wall. I played with Scott and Todd, got supper for the family, and took a break. Later I slid the remaining pages from the Flo Crit package, more to finish what I'd started than to get immersed again. It was not a fun read, especially when I thought of Michael inside me while I was on my not-so-merry-go-round. I hoped the amniotic fluid acted like insulation to protect him from some of it. But I wouldn't know if it had until, and if, I got to know him well.

Since my medical Intake indicated I had been exposed to tuberculosis through my mother, Flo Crit sent me to the clinic for a lung x-ray. There, the record states I "fainted" and was told to "rest." As it turned out, fainting was a symptom of the flu. Stress from my pregnancy, being separated from my family, abandoned by Tom, and rumored to death probably lowered my immune system. It didn't help that I now lived with about 40 new girls under the same roof and was being taken care of by professionals who somehow expected me to be easy-going.

Flo Crit gave me a private room to recover from the flu. It was tiny, not much bigger than a closet. Now Michael and I were each in wombs: I nestled in my closet; he, in me. The tiny stooped housemother, Mrs. Gamble, brought me a small cup of tea, my first of what would become my favorite beverage. The smallness of everything—the room, the cot-size bed, the tiny sips of tea, Mrs. Gamble—was at last the right-size environment. Finally, I was able to absorb things little by little.

After I recovered, the family for my new wage home came to Flo Crit to meet with me. There wasn't instant rapport but it had been a long time since I'd enjoyed rapport with anyone, so I figured it was my fault. Even so, before long I wanted out of the wage home.

In the Flo Crit packet, there were copies of letters I had written to Mrs. Wallis about getting a reprieve. "The people are very nice," I wrote, "but I find I can't keep up with the chores and the hours I work." I explained their baby was up at least twice a night and my rest period during the day was limited to when he took his nap, which he didn't always do. I listed my daytime chores: "I rise at 6:00, change the baby, dress him and the older boy, cook their breakfast, wash the dishes and counters, sweep the floor, and vacuum the rooms downstairs while I'm supposed to keep the boys busy."

There was more: "Later, I also fix everyone's dinner, do the dishes again, empty the garbage, wash the floor with a sponge on my hands and knees, iron the family's weekly wash, occupy the children, and re-vacuum every room. Then it's time to change the boys, put them to bed and rise whenever they wake up." It didn't help that the boys "bite me, kick me, hit me, all within vision of their mother who lets them have their 'fun.' They throw their plates on the floor after almost every meal."

The expectation that "I take all this in stride" was apparently too much for me. I added in my letter that "it's not a case of too much work; it's more that our upbringings are too vastly different." I admitted to Mrs. Wallis that "I am taking sleeping pills but I just can't cope with the strain." And I told her I accept "80% of my unhappiness (as) my own fault." Yet I offered a defense. "From what I understand I am not the only one to be dissatisfied under their employment. Previously, they had 2 girls who lasted 2 or 3 days each." I apologized for burdening Mrs. Wallis with my problems and concluded with my hope to return to the home where I "loved the girls and enjoyed it. So, you see," I concluded, "I'm not completely hopeless."

When I returned to Flo Crit I learned they were a supplier of hard workers for some well-off families. I met other mothers who had worse wage homes than I had. Others reported their wage home experiences were good ones. Wage homes were a mixed bag.

My Flo Crit packet had nothing in it about Michael's birth; no comments or documents to confirm they knew it happened. I checked the packet a couple of times to make sure nothing was misfiled. Everything about Michael's birth was apparently limited to the hospital medical records, to the pages of my Journal, and, thanks to that Journal, they were now touchstones in my memory: the too-early induction of my labor; his near-incubator weight; the hospital allowing him to stay in my bed with me so I could feed his lusty appetite; his oversized burps; the indescribable smell of him; his dark head of hair; the name "Michael" written all over his face; and, the limb-tearing pain of leaving him behind.

Although I was happy I had so much caring time with Michael in the hospital—nurturing no one could take away from me—-remembering how we parted still made me deeply sad.

I knew the next section of Flo-Crit materials would also hurt. I stopped reading and brewed myself a fortifying cup of tea. With one hand wrapped around the appropriately-scalding mug, I re-settled in my chair.

There was a letter from Carole. Dated January 10th, the first four paragraphs droned about the money situation:

how much I owed Flo Crit and the hospital and how that balance might be resolved. But the last sentence made me suck air:

Carole wrote: "On the lighter side, the baby is lovely and should be excellent material for adoption."

Lighter side?

Material?

"Lighter side!" I repeated as it sunk in. Money was heavy fare, and Michael's fate was light 'n easy?

While I wouldn't surrender for a couple more months, in Carole's mind, Michael was already on the adoption assembly line. After all, he was **"material!"**

When Mrs. Wallis replied to Carole, she wrote she, too, was "delighted that the baby is so lovely and desirable." I thought: others could desire him, but I couldn't? I wanted to shout back through time, why didn't it matter that I desired him? I took deep breaths as if I was in labor.

Calming down, I turned to the last letter in the packet. Carole had again written to Mrs. Wallis. This letter was dated March 27th, more than two months after Carole's letter indicating the adoption chute was ready for my "material." It read: "Lee has officially surrendered her baby and we expect to have him placed within a week or so. It was touch and go for a while as to whether she would release him and finally she decided to do so."

"Touch and go?" Half-right, I fumed: my "touch;" her "go." The word "release" and "decided" also grated. "Release" implied I held him captive while "decided" implied that, among several choices, I had selected the best one. Neither fit my experience. But Carole had at least partly acknowledged I had tried to hold on.

Looking again at the March 27th date of this letter, I recalled a different letter, one I received from the state after I got copies of their files on me. I set aside the Flo Crit packet and dug out the state's letter, which was dated April 15th. In it, Carole wrote that Michael's parents were now being approached about his "availability." A connection between Carole's two letters insinuated itself.

I recalled the day I surrendered in Carole's office, the day she gave me that yellow-lined paper with two columns—one column for the "things" I could give Michael and one column for the "things" adoptive parents could give him. I'd broken her rule for "things" when I wrote "love" under my column. But Carole had dismissed my "love," saying the adoptive parents had already seen him and loved him.

Sitting in my house now, I realized Carole's assertion the adoptive parents already loved him had been tool, not truth. According to Carole's letter in the state files, Michael's parents did not lay eyes on him for another month.

I had proof of a lie. Not just any lie. It was The Lie. It was The Lie that negated my love for Michael by offsetting

276

it with love adoptive parents allegedly already had for him. It was The Lie that caused me to collapse in surrender. Now, more than a decade later, there was nothing I could do about it. I felt fiercely impotent.

Then I realized there was another lie in the paperwork. I shuffled through the state paperwork a second time. Yes, there it was: in official documents Carole filed with the state, she wrote: "Lee had no maternal feelings for the child and felt that keeping him would not be in tune with her lifestyle."

Good God! I realized if Michael petitioned the Court for his records he would read that. He wouldn't know to ask Flo Crit for their materials. He wouldn't read Carole's letter in the Crit file admitting she knew the real truth: that I had tried to hold onto him.

I needed a support group—now—but Betty's group wouldn't meet for a couple of weeks. I was so furious I didn't immediately realize I could phone Betty. When the fury subsided enough for me to think straight, I called her.

I brought the packets of material to Betty's next meeting. I pointed out the "lighter side," the "material," The Lie, and the "touch and go" versus the "no maternal feelings." Mary Anne looked over my shoulder. I could feel her shudder. Yet, there was no choice except to move on.

But move on to what? Adoptees suggested I subscribe to Michael's local newspaper. Maybe his picture or information about his family would be printed there someday.

It was a turning point. I pivoted from securing information about back-then, to securing information about Michael now.

Almost at once, two photos of people with his last name appeared in their local paper. Knowing his adoptive parents' first names, I surmised these were relatives. A "Shirley" had helped to dedicate a bank. A "Norman" had earned membership in some special club for selling a certain number of automobiles. I clipped and filed these.

When Betty heard about this, she murmured, "Pathetic."

I laughed, then I said seriously: "Crumbs are better than nothing."

She promised: "I'm going to get you some good pictures."

At the next meeting, she showed up with Xerox copies of old yearbook pictures of Pat and Bob. They had gone to the same high school in the same city where they continued to live. I wondered if they had been high school sweethearts like Tom and me. I promptly stored these in my wallet with my other relatives' pictures, for that was how I had begun to think of them.

Then Betty handed me a blow-up of a color photograph. I saw the profile of two young boys pivoting into a driveway that was solidly banked with knee-high snow. The shorter boy was behind the taller one, but he partly looked at the camera, offering me a slice of himself to feast on. He seemed dark, like Scott. His posture was like two photographs I had of Tom: when he walked, Michael was a little stooped.

"The shorter one . . .?" I asked Betty, holding the picture close.

"Yes."

As I held Michael's picture, Betty beamed, and the adoptees and Mary Anne elbowed each other to "ooh" and "ahh." I remembered being on a hospital gurney and new mothers filing out of Flo Crit wards with their "oohs" and "ahhs." I also realized I was mothering from afar. Restraint was a form of mothering, denying myself the opportunity to know him was a form of mothering. But instead of feeling sacrilegious, like I had broken a taboo, as I once feared, I felt the opposite—as if I had been elevated to some special state of grace. Without being in a church. Without the intercession of a male priest. Despite being indoctrinated throughout my life on the divinity of religious men, I now believed a decidedly feminine spirit was working through my female-dominated second family.

But Michael's picture showed me almost nothing about how he really looked. I hungered for a close-up. I wrote to the local paper's sports editor asking for the names of the coaches of youth teams. Maybe there was a baseball team picture somewhere. With the coaches' names in hand, I wrote each of them. No luck. I decided to try the Junior High. As one school secretary to another, I enclosed $10 and asked for an extra copy, or even a Xerox copy, of the previous yearbook. She sweetly wrote back to say she was sorry but even their library copy had been lifted. I hoped the thief really needed it because he or she had deprived this mother of the only good look at her son she could get. I asked the secretary to hold onto the money for the next year's book.

* * *

Susan, Mary Anne and I had other children whom we had not yet told about their missing sibling. We wondered the best age to tell them. Although I was more closeted than they were, we three also wanted to know the best way to "out" ourselves to friends and relatives who had never known or who had brushed off our motherhood as a closed chapter.

Adoptees didn't have these same issues, not anymore. There was little, if any, stigma about being adopted, thanks to the "chosen child" story that everyone wanted to believe. Our motherly questions and issues were becoming clearer and I could see they were different than what adoptees had.

When a mental health professional attended one of Betty's meetings, I asked her if she could offer a "clinic" during which we mothers could focus on some of our questions. In addition to our questions about "outing," we wanted help in coping with our peculiar loss.

We were lost to that part of ourselves that had birthed our children. How could we reunite with that lost part of ourselves so we could be healthy and whole when our children found us? And what if our children chose *not* to search for us; what would we do with that now-integrated self? How could mothers whose children were "out there somewhere" live with not-knowing their whereabouts? How could we live in limbo if we did know? What were the boundaries of mothering from afar? Telling others who were in the dark about our secrets was one thing. After the outing, how could we help them accept what they now knew? There were many other questions for which we didn't yet even have words.

But when Susan, Mary Anne, and I attended our clinic, the mental health professional was as lost as we were. Even she admitted she didn't know how to help us work on such complicated issues.

It then seemed to me the agencies that had given us the advice to surrender, forget, and move on should devote some time now to our after-care. What did they suggest we do? In this changing climate, what advice would they offer?

I had kept Arthur at New Hampshire's state capital informed about everything I did. He had become one of my pen pals. Even though the other New Hampshire social workers—my first contact and the social worker who had talked with Michael's parents—weren't keen about knowing what I was up to, I copied them too. Art wrote to say he wanted to meet with me to explore "post-adoption services" for surrendering mothers. Even that phrase was new.

After I traveled from Cape Cod to Concord, New Hampshire, Art welcomed me in his cluttered office. He was as warm in person as he was in his letters. His suit was frumpy, his glasses greasy, but I was still impressed. Art freely admitted he didn't have advice for any of my clinical questions and he admitted he would like to have some answers, too. He hoped I would continue to share with him what I learned. He treated me as respectfully as if I were gathering information for an in-service training for his staff.

While I was there, Art called the social worker who had met with Michael's adoptive parents and suggested she meet with me. I traveled from Concord to the city where she had her office, which was where Michael lived. There was significant contrast between her and Art. He looked open and interested while she looked threatened and guarded, and, unlike Art, she wasn't about to relax access to her first name. At the end of the meeting, she frankly asked where I was "going with this." She sounded like David.

Leaving her office, I decided I would indeed go somewhere with "this." If she had tailed me, she would have seen me re-trace Michael's life. I went by his first house, the address on an early record Betty had found. It looked a lot like one of the houses I had been raised in. A neighbor happened to be in her yard. I asked if she had known the people who once lived there. She wasn't sure, she mused. As if to herself, she murmured: "Was that the woman who kept having all those miscarriages?" As I looked again at Michael's first house, I felt protective of its earlier mistress. I also felt a little gratified; maybe my pain had eased some of hers.

I then drove by the address where Michael now lived. I drove neither fast nor slow; I drove as if I intended to go down the road apiece. Glancing, I noticed his mother had chosen the same type of country curtains in her windows as I had chosen for mine. Diagonally across the street from their house was a small general store. I imagined Michael frequenting that store.

Small general stores had long been a part of my neighborhoods. Tom and I had spent a lot of time at the one across from my Manchester house while we waited for my mother to arrive home. Tom had also bought cigarettes for his mother at the general store across from her house. And Scott and Todd were always trotting to the general store around the corner to buy baseball cards in bubblegum packets. I was happy Michael's family shared the same touchstones I did.

I left Michael's city, knowing it was *their* city. A part of me felt like a trespasser but another part of me felt like I had only tested what a "swing by" would be like, as if his parents might someday throw me an off-handed invitation to see their fair city. In running a circuit of Michael's life, I oriented myself in a few ways that were exquisitely satisfying, even if they were fleeting.

* * *

Betty had been approached by the producers of a Boston news show featuring a rising young female reporter, Natalie Jacobsen. Betty wanted me to do the show. It was hard to say no to Betty, my Finder. I agreed to do it, but with certain conditions: I would be interviewed in silhouette, my voice would be distorted, and they would use a pseudonym for me. I picked a name out of thin air: "Lenore Hatch." Betty and Natalie agreed to those terms and that's how I was taped.

I shuddered to watch the tape when it played on television. I didn't like looking like a criminal. But most people still didn't know; most importantly, my boys. "It would be too big a secret for them to carry," Dave had stressed. "Even innocently, they might spill the beans to their friends, who would tell their parents. The whole thing could blow up," he had warned. I had promised Dave I wouldn't tell them.

After the show aired, I told them. They were overhearing me use the word "adoption" on the phone. I didn't want them to think they were adopted. One of the few useful things that came to me from the clinic was the danger of secrets in a family. I learned secrets have a bad vibe that is highly detectable to sensitive children. Also: I worried that my keeping secrets from them might give them permission to keep secrets from me. I prized my relationship with my boys too much to chance it. Besides, I was ready.

When Dave was at an evening meeting, and after the boys had had their bath, I invited them to join me on the floor of the sitting area of my bedroom. This was different staging than their nightly story, each in their own bed, so they looked at me expectantly. However, I was my usual casual and cuddly self and soon we were talking the way we always did. When the moment felt right, I told them I wanted to share some news with them.

I began: "Before your daddy and I married, I had a baby. I couldn't raise the baby because I wasn't married then and because they said I was too young. The baby was given to an older married couple in New Hampshire. When that happens, it's called 'adoption.'"

Todd interrupted. "Was it a boy-baby or a girl-baby?"

"A boy-baby. You have an older brother. He and his parents love each other very much. I love them, too, but I can't see them for a long time yet."

"When you see him, can I see him, too?" Scott asked.

"Oh, yes, pumpkin. I hope that can be arranged."

"Me too?" Todd wanted to know.

"You bet."

While digesting this, they each reacted in a way that was typical of their personalities. Scott stared intently with quiet interest. Todd fell over backwards yelling "Wow."

"I wanted to tell you this now," I continued, "because I am working to help people understand adoption. I know you have heard the word and you might think you are adopted."

Scott and Todd looked meaningfully at each other as if to check in.

I saw with relief I had caught any speculation before it got legs. "You aren't adopted," I assured them. "You grew inside me."

Todd grandly patted his belly.

"What's his name?" asked Scott.

I was glad I could tell them.

"Does he play baseball?" Scott asked. They had concocted elaborate rules for games with a whiffle bat and ball. I could see Scott's mind working out how to adapt the rules from two to three players. In a few seconds, his face relaxed; he had figured it out.

"I'm afraid I don't know whether Michael is interested in baseball," I answered. "There's a lot I don't know. I do know I will ask him someday if he would like to know more about us. And then maybe we can all know each other. In the meantime, we will wait for him to grow up a little more."

"Anyway," I added, stretching out my legs and leaning back on my hands. "Until Michael is a little older, your daddy thinks it's better if we don't tell anyone else. You have each other to talk to about this, if you want to. And, me, of course. And," with fingers crossed I added, "your daddy, too. Okay?"

"Okay, momma," said Scott seriously. "Will you read 'Little Toot' now?"

"You sure you wouldn't like me to read something else tonight?" I laughed. Even the school librarian had joined my campaign to try to talk him out of his obsession with "Little Toot." But while he would give other books a try, the "Little Toot" series remained his all-time favorite. And this was not a night to push more change.

I turned to Todd. "While I read to Scott, why don't you find a book you want me to read to you? How about that?"

"Okay" he agreed. He scampered off in search of one of his favorites: "The Little Train That Could."

When I told Dave later, he was not happy with me. However, when he saw the boys playing as usual with each other, and their ongoing comfort with me and with him, he began to relax. No doubt, though, the possibility of "the whole thing blowing up" still worried him.

* * *

I didn't want to continue to pile things on David. But there was one more telling I had to get out of the way. Tom. I thought I had become strong enough to hear his side of the story.

Over time, I talked with adoptees about their interest in their natural fathers, and I hedged about Tom when Natalie Jacobsen questioned me. My professional mentors in adoption reform—Annette Baran, Reuben Pannor, and Arthur Sorosky—encouraged me to begin to prepare Tom or at least to find out whether he would reject Michael or his adoptive parents.

287

In the back of my mind, I had replayed countless times what Donna told me after the family reunion. Tom had asked about me, she said. He had also volunteered he wouldn't let his mother "do that again" to him when she had tried to block his marriage to his pregnant girlfriend.

Dave was anything but pleased about the thoughts I was beginning to have about contacting Tom. But maybe he had become punch-happy, for he reluctantly came around after I explained what I had learned from others and shared the study the Baran team had conducted, which revealed, in the black-and-white Dave preferred, that 75% of adoptive parents wanted more information on the natural father. I also told David this was the last past-thing I would have to do. My return to the simple life we had known together was around the corner. I was exhausted from all the interior work I had done and I assured him I looked forward as much as he did to resuming our normal life.

* * *

For both Michael's sake and my own, I needed to finally understand where Tom stood about his paternity. Why had he denied his fatherhood after our years together? What had happened? Was he scared? Did he really have doubts? Did he now want to know about Michael? Like a snowball running downhill, I indulged a fantasy: Would Tom, maybe, want to go to just one ALMA meeting with me and learn some of what I had?

I phoned Donna. Would she call Tom for me? Ask him if he was willing to talk with me?

She didn't hesitate. A seemingly scant second later, Donna called back. "Tom said to call. He's waiting by his phone."

Suddenly I felt like throwing up. I began to get such chills that I put a blanket over my shoulders. Hunched under the blanket, I dialed his number. His voice was the same. The 14 years since we last talked disappeared. Our communication style was the same. We talked as we had as teens, finishing each other's sentences. Except this time, I finished more than he did, since I had given the matter more thought.

When we hung up, I was flying high. Finally, I had a few answers. The rest would come tomorrow. Tom wanted to talk as much as I did. For an anchor, I typed our conversation. By now, writing about my experiences had become second nature.

I wrote that Tom used short, broken sentences urging me to understand.

"Everything was so confusing to me. My parents. When you're that age, you listen. They were like…brainwashing me…telling me I was being framed…so confusing…. I was like at the bottom of this pit. No, I didn't know about a son. I never knew anything.

"Yes, I want to talk. I wouldn't want your husband in the room. I couldn't talk freely with anyone there. Not even Donna."

"I usually work weekends but not tomorrow. And then I'm free so far next month. I'd rather do it tomorrow! I'll cut short my rehearsal tonight and talk to my wife when she comes home from work. I suppose you'd be fast asleep? What's your number? I'll call you at 7:00 in the morning."

Sounding sincere, he returned my "Good to talk with you." He was as reluctant to hang up as I was.

But Tom didn't call the next morning. My wings suddenly clipped, I crashed. David called Tom for me, waking him up. Tom explained he had been up until 3:00 in the morning with his wife. Anne didn't think it was a good idea for Tom to see me. Dave then talked with Anne, urging her permission. I talked with her too.

Anne told me Tom did not believe he was the father of my child.

I couldn't believe it was happening, not again. Especially not after the night before. Turning away from the mouthpiece of the phone, Anne gave Tom an alternative. "You can talk to her on the phone," I heard her order, "or in person, if someone else is in the room."

With an abrupt about-face from strong-willed to timid-Tom, he answered, "I don't know. Whatever."

Tom had told me the night before he couldn't talk freely with anyone in the room. And, now, there was no way for me to last a three-hour drive. I had to know, immediately. I had to get this over with. Now I had even more questions. Why the change of heart? Where had last night's Tom gone? I looked at David, sad and worried about me. I couldn't deny he had good reason.

Even the tone of Tom's voice had turned around. I saw his repulsive underbelly, looking even uglier now that he couldn't be excused as a teenager. He was no longer interested in having a meeting of the minds. Just the opposite. He was on offense.

Later, I transcribed that second call.

"It seems to me that if I was the father you would have gone all the way to court to prove it. Why did you take a settlement?"

Dumbfounded, I answered I was exhausted by his denial of paternity. I wanted the awfulness to go away. I also stated what I thought should have been obvious: I didn't pursue the paternity suit in order to make money. When his parents offered enough to take care of sending me to a home for unwed mothers, I stopped asking for more. I shot back: "If your parents were so sure you weren't the father, why didn't *they* go all the way to court to prove it?"

He didn't have an answer for that. Instead: "One of your old *boyfriends*—the one who loaned us the book on state laws—asked me to meet him. He offered to set us up in an apartment and to set me up in a job. It seemed like a set-up, period."

I was surprised, and I told Tom I hadn't known about any of that. It went over his head.

He barreled on, squashing any hope we could be civil: "If I were the father, I would have wanted to see him back then. If he looked like me…my girls, I couldn't deny them. They look just like me."

He sounded conceited and self-involved. He would only admit paternity if a child looked "just like" him? Still, I tried to understand. Maybe his need for proof-positive came from doubts his mother had instilled long before? I told Tom I had a picture of Michael but it wasn't a clear shot. I said I was trying to find a better one but it would take time. I added bitterly, "I'm not about to snap a photo of him after school, you know," being reminded as I said it that Betty had done that very thing.

As a last ditch effort, it seemed to me if I could get Tom to remember our "first time," he would recall I had been a virgin. I tried, offering humiliating details.

"I don't even remember our first time," he slammed, unlike any other male I ever heard of.

Wherever the Tom of the night before had gone, I couldn't reach him. By now, I was using the heel of my free hand to wipe away tears—tears of frustration, of disappointment—tears about him I should have shed 14 years before.

"What should I tell Michael?" I asked, feeling the pain I would have to pass along to our son.

There was a long pause. As the silence grew, my system suspended. I wondered if the Tom I had talked with the night before—the Tom I had once known—the one who had talked with Donna—would circle back. But he only answered: "Tell Michael whatever you have to."

There was nothing left to say. Still, I didn't hang up and neither did he. This new silence stretched. Reluctantly, I brought it to a close. It seemed he was equally reluctant, which only confused me more. If he really didn't think he was Michael's father, wouldn't he be dying to get rid of me?

Later, the disappointment and sadness stepped aside, making room for anger. Where Tom was concerned, these were familiar feelings. Tom had married his mother. Anne was like Ellen. I could almost see her wagging her finger at Tom in the wee hours of that morning, badgering him, putting him, as Tom had told me the night before about his mother, "at the bottom of a pit with no way out." Anne, like Ellen, apparently made decisions for him, said things for him, told him how to feel. Although the cast of characters had changed, the script was the same. I was back to figuring things out on my own. Only now I had more to figure out.

The good news was, I had support. I hugged David to me like the dear he was. He was genuinely sad for me that I hadn't been able to tie that loose end, and maybe he was also sad for himself. He knew I didn't do well with dangling threads. I had proven I was one to pick them apart until I could laboriously weave them into some new whole of understanding. He might have wondered, rightly, what came next.

* * *

A few days later, I received a reward for my patience. Michael's local paper posted a list of students who made the Honor Roll. With hope, I traced my index finger down the list of names. I telepathed:"I hope you've been smart this quarter. You need to be a good example for your brothers!" His name was there.

Good news helped me stow some perspective on Tom. Apparently, I might never know what happened with Tom-- not 14 years before and not more recently. I had lived with that uncertainty for a long time and, since it was apparently necessary again, I would "just" return to that state. It wasn't ideal but everything else had sorted itself out. It was the one remnant I would have to live with, at least for now.

I shared the good news about Michael and the bad news about Tom with Betty on the phone.

She told me not to worry. "Some natural mothers don't even know who the father is. Adoptees adjust. Some adoptees don't even want to know their father. Their need is satisfied with the mother."

For reasons I couldn't explain, I strongly doubted Michael would be satisfied with not knowing about Tom. If Michael was anything like me, he would pursue the Tom in him. But maybe Michael would be more like Tom and not care? Although not caring was possible, it didn't ring likely to me. [15] I sighed deeply into the phone.

"So" Betty recapped, ignoring me. "You have come such a long way. A couple of years ago, you were in la-la land," she laughed, "not remembering a thing. Since then you have written that Journal. How long is it, 500 pages?"

I laughed. "I wrote that twice, no less. Once wasn't enough. I had to clean it up, you know. In case Michael wants to read it someday."

"Exactly my point," Betty continued. "You get to the bottom of things. You dot your 'i's and cross your 't's. You've picked adoptees' brains. You've gathered information on adoptive parents. You've reconstructed your experiences with the hospital, your agency, and Flo Crit. You petitioned your agency to Release your Protection. May I remind you, by the way, you were successful with that? You broke new ground, Lee. You even put a clinic together for a few birth mothers so you could help each other out. . . ."

"That was a joke, Betty," I interrupted. "I mean, the counselor was very nice. She tried. But she just didn't know how to help us. My New Hampshire social workers didn't know how to help us either; two of the three NH social workers were even rude. Heck, I don't know how to help us."

"Maybe not…yet," she trailed. "But you know more than any mother I've ever known. You have good instincts."

Except for the Tom threads, I couldn't dispute my instincts were often on target. As I thought about those times, my end of the conversation slacked.

Betty stepped into the opening. "You did all this while you were…are…a wife, a mother, a school secretary…."

"Stop it, Betty." I smiled. "You're making me tired."

"You have more energy than anyone I know. Add that to your good instincts. You know what you get?" she asked.

"A partridge in a pear tree?" I joked.

"Seriously, Lee. Are you ready?"

"Ready for what?"

"To start an organization for mothers who have surrendered children for adoption?"

* * *

With Betty's flattering assessment of my accomplishments still ringing in my ears, I told Dave what Betty said. To my surprise, he agreed. "I have to hand it to you, Lee," he said, mangling an axiom as he often did: "You've gone from negative numbers on the speed dial to a speedy demon. You've rounded corners that left me in the dust. But I've watched you from the sidelines and I have to applaud."

I gaped. "You think I've done the right thing?"

"Feeling as you do, you've done the only thing you could. I know how much you love Scott and Todd. I don't know how you lived all these years without acknowledging your love for your first child. [16] I also agree with Betty that you've shown you could start this organization she proposes. I don't think anyone could top what you would bring to it."

I knew it was hard for Dave to admit this much. He may not have meant it as permission but that's what it sounded like to me. In a way, this permission, if that's what it was, complicated things more. How could I risk hurting this man of grand gestures by taking what I wanted…if I wanted to start an organization in the first place.

Could I protect Dave if I started a group? Thinking out loud, I wondered, "Maybe my group could become a branch of ALMA?" I could imagine hiding under that foliage, rather like I did with the Natalie Jacobsen interview. I reminded Dave—and me—"I used a pseudonym then. Maybe I could continue with that pseudonym?"

"Think about what you really want," Dave answered, his eyes clouding in a warning that did not match the go-for-it encouragement moments before.

* * *

I had now attended ALMA meetings for more than a year. In that time, I had only met two other surrendering mothers. What if Mary Anne, Susan and I were unusual?

What if most mothers were truly able to put the experience behind them? If our numbers were small, there would be no need for a group. I needed to test the waters.

I wrote to the Editors of the "Confidential Chat" section of the *Globe*. I wanted to know: If I posted a letter asking women to contact me directly, and if those women gave permission to the editors to forward their responses to me, would the Editors send their letters along? Yes, they would forward letters to me, they said.

The following week a letter from "Biological Mom" appeared. In that letter, I said I had not been able to maintain the memory loss my social worker had prescribed. Was I alone? Were "you" a reader who surrendered a child only to discover you couldn't forget? "If you would like to discuss your situation," I wrote, "please reply and include a note to *Chat*'s Editors that you would like your letter forwarded to me."

I liked the idea of letters coming my way. It was a lot safer if no one personally arrived on my door step. Although I met many lovely young women in the home for unwed mothers, I had heard all the rumors about women like me. Some trashy women could come out of the woodwork. The women at Flo Crit and the women at ALMA meetings could be exceptions.

The first letter to be forwarded to me came from "Joanne." Unbelievably, she lived in Orleans, the next town. It was too close for comfort. Still, a neighbor in whom I could confide was an irresistible draw. I decided to chance it.

On the phone, Joanne sounded strong, intelligent and funny. Even so I didn't want her to know where I lived. Instead, I wrangled an invitation to her house. I dressed extra-conservatively so she wouldn't think *I* was trashy. But when Joanne opened her door to me, all bets were off. She definitely wasn't conservative...and she was proud of it. Forty or so extra pounds ballooned her shapeless muumuu. Her house reeked of a musty odor she later told me was pot. She was unkempt. Her hair needed a good scrub. She happily, almost lovingly, ushered me into her kitchen, sidestepping her pre-teen son and daughter who were horsing around. "Adolescent foreplay," she explained.

She swept aside a mound of clutter on the table so she could make me some tea. As she lowered her bulk into a chair, she hiked the hem of her dress and then raised her arms above her shoulders to cup her palms behind her head. That is when I saw that shaving her legs and pits also wouldn't hurt Joanne's appearance. I didn't know how to escape without hurting her feelings, so I endured the tea.

Over her steaming cup, she told me her story. [12] She was 15 when she became pregnant with a daughter she named "Bettina." Her baby's father, whom she dated for more than a year, said he wanted to marry her. But he soon dropped out of sight. Joanne's bulk shielded her pregnancy until she was six months along. Then her parents "whisked" her off to Flo Crit, the same home I went to. "It was like being in jail," she told me. "My family lived in the same city and I

299

wasn't able to go out in case someone who knew our family would see me. My parents insisted on secrecy."

Like me, she pleaded with her family for help to raise her child. But "at no point did anyone but me consider the possibility of me keeping her. All of the so-called counseling I received was geared to make me sign the baby away." Her parents were the least help of all. She explained: "There was a veiled threat I would be signed away myself—as a 'stubborn child'." As she talked, she threw out the word "fuck" a lot. She was unconcerned her kids were in her listening area. At that time, I wouldn't have dared to use That Word in a nightmare.

After I extricated myself politely, I dashed for my car. I decided if I saw her on the street, I would cross it and go in the opposite direction.

Joanne, however, had different ideas. Thank goodness. She latched onto me and wouldn't let go. Since refined little me didn't know how to graciously tell her to kiss off, I politely answered her regular phone calls. Before too long, her irreverent humor hooked me. I began to call her to get another dose of the genuine article she clearly was—that I had not been for a very long time, if ever.

Much later, whenever I taught a module on "first impressions" I told my students about Joanne and the importance of not judging a book by its cover. I credit Joanne more than anyone with modeling for me how to be myself, even though, I realize at this point, it will never come as easily for me as it seemed for her.

Another *Chat* letter came from "Gail." She lived in Maine but planned to move soon to Massachusetts with her, what sounded like, normal family. Gail's surrendered daughter was very young. Gail told me she had also gone to "Flo Crit" several years after I was there. I wondered if she had slept in my bed, sewn on my machine, taken out the same book in the library. I wish I had been able to leave a note behind—under the mattress, in a sewing basket, among the pages of a book—like some kind of time capsule. Maybe the note could have read: "Listen only to yourself."

Kathy was a third writer. She surrendered a daughter who was younger than Michael. Living south of Boston, she promised to come to a meeting either on Cape Cod or in Boston, if I held one.

Other mothers wrote, too. One said she had buried her pain in order to survive. "I blanked out a period of my life to the point I couldn't consciously recall what happened." Reading this, I realized she sounded just like me, especially when she continued: "There was a price to pay. I developed a habit of turning off my feelings and memories, a kind of psychic numbness that started with surrender and spread to other areas of my life."

Another articulated a different part of me: "I've had to act like everything was fine. I had to pretend and live a lie. I must have done it very well because I believed it myself."

* * *

During my next phone call with Betty, I brought her up-to-date. "So, you can see, Lee," she announced, "you are not alone. There are probably thousands of women who are thinking they are the only ones who can't get past this. They need you."

She overstated the need for "me." I wasn't anyone who was any more special than anyone else. Probably less special, since I was very much in the closet. I reminded Betty of that.

She ignored me. "Just play around with the possibility, Lee. If you did this, what would you call your group?"

I told her IF I did it, I would like to set it up as a branch of ALMA. She thought that would work but that the branch would still need its own identity. She knew—perhaps intuitively, perhaps craftily—that I was a goner when my creativity button was pushed.

"Well, for starters, I think we need to be known by a single term. We've been called by every name in the book—other mother, first mother, surrendering mother, birth mother—you name it. Many names are not very flattering, if you know what I mean."

She said she did. "So which term would you select?"

I admitted I knew them all. I had used most of the terms interchangeably myself. I thought through "natural mother." "I like that," I told Betty, "since our relationship with our children comes from a natural process but it may make adoptive mothers feel unnatural. I want us to end up on the same side: the side of our children. So I don't want to hurt their feelings. As for "biological," I'm sorry I ever used the term 'Biological Mom' in my *Chat* posts; after all, we are not just procreating protoplasm."

Betty laughed into the phone. "You have such a way with words," she encouraged. "Keep going."

"I have reservations about the term 'first mother.' I like it but adoptive parents might feel it makes us the primary parent; you know 'first,' as in a contest or something where adoptive parents come in "second." And what would that make them? Secondary mothers? As for 'original mother,' it reminds me too much of Eve and her original sin." I shuddered. "As a recovering Catholic, I couldn't stand that."

I thought some more. "I do like the term 'birth parents,' which the Baran team uses in their articles and book. We are connected to our children through the birth process, so it has the same feel as 'natural' to me but without being negative to adoptive parents."

"That sounds good, Lee. What else? You need a few more words for the title of the group."

I thought. "How about 'concerned?' We are 'concerned,' right?"

"Right," she agreed.

"And I hope we can be 'united'. So, how about 'Birth Parents United in Concern'."

"The acronym would be BPUIC," she said, expressing it phonetically.

We laughed, realizing it sounded too much like a "Buick" on a bumpy road. "Yes, you're right, Betty. Sounding like a car with hiccups would never do. What would we use for a logo? Something from the TV show, *My Mother, the Car?*"

As our laughter subsided, we thought in silence. Then inspiration struck. "What if we combined the words 'birth' and 'parent' to one word: 'birthparent.' You know," I said, getting excited, "like 'grandparent'. Like grandparents, we are the child's progenitor."

"Hmm," Betty mused. "So BUIC? Nah, that sounds even more like the car."

"What if," I said slowly, still thinking out loud, "we changed the title around so that it was 'Concerned United Birthparents'!"

"Now you're talking! And the acronym would be...."

Like a duo, we sang together: "CUB."

"Wow!" Betty exclaimed after a moment. "That's it!"

"Yes, that is it." And: "You tricked me!"

"But you would be so good."

"I'm not going to do this, you know. I can't."

"Why not?"

"My husband, for one. He'd lose his job. We'd end up on the streets, on welfare."

"You really think so?"

"I know so. You don't know these people. Image is everything to this bank. I mean, they even interviewed me and our two-year-old before they offered David a job."

"Well, you could use a phony name, like you did before. Maybe you could get other people to take the spotlight. What this organization is going to need are your leadership skills."

This was the same out—a pseudonym—I had used earlier with Dave and Betty. Still, it was a pretty far-fetched idea. "Betty, be serious. I've never led anything in my life. I keep a clean house. Raise great kids. Bake all my own bread. I'm kind of clever with decorating. But lead? Not me." I did not mention that I had been president of the "girls' council" at Flo Crit.

Betty continued to ignore my arguments. "You'd be a great leader. I can tell."

Within a few days I also had the perfect logo of a mother bear and cub, which was placed in my hands quite serendipitously.[17] I also had a meeting place and a date for the first meeting. Meanwhile, Betty said her ALMA newsletter was about to go to press. She wanted to include a notice about our first meeting. I gave her the information but in the back of my mind I left the door wide open so I could easily back out.

* * *

Joanne exclaimed "Far out!" when I told her my ideas. She offered to serve as Treasurer, saying it was the only way she'd get to touch any money. I wrote to Gail. She wrote back, saying to count her in. She promised to be CUB's secretary. Susan said she'd be Vice President until someone else came along. Kathy said her husband/lawyer would advise us on legal stuff. Mary Anne wasn't sure she believed in officer positions. She thought everyone should be equal. But she wanted to be a member.

* * *

Reading a newspaper clipping to me over the phone, Joanne told me someone named Betty Jean Lifton was scheduled to speak in Orleans. Explained Joanne: "She wrote a book called *Twice Born: Memoirs of an Adopted Daughter*. It says here that she summers in Wellfleet. It should be interesting. Let's go."

Before I drove to Joanne's to pick her up to hear Betty Jean Lifton, I pulled a wide, thin packet from my mailbox. It showed the postmark of the city where Michael lived. Obviously, the packet had something to do with him. I wondered what it could be. At my kitchen table, I opened it up."Oh, my God!" I cried out loud, clutching the envelope to my chest. Michael's seventh grade yearbook. His school secretary had kept the $10 I sent her the year before and remembered to send me a copy. Meanwhile, I had done so much during the year I had forgotten about it.

306

I quickly gathered the boys in the car and took them to Marie's for a play date with her kids. Then I sped to Joanne's. It was now a ritual for her to sweep clutter from her table and I not-so-patiently bounced on my heels. "*Oy vey,*" she laughed. "What's the rush?"

I held up the packet. She glanced at the postmark and her eyes popped. Now as much at home in her messy kitchen as I was in my own spotless one, I quickly wrung out a rag and wiped off the table. When it was as clean as an altar, we carefully opened the book.

Eighth graders were featured in wallet-sized photos at the front of the book. Quickly flipping to the back pages, we discovered that seventh graders were lined up according to homeroom. Homerooms, we figured out, were ordered alphabetically by kids' last names. I was so full of anticipation there wasn't enough room in me for my lunch. It rose in my throat.

To my left, Joanne giggled with delight. "Here's the name," she exclaimed, pointing. "And, Lee, here's the face. Oh, my God, the face. He's beautiful. *Oy vey,*" she repeated.

Tears pooled in my eyes, blurring the picture. I blinked them away and mentally prepared to follow Joanne's lead. I hadn't feasted my eyes on Michael's full face since he toyed with my finger as a baby. Joanne moved her body so I could lean into the yearbook.

Joanne was right; he was beautiful. Dark like Scott. Smile like mine. A look of Tom's older brother about him.

His face, rounder than Tom's. Eyes? Although they looked almond-shaped in the picture, it was hard to tell what they looked like when he wasn't smiling, as he was in the photo. Even if I didn't know who he was, I would have been drawn to him. He had a special, sweet presence. My arms grew heavy, as if my bones had suddenly filled with lead. It was the way I'd felt when I'd left him behind for the last time, knowing I wouldn't be able to hold my baby again. And I wouldn't. He was a boy now, and I was still years away from being able to reach out to him.

* * *

BJ Lifton used her hands to talk. Light feathery strokes underscored her soft, cultured voice. She talked about her book, which was based on her experience as an adoptee. She had also written an article about teen adoptees for *Seventeen* magazine. Teen adoptees, it seemed, were of special interest to her. For her next book, she wanted to write a fictional story about adoption for teens. She already had a title: *I'm Still Me*.

BJ talked about the developmentalist Erik Erikson. His theory proposed, she said, that we are challenged to greet particular life tasks when we reach specific ages in our lifespan. During our teen years, BJ explained, we need to settle our confusion about who we are by learning our social roles. She said Erik Erikson called that task "Identity versus identity role confusion." She continued: "We don't want an identity so firm we stop amending it. Nor do we want our confusion to be so dense we can't work through it. We need to strike a balance."

I had an "Aha." She had given me another answer to my "why now?" I had been in the middle of figuring out who I was when an untimely motherhood became part of the mix. Becoming a mother further confused my search for a self. Before Carole or anyone else said "Boo" I was already muddled. Then, with surrender, my role as Michael's mother was suspended. In some ways, I was picking up now where I left off then. I thought about my counselor saying I was remembering because I finally felt safe enough to remember. As an adult, I was now far enough along in my search for self that I could safely backtrack to the role I'd left behind. I only had the barest outline of how this all worked but I felt I was onto something. I wondered if BJ could help me put this together.

When BJ finished autographing her books, Joanne and I approached. We told her we were birthmothers of teen adoptees.

"Reallllly?" BJ smiled. She smiled with her lips together, the corners turned up. Her wispy-soft Dutch-boy haircut peeked from under a black newsboy cap. Her eyes danced merrily. She looked long at Joanne and then hard at me, taking us in as if we were hors d'oevres whose presentation she wanted to appreciate before she daintily tasted each of us.

"And Lee is going to start an organization for birthparents, one word," laughed Joanne. She was already into the party line.

"Reallllly?" BJ said again. "You must tell me all about being birthmothers of teenagers. You must tell me about this organization. What do you call it?"

"*If*," I stressed, looking meaningfully at Joanne to remind her I wasn't fully committed, "If I started a group, I'd call it *Concerned United Birthparents*."

"CUB for short," interrupted Joanne. "With a mother bear and cub for a logo."

"Parent bear," I revised.

Chin down, BJ darted her eyes between Joanne and me, as if she were watching equally matched tennis players. "I want to know every…thing. You must come to my house in Wellfleet. You must read the letters I've received from teen adoptees." She spoke with a Barnard-educated New York accent. And everything was "you must."

Normally, a "must" would have made me bristle. But she was right. I "must."

* * *

Bucking stop-and-go tourist traffic, Joanne and I headed to Wellfleet the following week. The first thing we heard as we pulled into the long dirt driveway was the barking of dogs. As we parked, two black standard poodles bolted our way, BJ behind them. She wore what I would learn was BJ's standard issue: black silk Japanese "pajamas" and that newsboy cap she had worn the week before.

310

BJ greeted us warmly, lovingly chided her dogs, and then gracefully led us through the xeriscaped front yard to a one story house with weather-worn shingles. The house was so nestled in the dunes it looked like darker sand had blown in for a visit and settled down.

BJ ushered us into a long, informal living room with a broad expanse of glass sliders that provided a stunning view of the ocean. She plopped on the wooden seat of a swing suspended by thick ropes from the rafters. Swinging there looked like fun and I debated whether to go for a turn but she quickly slid off and asked her *au pair* to bring us iced tea. Opening one of the sliding doors, she suggested we make ourselves at home on her back deck.

This was not a slice of life with which I had any experience. Yet I wasn't intimidated. BJ was endearing, approachable, interesting…and interested.

On her deck we sipped our tea and took dainty bites from butter cookies her *au pair* had made. In the distance to my left, sea grass poked from sand dunes like week-old whiskers. Just beyond the dunes, the Atlantic reared so high, I could almost hear it roar. Meanwhile, BJ quizzed us like the journalist she was, making scratches on a small pad she kept on her lap. She reminded us she wanted to know "everything."

"What do you call it?" she asked with a smile of apology for not remembering. She leaned forward as if to promise she would never again forget my answer.

311

"Birthparenthood," I supplied, capturing our complicated situation as a condition and putting a label on it.

She looked thoughtful. "I like it. It's really very clever. I prefer 'natural parent' but it's so upsetting to some adoptive parents, it's not worth it."

I nodded, remembering I had said the same thing to Betty. I told BJ as much.

"Really?" she said again, using her obviously favorite word. "A birthparent organization is necessary, you know. All the opposition keeps talking about is protecting *you.*" Sweeping her hand to indicate Joanne and me, she laughed lightly.

"Tell her about your Release of Protection with the adoptive parents," Joanne coached.

I filled in BJ.

"Interesting," she commented, leaning back. "Yes, you must start this organization. I think you would be very good at it. Don't you, Joanne?"

Joanne agreed.

I was cornered but I discovered I kind of liked it there. It felt a good place to be. From there, I could go places, do things and meet people who could teach me whatever it seemed I was destined to learn, like it or not.

BJ then led us into a small guesthouse with two rooms. One room held twin beds. The other room faced the water. Colorful birds perched in cages were suspended from low ceilings. BJ greeted each, clucking their names. An iguana clung to an upright branch in a tall cage in a corner of the study. This room also held a messy assortment of books, a typewriter, stacks of paper, and a litter of boxes tucked under this and between that. Clearly, BJ worked here, hard. She drew out one of the boxes. "Here are letters from teen adoptees."

Joanne and I looked at the stack like it was an oasis in our desert. We began pulling out the letters and reading passages aloud to each other.

"I wonder all the time who I look like".... "I want to know, more than anything else in the whole world, who my real parents are".... "We had to trace our hair color in school through the generations and I couldn't do it. I was embarrassed".... "I want very much to understand why she didn't keep me".... "They say I'll have to wait until I'm 18. I may only be 14 but I'm human too".... "My parents ask me if I have any problems with my adoption. I tell them 'no'."

We picked BJ's brains. Why were they afraid to tell their parents how they felt? Given her lecture the previous week, I knew she, like Deb, was savvy about the unconscious and other psychological concepts. "I think," she offered, "adoptees feel they must protect their parents from the stigma of infertility."

Joanne and I looked at each other. We could weigh our stigma against theirs any day and come up heavier. It also cast my Release of Protection in a new light. If Michael wasn't expressing his needs, how could his parents meet them?

We discussed the underpinnings of adoptees and adoptive parents. BJ probed our psyche.

"Birthparenthood," she mused, proud of herself for using the term I had just invented, "is uncharted. There's no research. You must publish. Your experience must get reported."

I felt a shimmy down my spine, like a firefighter on a pole. BJ was right, again.

Since research and reports dig up answers, I had more than enough questions to get CUB started. Although I didn't know *how* to get started, it seemed BJ was on board. She was a published writer who had pillow talk and daytime chats with her husband, Robert Jay Lifton, a Yale psych professor who was internationally respected for his work on war and genocide. Alongside BJ were my California mentors who were also writers and researchers. They were asking my opinions too. Others' belief in me suggested they saw something in me I didn't know was there. That sense was becoming all too familiar. By now, it was clear I didn't know myself all that well. For that reason alone I had to take their assessments seriously.

Meanwhile, my tests and trials on the home front weren't going away any time soon. There was the matter of

Michael for whose sake I felt I would have to someday resolve the situation with Tom. Begging for more resolution—at least within me—was the matter of Michael's grandparents and aunts and uncle. The question of my friendships would also have to be explored: who would stick with me and who wouldn't? Above all this loomed the overwhelming need to protect my innocent boys and husband, including his career.

With a long to-do list, I needed all the help I could get. I didn't trust professionals—not even BJ and my California trio—to be able to deliver. Only by talking with other birthparents—those who were going through the same thing—could any of us hope to figure things out.

The bad news was, over the previous four years I had had to pry myself open again and again. The good news was that, although this new type of exercise had been exhausting, I was beginning to feel a little pumped. Maybe some muscle was developing under my skin.

As I left BJ's seaside home, the wind picked up. While I walked to the car, the sand in the xeriscape peppered my legs like stinging nettles. Closing the car door against it, I caught a whiff of hope in the salt air.

2013

Age: 68

Florida

Looking back from the age 68, I see I may have begun that day to prepare myself in earnest for my next move. I wouldn't start over geographically. I would stay put on Cape Cod. But I would draw from my experiences of moving around as a kid. I would re-invent myself yet again.

I didn't know if I'd feel the same way about starting CUB the next day or the day after. But at that moment--that "now" moment I had finally seized--I was open to giving my life some leeway.

MORE
A (Too) Simple Sociological Timeline

World War II ends and the government reverses its war chant. Women are no longer encouraged to become Rosie the Riveters while their men soldier on. Now, married, white, middle-class women must return to the home fires, turn over their position as heads of household to their returning husbands, and add babies to the new houses the government helps to finance so the economy can re-focus on the domestic front.

*

Religions that foster hierarchical values command central stage in the lives of most households.

*

Those in popular culture who do not live a "proper" life suffer reproach. Pat Boone with his soft voice, sparkling white buck shoes and squeaky clean image is admired by the older generation. Not so Elvis Presley. His greasy side-burned hair which brushes the collar of his flashy jacket is loudly condemned. His rock songs, inspired when, as a southern boy, he listened to Blacks pick cotton, confuses the elders. Meanwhile, when he accompanies his guitar-playing with pelvic gyrations, the camera man on *The Ed Sullivan Show* is instructed by the censors to cut him off at the waist.

*

While reproduction is encouraged within marriage, birth control for singles is limited to saying "no." If she says "yes," he uses nothing, "withdrawal," or condoms, but only if he's willing to risk his "manliness," which he usually isn't, since traditional gender roles are strictly adhered to. If she gets pregnant, she goes through with it; it is illegal for her to control her reproduction.

*

The number of "homes for unwed mothers" expands to conceal single pregnant women, especially high schoolers who are kicked out of school and must look for ways to hide their shame. Their friends' mothers disallow their daughters to hang out with them. Peers gossip. Pregnant girls "get a reputation." It is acceptable for single fathers to be pushed off the scene or to walk out on their own. In a double standard, peers admire them for the deed.

*

Because wives are expected to become mothers, those who are infertile seek ways to achieve that ideal.

317

*

Reaching beyond the approved career outlets for women—teacher, nurse, secretary—a new round of mostly female, often single, women become social workers. They organize professionally to earn credibility for their delay into, or for their alternative to, their own motherhood.

*

Social workers find purpose, in part, by disarming single mothers and transferring custody of their babies to infertile wives. For wives with new babies, adoption is a way to experience motherhood, to cover their reproductive difference, and even to exceed social expectations since they choose to rescue "abandoned" babies. For retreating single mothers, adoption removes evidence of wrong-doing and masks tarnished reputations. These single mothers withdraw from view, hoping the social prescription—to forget and move forward—will perform as promised and ease their memories. Birth certificates are falsified and the truth is sealed.

*

A natural challenge by a younger generation of an older generation's social order becomes more potent than earlier generational shifts due in part to faster print production, to increased reports on social changes, and to more widespread television viewing.

*

The Vietnam War gives rise to a generation of young people who noisily and sometimes violently question others' authority to dictate the terms of their lives and the society they hope to influence.

*

Publicity for a "free love" (sex) philosophy," for hippy communes, and for Hollywood releases of increasingly suggestive movies portray that non-traditional lifestyles are possible.

*

A strain of women who balk at the social imperative to limit their lives to motherhood begins to get traction for equal access to and credibility in the workforce. To qualify for jobs, these feminists agitate for the ability to reliably control their reproduction.

*

In 1972, a medication that met FDA approval in 1960 undergoes more chemical adjustments that now make it safe for millions of women. It's called the birth control pill.

*

In 1973, the Supreme Court legalizes the right of women to personally make decisions about their reproductive lives and to end early pregnancies, if that is their choice.

*

318

Title IX of the Education Amendments of 1972 is judged to include the right of pregnant girls to remain in schools alongside the fathers of their children. The increased presence of pregnant girls in mainstream society reduces the stigma.

*

For the mothers whose children were taken for adoption in previous decades, time disproves the promise they will forget and move on. These mothers find each other, organize, and agitate for a reform that moves adoption from a sacred institution to one that is reality-based.

*

While some power-brokers embrace the shift, most continue to resist changes to adoption practice and state law. Some worry birthparents' visibility and the work for adoption reform will now influence some single mothers to keep their families together. They are right.

AUTHOR'S NOTES

If you typically read a book from front to back, you probably have finished reading *STOW AWAY*. It's the first of the two books I have for you. (The second is *CAST OFF*, which will be ready in 2014.) I want to describe the three sources I used for *STOW AWAY*.

One source was a three-ring binder. It's five inches thick and is stuffed with personal letters and documents written by, to, and about me between1960 and 1996.

Another significant source was a Journal I wrote in 1974—the one you read about in **STOW AWAY**— which I updated in 1996 so I would have a record of my shenanigans between 1974 and 1996. This Journal is about three inches thick, printed on both sides, and is spiral-bound. Let's call that my 1974/1976 Journal.

Some other material came from my decades as a full-time social science professor in which I taught a garden variety of courses in the Social Sciences.

The binder is self-explanatory, but here's more about my 1974/1996 Journal and a little about the academic in me that surfaced on some pages.

As I just implied, my 1974/1996 Journal covered two distinct time spans: 1958-1974 and 1975-1996. *STOW AWAY* covers the first and a little of the second.

In *STOW AWAY*, I showed how my memories as a teen and young mother charged from their hold a dozen years after they had taken refuge. I described how these memories took over what I now see was a kind of ship-in-a-bottle life, a life that was ideal but not real. At the time, my memories were completely unexpected and decidedly unwelcome. But they had a mind of their own. Eventually, I lost control of my own ship and hoisted a bloodied rag of surrender. Then my younger self dictated the memories she should have purged and integrated with the rest of me long before.

But how accurate were those memories? Amazingly, dead on! I later learned my teen's memories had been flash-frozen in a process called "dissociation."

Dissociation happens when your psyche keeps some parts of you secret from other parts. Your psyche is a neural device that is formed by nature and nurture. It has many functions, including protecting you from being overwhelmed. Since everyone needs to be protected in unique ways, being dissociation will present differently from one person to the next. But there are some commonalities. In End Notes, I offer an admittedly simplistic view of this disorder and one of its syndromes, Post Traumatic Stress Disorder (PTSD).[18]

Now, full disclosure here: excerpts from my 1974/1996 Journal did not carry into *STOW AWAY* with 100% accuracy. That was due to space. In order to accommodate other material, I only excised those portions of my Journal that preserved the *zeitgeist*—the spirit of my time—which might help you to understand the culture in which I surrendered. Compared to the full Journal, the excerpts seem to me like bones without flesh. Still, I did my best to honor those bones.

I also made some other changes. To keep my cast a wieldy number you can more easily follow, I merged some people and their stories into composites. To preserve the privacy of anyone who may want it, I have used either their first names or invented some new names. The timelines of some events may also not be narrated the way they were actually lived. Some events were collapsed or re-ordered.

I have one more source to introduce. I taught social science courses for more than 30 years at the college level. I couldn't tell the professor in me to disappear; nowadays, I strive to be one whole person. But since I didn't want *STOW AWAY* to be a textbook, I only judiciously used academic stuff—like in post-Chapter vignettes I call "MORE;" in this "Author's Note;" in "Afterword;" and, in "End Notes."

I wanted *STOW AWAY* to be a story, a narrative. But even that has an academic flavor. Social scientists call real life experience "anecdotal evidence." And anecdotal evidence suggests things that deserve more attention.

Lee Campbell
2013

AFTERWORD

2013

AGE: 68

FLORIDA

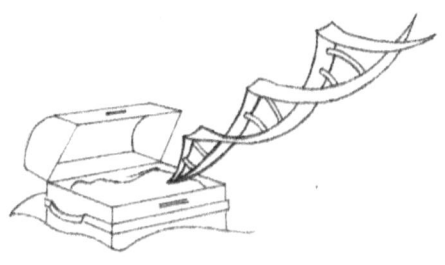

In my first e-book version of STOW AWAY, the Introduction was hefty. Some readers told me it was a speed bump for them, as they had been eager to get to Chapter One and the meat of the story. So, for this newer version, I divided the original Intro. I put upfront the part relating to "Why I wrote the book." I also reserved some parts for this "Afterword" and others for "End Notes."

This "Afterword" does two things: it updates you on adoption reform and it honors some early adoption reformers who are no longer with us (at least not in the way I was privileged to know them).

Like most updates, a little back-up is in order.

Prior to World War Two, birth certificates of people who were adopted weren't uniformly sealed, and "amended" birth certificates were not always issued. In fact, major welfare agencies argued the value of keeping birth certificates truthful.[19] After World War II, American society became very pro-natal, very pro-make-a lot-of-babies (see Chapter Nine's "MORE").

To satisfy infertile couples' desire to be the same as others who were reproducing like crazy, most states began to transfer custody of children of errant single mothers to ideally-married couples. To maintain the couple's façade of sameness, most states fictionalized birth certificates. The "amended" certificates claimed that adoptive mothers had given birth to, and adoptive fathers had sired, their adopted children. To give further credence to these legal revisions of personal history, factual birth certificates were sealed.

To their credit, Kansas and Alaska never sealed the original birth certificate; truthful birth certificates have always been as accessible to these states' adopted citizens as they were to their non-adopted citizens. But that leaves 48 other states. At various points in time each of those 48 states has sealed—and sometimes unsealed and re-sealed—the truth. Adoption reformers have focused on these truth-sealing states, arguing factual birth certificates should be as accessible to adopted persons as they are to non-adopted persons.

When I returned to CUB as its Curator (see "Why I Wrote This Book"), I wanted to find out how reforms were going. Since I had been "out of it" for decades, I was able to see things through "fresh eyes."

It was both sad and frustrating for me to see that reforms had advanced only a little for adoptees. Of the fifty states, only ten states in 2012 — including Kansas and Alaska— allowed adoptees access to their true birth certificate through the same process used by non-adopted citizens. Another nine states had created convoluted access, which made adoptees second-class citizens since they have more hoops to jump through than others. During the 2012 legislative session, four other states considered and denied some kind of access.

In New Jersey, the state legislature approved access only to have its governor, Chris Christie, veto it and submit his own fettered proposal. I read that Mr. Christie has an adopted sister and is Catholic. It's probably not too far a reach to assume he asked their opinion. If my presumption is right, allowing his sister to weigh in could have been like asking a woman in a co-hab relationship if she thinks it's a good idea to marry her partner and, if told no, then denying marital rights to every other cohabber. As for any resistance by the Catholic Church, I could see they didn't need another scandal. Although access to a right doesn't necessarily mean the exercise of that right, with access more adoptees could find their birthparents and learn about the tactics some church-affiliates used to get their mothers to part with them.

At first, it seemed to me that things were different for new mothers than they had been. By the time I left CUB in 1984, a few agencies had begun to listen to our plea for more openness in adoption. Now it seemed open adoption was fairly standard practice, especially those adoptions where the internet played a role.

Today, mothers with untimely pregnancies, who are convinced they want adoption for their children, can usually participate in the selection of their child's adoptive parents. With these prospective adopters, mothers could collaborate on a contract for an open adoption that allowed them some ongoing contact or information.

But things weren't as rosy when I looked deeper. I learned many adoptive parents promise mothers the moon to get their children, only to later pull the plug on the contract. Only 26 states and the District of Columbia have laws that enforce open adoption contracts to some degree. [20]

If a new mother surrenders in some other state, she can be left by the roadside without a crash kit.

As a sociologist, I also looked at the bigger picture. Some states were stepping up control over women's reproductive lives. Access to abortion was becoming more complicated. Funding was being threatened in some states for Planned Parenthood. The definition of "rape" was narrowing in places to fit political purposes. The Commonwealth of Virginia even tried to mandate that instruments be inserted into pregnant women without their permission. About this, I felt like screaming. I had heard too many stories from too many single mothers about brutal vaginal exams, prolonged deliveries without anesthesia, snide and rude medical attendants, and even shock treatments, sometimes also accompanied by explicit statements along the lines of "I hope this teaches you a lesson." In a reminder of the '50s, some politicians even suggested that contraception should be less available.

If these proposals could be seriously considered in our 21st century, what else would we debate and perhaps execute? Looking at latent functions—unforeseen ripples of change—would these proposals lead to an increase in the number of untimely pregnancies and, to extend this possibility, an escalation of forced surrenders? Such proposals would dim the optimism of any card-carrying feminist, and, although I hadn't always been a feminist, birthmothers' stories had made me one.

Zooming further out, I could see that, elsewhere in the world, change seemed brighter. With the exception of the

327

Northern Territory, every state and territory in Australia—including, in March 2013, the Australian national government—has apologized to its birthmothers[21] for the coercive practices that were used to get them to part with their children. In Ontario, Canada, legislation in 2009 allowed birthmothers and adoptees to obtain identifying information about each other. Court cases and legislation elsewhere in Canada hold promise, too. England, Spain and Ireland are also studying their treatment of birthmothers.

I did see some hope for change within our own borders: A Dan Rather expose—*Adoption or Abduction?*—aired in 2012 on American television. Here, too, though, were disappointments. The Rather team expressly stated birthmothers were only now coming forward with their stories. With this, those who had been telling their stories since 1976, and risked everything to make adoption accountable, were tossed in the dustbin of history.

It seemed to me that CUB itself had grown quieter; its organizational focus seemed to focus now on an annual Retreat and member support, both valuable thrusts but different from the noisy CUB I had known. But something even more fundamental was missing in CUB. While CUB had been founded, in part, to honor the whole truth of people's lives, CUB, like me, had ignored its own past. This omission made it too easy for Dan Rather types to hype less-than-truthful claims.

The good news on that front is that CUB's past is now digitized, is available on CUB's website (www.cubirthparents.org), and awaits processing by

Harvard's Schlesinger Library. It remains to be seen whether journalists, historians, and researchers will help CUB to set the record straight.

As I close *STOW AWAY*, I must turn my attention and yours to adoption reformers who are no longer able to fight materially for truth and equality. Jean Paton, whom I mentioned in the Introduction, deserves another mention here.

In addition to Jean, I mourn the loss of colorful Joanne McDonald, whom you met in STOW AWAY. I also ache for sweet Susan Daggett, CUB's early Treasurer, and for Libbi Campbell, CUB's full of grace Massachusetts Coordinator. I'm also still raw about the loss of Mary Jo Rillera. You will meet Susan, Libbi and MJ in *CAST OFF*.

It still stings, too, that Annette Baran has died. She was one of my personal mentors and a powerful yet love-ly thinker. The great Reuben Pannon, who co-wrote *The Adoption Triangle* with Annette, recently followed her in death. I told you about their importance to me in Chapter Eight.

Between Annette's death and Reuben's was the loss of the singularly special Betty Jean Lifton. You met BJ in Chapter Nine. BJ became a professional adoptee of sorts (a good thing) with her books—*Twice Born, I'm Still Me, Lost and Found*, and *Journey of the Adopted Self*. Taking a cue from her famous psychiatrist husband, Robert Jay Lifton, who analyzed the Holocaust, Nagasaki, and Hiroshima, BJ also became what I would call a profiler of criminals who were adopted. Among her most notorious subjects was the New York murderer and rapist "Son of Sam."

As you might imagine, I celebrate to the high heavens that I can still count some of my dearest former colleagues among my friends today. I'll name three.

Gail Hanssen Perry, CUB's first Secretary and my indispensable right hand, personally helped mothers to retract surrenders and opened her home to shelter a few. Sandy Musser, CUB's first branch coordinator in Pennsylvania, wrote *I Would Have Searched Forever* and *What Kind of Love is This*? Later, she went to federal prison for four months for the "crime" of reuniting adoption-separated family members which prompted her third book, *To Prison With Love*. And, Alison Ward held several positions in CUB, including support for members who had been involved in a New Jersey sting operation initiated by Betty Furness, a then-NBC commentator. Alison also supported Mary Beth Whitehead, the nation's first surrogate mother.

Despite the four of us being early reformists, our lives have evolved way beyond the surrender of our children. Many times we meet—now rounder and grayer—and talk our heads off without once saying the "A" word.

After you read more about them, and others, in *CAST OFF*, you'll appreciate how remarkable it is that our lives have somehow become normal. And probably a lot like yours.

END NOTES

1. I often used self-disclosure in my teaching. Revealing parts of my life experience was, as I explained to my Psych students, a way for me to model Carl Rogers' Humanist approach to counseling. Getting "professionally personal" with my students also created a level of trust between us, which inspired them to volunteer their own experiences. Our class discussions were a rich and lively exchange.

From time to time, I introduced birthparenthood to my Sociology students. For some examples, when we discussed…

Emile Durkheim… who believed people need moral regulation from society in order to manage their own situations. When society has not established norms—expected behaviors—"anomie" sets in. If this normlessness is combined with a lack of control and a perception of being alienated from others, suicide can result literally or, I submit, figuratively (as in trying kill off parts of a self) .

Robert Merton… who believed society can create stress for its people when it promotes values but not the social structure where those values can be performed. On the one hand, society promotes mothering but, on the other hand, it denies a sub-section of mothers the opportunity to exercise that mothering.

Robin Williams Jr… who believed some western core values conflict with other core values. For example, our culture wants us to be responsible for our own success or failure ("individualism") at the same time it wants us to help others who lag behind ("humanitarianism"). Social workers in the early 1960s were supposed to help clients achieve their personal goals (humanitarianism). For many mothers, that goal was to mother their children. But for a subset of clients the social workers instead stressed individualism. Mothers should surrender motherhood in favor of the schooling, careers, and "normal families" that would make them "successful."

Gordon Allport who believed...members of divergent groups will get along if they receive positive feedback when they interact with each other in non-discriminatory ways. There were several social structures in the early '60s that withheld positive feedback to single mothers. Such structures included schools that booted out pregnant students; maternity homes that sequestered pregnant women in a way that made them feel as if they were wrong-doers; and, adoption agencies with the credibility and wherewithal to discriminate against single mothers by denying them options.

Charles Horton Cooley who believed... it is part of social conditioning for an individual to develop a "looking glass" self. With a looking-glass self, you assess how others regard you. With the development of a "looking glass" self, a person internalizes—takes as their own—others' perceptions. Most mothers who surrendered in the early '60s were younger women in the process of assessing others' regard. They discovered their pregnancy reduced others' opinion of them, which they tended to accept as truth.

Abraham Maslow who believed…an individual can't become their "best self" (self-actualization) unless they have satisfied lower-level needs (such as: "belonging" and "esteem"). An early '60s, middle class young woman was often removed from her environment and sent away. Her belongingness was suspended until the evidence of her transgression was removed. Meanwhile, issues of low self-esteem plagued her before, during, and, to the extent she fully understood her situation, after she surrendered.

2. E. Wayne Carp. (2013). *The extraordinary life of Jean Paton and the struggle to reform American Adoption.* University of Michigan Press. Print.

3. For more about Steve Jobs' quirky personality and his adoption, see: Walter Isaac Citation. *Steve Jobs.* Simon Schuster. 2011.

4. *Nolo Contendre.* I probably would have felt better if someone had explained to me what Tom's plea legally meant. I assumed it meant he was saying he wasn't guilty. Instead, *Nolo Contendre* means he did not submit either a guilty nor a not guilty plea.

5a. Here is a copy of my own surrender document. Notice there is no "promise of confidentiality."

COPY

NHDPW-13

State of New Hampshire
Department of Public Welfare

SURRENDER OF CHILD TO DEPARTMENT OF PUBLIC WELFARE

FOR ADOPTION

I, ...Leona Ann Horrocks......, a resident of the town of ...Manchester...

in the county of ......Hillsborough...... and State of New Hampshire do hereby affirm

that I am the mother of ......Ronald Thomas Horrocks...... who was born out

of wedlock on the ....twenty-first.... day of ...December...... 19.62., in the City

of ....Boston.... in the county of ......Suffolk...... and said State of Massachuset

I hereby abandon all claim to the said ......Ronald Thomas Horrocks......

and give him/her up to the Department of Public Welfare of the State of New Hampshire for

adoption in some home deemed suitable by said department. By this instrument I give up and

release all my rights, privileges and responsibilities pertaining to said ...Ronald......

......Thomas Horrocks...... and I give my consent to the change of name of the said

Ronald Thomas Horrocks

This surrender shall operate as my consent to any adoption subsequently approved by said department and I am fully aware of the gravity of the step I am taking in making this surrender.

Signed and sealed in the presence of: _Leona Ann Horrocks_ (Seal)

State of New Hampshire
Hillsborough SS.
Personally appeared the above named ...Leona Ann Horrocks...
and acknowledged the foregoing instrument to be her voluntary act and deed.
Before me,

March 16, 19 63

Sophie D.
Notary Public
My commission expires: Jan. 31, 1966

5b. In 2013, Dr. Elizabeth Samuels, Professor at the University of Baltimore's School of Law published a paper that analyzed 75 mid-twentieth century surrender documents from 26 different states. She did not find any

documents to support the claim that confidentiality was promised to surrendering mothers. See:
http://papers.ssrn.com/sol3/cf_dev/AbsByAuth.cfm?per_id=280573

6. This "fake it till you make it" approach is controversial. Some studies find that if you smile even when you are not happy, you draw an "inference" from your smile that you are happy, and *voila!* you become happier. Psychologically-oriented people call this the "facial feedback hypothesis." I sometimes encouraged my students to experiment with smiling in college hallways, cafeterias and libraries to prove or disprove the theory. More often than not, students reported they felt happier, at least temporarily.

To explain why this works, some say that "putting on a happy face" prompts others to smile back at you, which, in turn, makes your smile more genuine. Others suggest that the upward turn of the mouth depresses certain nerves in the brain that, in turn, trigger a shower of feel-good neural chemicals. For more about such experiments, see, for example: Strack, Martin, and Stepper's. *"Inhibiting and facilitating conditions of the human smile: A nonobtrusive test of the facial feedback hypothesis."* Journal of Personality and Social Psychology, 54(5), May 1988, 768-777. doi: 10.1037/0022-3514.54.5.768

7a. In a number of studies, the variable "frequent moves" has been positively correlated with an increased likelihood of teen pregnancy. One hypothesis is that teens who were nomadic in childhood may unconsciously (and prematurely) try to create their own households. In their own households, they could have greater control over where they live and how long they live there.

Because I can no longer find this study, I can't answer follow-up questions you probably have, such as whether it mattered if the moves were sudden, or if the moves were planned and expected, such as with military families.

7b. According to Schug, Yuki, and Maddux in *Self-Concealment*. Psychlopedia. psych-it.com.au . (2010), moving frequently in my youth should have been a plus in discussing my surrender with people in my new life.

The trio wrote: "the sense that one can form new friendships and terminate older friendships…eases self-disclosure, since rejection is not especially distressing.

I don't know whether to beg to differ, or to point out this premise only shows how strong the taboo was against me divulging my secret, since my fear of rejection was indeed distressing.

8. For an historical overview, see, for example: Fershee, Kendra Huard, Hollow. (August 22, 2009). Promises for Pregnant Students – How the Regulations Governing Title IX Fail to Protect Them from Discrimination in School. *Indiana Law Review*, Vol. 43, No. 1, p. 79, 2009. Web.

9. For more on women uprisings at *Newsw*eek, see: Lynn Povich. *The good girls revolt*. Public Affairs. 2012. E-book.

10. As I cut-and-pasted the Journal entry on the river scene into *STOW AWAY*, I could clearly see the features on Tom's face. This is interesting, in an academic kind of way.

In my courses in "Marriage and the Family", we, of course, discussed "love." As I read studies and articles for information I could use to spice up my lectures I came across a study that found most divorced individuals cannot recall the details of their ex's face after two years. Because I can recall such details fifty years later, I could be an "outlier," an oddball with unusual recall. But the two year shelf life for facial recall may not apply to first loves, since first loves, like footprints in fresh concrete, may make a more lasting impression than other exes.

11. Trying to find a comfort zone in "yesterday," "tomorrow," or "today" loosely fits a psychological concept called "opponent process theory" (OPT).

In OPT, after you experience something dramatic that resulted in unpleasantries, you seek an opposite experience, thinking you will now experience a pleasant result. However, it is likely that you will not be happy with that extreme either. So you now set out to find an experience that is somewhere between the two. For example, you partner with a spendthrift, which doesn't work out. So, you partner with a miser, which also doesn't work out. Now that you know the parameters of the two extremes, you can seek someone in-between. OPT applies to relationships, to behaviors, to types of cars, homes, to most things, even including to the color wheel.

12. For context, see CUB's publication *Understanding the Birthparent.* (1977, 1978, 1979) at www.cubirthparents.org or Radcliffe's Schlesinger Library at Harvard University.

13.. See: Baran, A., Sorosky, A., and Pannor, R. Adoptive parents and the sealed records controversy. *Social Casework* (1974) 55:531–36.

14. Scientific research has now proven that emotional tears and emotionally-neutral tears (e.g. peeling an onion) have different chemical properties. Emotional tears include the stress hormone "cortisol." Crying, then, helps to rid the body of stress. See, for example:
http://drsherylwagner.blogspot.com/2011/03/tears-natural-stress-release.html

15. Biologists have discovered fetal cells remain in 50-70% of mothers for many decades after they are conceived. In a process called microchimerism, fetal cells have been variously reported as (a) having an effect on the mother's auto-immune system, (b) serving like stem cells to repair her damaged cells, and, conversely, (c) having no purpose whatsoever.

I propose something far-fetched but intriguing, since it may suggest how I knew Michael's interest in his birthfather would be strong, before I even knew Michael.

Since cells carry signals, it may be possible for fetal cells to contain information about a fetus' personality traits, which a sensitive mother could intuit.

For another application of microchimerism to birthmotherhood, see: Meredith Hall. (2007). *Without a map.* Beacon Press.

16. In the 1999 *Handbook of the Sociology of Mental Health,* edited by C.S. Aneshensel and J.C. Phelan, Thoits wrote: Prominence of identity may exacerbate stress because the more an individual identified with, is committed to, or has highly developed self-schemas in a particular life domain, the greater will be the emotional impact of stressors in that domain."

I was a Catholic girl who grew up in the late '50s and early '60s. I was raised in a family where I was built-in babysitter for a frequently ill mother. All my social and personal upbringing primed me for motherhood. From the time I can remember, I looked forward to it. When I finally became a mother to children I could raise, I was more than ready. I adored the role. To me, Thoits is saying all those factors made me a strong candidate for exceptional stress about my child missing in adoption.

17. The sequel, CAST OFF, reveals the serendipitous way I literally bumped into the logo.

18a. Here are a couple of vignettes on "dissociation" from my Psychology course.

Your psyche is sensitive to conflicts in the emotional and thinking parts of your mind. Because your psyche prefers harmony, it tries to mediate whatever it perceives as threats. If you have had a painful trauma that arouses serious conflicts—between emotions, between thoughts, or between emotions and thoughts— the psyche can use complicated ways to try to resolve them. Dissociation is one such way, and it *is* complicated. Let's try to break it down.

First, there are the pain-riddled emotional components of a trauma. If your psyche senses that a trauma poses an actual or even a potential threat of serious emotional distress, the psyche can use dissociative remedies.

One remedy is like anesthesia. The psyche takes a kind of divide-and-conquer approach to dispensing anesthesia. It's as if your psyche says "This emotional part of you will feel this emotional pain; that other part will feel a different piece." Therefore: "Here's some anesthesia for the pain this part of you feels." And: "Here's a pain-killer for the part of you that feels a different pain." (Examples are coming up.)

In addition to dissociation divvying up remedies for emotional pain, dissociation compartmentalizes your thoughts. Your very busy psyche can assign some thoughts to one part of you and some thoughts to other parts. When it comes to passing out thinking roles, the psyche is like a director: "You read from this script." "You, over there, you read from this one." Most actors try to find the motivation behind the characters they play, so your psyche, as your casting director, also invents reasons you can use to justify to yourself why you act the way you do in this situation or that.

With dissociation, some feeling parts of you are numb; some thinking roles are assigned. Since the way you think and feel influences the way you act, dissociation can also impact your "social roles," the way you conform to others' expectations.

Meanwhile, there is a part of you that hasn't been monkeyed with "too much." The part of you that is relatively intact can interact with familiar people; it can also meet new people. The intact-you can manipulate info to manage your day; it can also learn new things. Further, the intact-you can chauffeur your body where it needs to go.

The psyche monitors all this. Your psyche took a lot of energy to protect you from a trauma's aftermath. So your psyche is actively invested in making sure its protections do not get disturbed.

Now, depending on how resilient you naturally are, and on the actual or potential fallout from a trauma, your case of dissociation could be extreme, mild, or anywhere in-between.

An extreme case of dissociation might be multiple personalities, the stuff of several fascinating movies (see "Sybil," and "The Three Faces of Eve."

Let's drive this home by talking about a victim of child sexual abuse. She doesn't have the wherewithal to make sense of that kind of assault, so her psyche divides her emotional and thinking selves, and, thus, her social role.

With a trauma this potentially devastating, the psyche can re-arrange and mesh some of the parts it created. Like a sculptor working with bits of clay, the psyche can form fully-developed personalities. Each persona can assume some responsibility for a share of the trauma.

A persona can present herself to the outside world with her own name and style (such as accent, gait, and even preference for clothing and hairdo). And, with such unique attributes, each share of the trauma can have its own personality. One might easily fly off the handle; another might be analytical.

One may carry the memories of the initial abuse and act as a proxy for future hits. Meanwhile, another may vent the abuse by being overly promiscuous or overly prissy. If a case is complicated by many whole selves, a psyche may delegate management of everyone to a bossy pants.

Like living in a condo complex, a persona may not know its neighbor. If awareness develops, it may be a long process of (selves!) discovery.

Dissociation of this magnitude is not a disorder for the weak; usually only bright and imaginative people—most often women—have the wherewithal to do this.

Not all dissociations are this dire. Dissociations can also be minimally invasive; can manifest in only one dissociative event; and can be short-lived. The sense of watching yourself from a point outside your body may be a good example. After a horrific car crash, you watch your body as ambulance techs attend to it. Sooner rather than later, though, you become realigned, and you are good to go.

Here's how the concept of dissociation applies to me.

On a scale of one to ten, where ten is multiple personalities and one is the car crash, my own experience with dissociation is hard for me, as the affected person, to rank (which explains why shrinks have shrinks). I may have been a four. I was initially semi-aware I needed to shut down and split off, but as splitting became second nature, my memories burrowed as if into the marrow of my bones, where they hibernated. They were quiet so I never gave them a second thought. But after ten years my divided natures were the only thing I could think about.

I now know I had a type of dissociation called Post-Traumatic Stress Disorder (PTSD).

18 b. PTSD is a two-step process. In Step One, someone does something way outside the social expectations she has internalized for herself. She didn't anticipate going so far off-course so it catches her off-guard, devastates her, and she doesn't know what to do. She doesn't split into separate and distinct selves. Instead, she divides into semi-related parts. To keep these disjointed parts moving, she becomes robotic.

We all feel divided from time to time; for example, maybe we are of two minds about a decision that needs to be made. But in such cases we are able to weigh and assess each option. In PTSD, she's too mechanized to weigh and assess. Like a drone, she's also not very articulate. She may feel the need to say something but can't summon the words; she's in a kind of "conscious coma."

Most people are uncomfortable when a decision "should" be made. If someone with PTSD can't make a decision, others will step into the vacuum. They will propose solutions and maybe even lobby for one in particular. Meanwhile, the trauma survivor may appear to agree with a proposed solution because she goes along with it. She goes through the motions. Others don't see her inner robot put one foot in front of the other and she can't feel the robotics either, at least not at first.

Later, though, it's a different story. In some cases, eight to ten years pass before the initial trauma re-asserts itself. When it rears up, Step Two of PTSD begins.

The former situation needs to be accommodated by whatever new situation has arisen in the interim. It's a little like being the widow of a soldier declared dead. After she remarries she learns the declaration was false and the previous husband is coming home. The need to enfold a long ago situation can be confounding.

Fortunately, today there are counselors who are well-versed in PTSD and know how to help if you commit an asocial act they have studied. If you are a soldier, they understand your situation. If you are a rape victim, you have trained people to turn to. But if your PTSD stems from an uncharted trigger, then you are on your own. And if you must figure out your PTSD by yourself, it helps if you know you have it. I didn't learn about PTSD until long after it had its way with me.

19. I have read several historical accounts of the sealed adoption record. I most trust the work of Dr. Elizabeth Samuels (see End Note # 5b). For another account see: Madelyn Freundlich's "For the Records: Restoring a Legal Right for Adult Adoptees." Published by The Evan B. Donaldson Adoption Institute. November 2007. http://www.adoptioninstitute.org/publications/2007_11_For_Records.pdf

20. For more about enforcement of open adoption contracts, see: https://www.childwelfare.gov/systemwide/laws_policies/statutes/cooperative.pdf#Page=2&view=XYZ

21a. Here is a copy of the Southern state of Australia's apology:

APOLOGY
for FORCED ADOPTION PRACTICES
18 July 2012

 he South Australian Parliament recognises that the lives of many members of the South Australian community have been adversely affected by adoption practices, which have caused deep distress and hurt, especially for mothers and their children, who are now adults.

We recognise that past adoption practices have profoundly affected the lives of not only these people, but also fathers, grandparents, siblings, partners and other family members.

We accept with profound sorrow that many mothers did not give informed consent to the adoption of their children.

To those mothers who were denied the opportunity to love and care for their children, we are deeply sorry.

We recognise that practices of our past mean that there are some members of our community today who remain disconnected from their families of origin.

To those people adopted as children who were denied the opportunity to be loved and cared for by their families of origin, we are deeply sorry.

To those people who were disbelieved for so long, we hear you now; we acknowledge your pain, and we offer you our unreserved and sincere regret and sorrow for those injustices.

To all those hurt, we say sorry.

Hon. Jay Weatherill MP
Premier *of* South Australia

Hon. Grace Portolesi MP
Minister *for* Education and Child Developm

21b. The State of South Australia created adoption rights in **1989**. See: Evelyn Robinson. *Adoption Separation: Then* *and Now*. www.clovapublications.com. 2010. Here are some of the rights that were given to members of adoption-separated families:

* Adoptive parents can, if they choose, add their names to the child's original birth certificate. In that case, the names of both the birthparents and the adoptive parents appear on the same document. After the birth is registered, each parent named on the document can get a copy of the document at any time.

* At age 18, adoptees can obtain their original birth certificates and other documentation about their adoption. Adoptees under 18 can acquire this information with the permission of both their adoptive parents and birthparents.

* After an adoptee reaches age 18 a birthmother has a legal right to obtain an adoptee's replacement birth certificate if one is issued. Before 18, birthmothers can get a copy of their surrendered child's birth certificate if adoptive parents elect the first option, above.

 * Birth and adoption documents are available to any other children of the birthmother if the mother gives permission, or after her death. The children of adoptees have similar rights.

MORE ABOUT THE AUTHOR

In 1976, Dr. Lee Campbell started the first organization in the world that was devoted to parents who surrendered children to adoption, Concerned United Birthparents (CUB). As proof of the need for CUB, parts of her story, and her members' stories, were repeated in countless broadcast and print media, one alone netting more than 10,000 letters.

In 1978, Lee was appointed by the then-Department of Health and Welfare to serve for two years on a panel of experts that developed model adoption laws for the country. With an ad hoc committee she organized, she also helped to promote the concept of open adoption as an alternative to the closed adoption policies of the day. To underscore the need for openness, she further co-authored four studies on birthparenthood and reunions, which were each published in professional journals.

During the time that Lee earned a Master's Degree in Education from Antioch University, a Certificate of Advanced Studies in Education at The Johns Hopkins University, and a doctorate in Clinical Sociology from the Union Institute. She also taught at the University of New Hampshire, the College of Notre Dame in Baltimore, and, later, at Edison State College in Florida. At Edison, she launched a program, "Risk A R.A.S.K." Through RASK, she collected 5,000 reports of Random Acts of Senseless Kindness to offset reports of violence. This landed her on *Oprah* and in other national and local broadcast and print media. She then devoted her energies to the college classroom where she taught courses in the social sciences for a couple more decades.

When Lee retired, she returned to CUB as its curator. Charged with re-assembling CUB's history, she has recently shipped her collection to Radcliffe's Schlesinger Library at Harvard University, where it awaits processing. Soon, it will be physically and digitally accessed. Meanwhile, CUB's own website (www.cubirthparents.org) offers access to many of these documents. Adoption reformists, women activists, and historians of every stripe-- as well as researchers, producers, reporters, and publishers- -are encouraged to view these resources.

STOW AWAY and the upcoming sequel *CAST OFF* offer a context for Lee's story and CUB's. They offer inspiration for further study and suggest some ways to extend the work of adoption reform and support for crisis pregnancies. Lee welcomes your interest and queries about CUB's history at cub.curator@gmail.com.

The mother of four sons, stepmother to two others, and grandmother to many, Lee now lives in southwest Florida with her husband, the late-in-life, love-of-her-life.

IN OTHER WORDS

Some Works Authored, Co-Authored or
Collaboratively Written by and with the Author

Editor: *CUB Communicator.* Concerned United Birthparents, Inc., 1976-1979.... *President's Column: CUB* Communicator. Concerned United Birthparents, Inc., 1976-1984....Editor: *The Birthparents' Perspective.* Concerned United Birthparents, Inc., 1976-1984. . . .Editor: CUB brochures. Concerned United Birthparents, Inc., 1976-1984. . . .Editor: *Understanding the Birthparent.* Concerned United Birthparents, Inc., 1977, 1978, 1979. . . .*Leaders' Handbook,* with a grant from the American Institute of Research, 1979. . . .*Living as a Birthparent,* with a grant from the American Institute of Research,1979. . . .*The Birthparents' Right to Know.* Public Welfare magazine, 1979, 37(3). . . .*Adoption Abuse.* Our Bodies Our Selves. Boston Women's Health Book Collective. Reprinted from *Women-wise,* 1983 5(3). . . .*Adoptive Parents Write to CUB.* Concerned United Birthparents, Inc., Circa 1980. . . .*Model Adoption Laws and Policies.* For the then-Department of Health, Education and Welfare, 1980.... *Birthparents and Pride.* Concerned United Birthparents Inc., 1980.... *On Language.* Concerned United Birthparents Inc.,1980. . . .*Choices, Chances, Changes: A Guide for Your Untimely Pregnancy.* Concerned United Birthparents, Inc., 1980-1984.... *New Beginnings: A Five Year Report.* Concerned United Birthparents, Inc., 1981....*A Search Group Directory.* Concerned United Birthparents, Inc., 1981. . . .*Reunited After 16 years: A Mother's Search for her Son.* Women's World, Nov. 10, 1981....*I Care Too: An Interview with Birthfathers.* Concerned United Birthparents, Inc., 1982....*Birthparents Searching: You Can't Have it Both Ways.* Concerned United Birthparents, Inc., 1982. . . .*National CUB Takes Legislative Stand.* Concerned United Birthparents, Inc.,

1983. . ... *Growing Strong with CUB: A Two Year Report.* Concerned United Birthparents, Inc., 1983. *An Introduction to the CUB Sister Program.* Concerned United Birthparents, Inc., 1983. . . . .*The Postadoption Experience of Surrendering Parents.* American Journal of Orthopsychiatry, April 1984. . . .*The Cabbage Patch Kids: The Birthparents' Perspective.* Guest column. USA Today, 1984. . . *Who Cares About Keeping this Family Together?* Concerned United Birthparents, Inc., 1984. . . .*Reunions between Adoptees and Birthparents: The Birthparents' Perspective.* Social Work, 1988. . . . *Collaboration between Teachers on Integration of Technology within the Curricula of Students with Disabilities*, for United States Department of Education, under federal grant with The Johns Hopkins University Center for Technology, 1989. . . .*Reunions between Adoptees and Birthparents: The Adoptees' Experience.* Social Work, July 1991. . . .Women and Mentoring: The Tradition, the Process, the Vision. Dissertation in partial fulfillment of a doctorate in clinical sociology, The Union Institute, 1992. . . .*Reunions between Adoptees and Birthparents:The Adoptive Parents' Experience.* Social Work, September 1994. . . . *RASKing 'Round the Town.* Charlotte Sun-Herald, 1994-1995. . . .*R.A.S.K. Report*, quarterly leaders letter. Edison State College, 1994-1995. . . .Student manuals for online courses. Edison State College, 2005-2011.

Some Presentations Offered by the Author
(In random order of recollection)

Key Notes: Adoption Connection, Nashua NH. . . .New England Home for Little Wanderers, MA. . . .Framingham South High School, Boston. . . .Adoption Forum Conference, PA (2x). . . .Department of Welfare, MA. . . .Florence Crittenton House, MA. . . .Harvard University, MA (5x). . . .American Adoption Conference, Washington DC (3x). . . . NY State Social Workers,

NY...New Frontiers in Postadoption Services, MN (3x)....Triadoption Library, CA. (2x) numerous women's groups in SW Florida....Rotary and other community groups in SW Florida....Students, Washington College....Women employees, CSX Transportation....National Women's Studies Association....Business and Professional Women's Association, Hunt Valley, MD....Catonsville Community College, National Secretary's Day, MD....Rollins Hills Women's Club, MD....Sociological Practice Association National Conference, RI....Bon Secours Center for the Elderly, MD....Antioch U, MA....NH Department of Welfare, NH....University of New Hampshire, NH....Open Adoption Conference, Traverse City, MI....PostAdoption Center for Education and Reform, CA....More.

Radio Broadcasts: National Public Radio...."Close Up"...."Action 4, Boston....Paul Benzaquin, Boston....Dayton....Christian Sciences, Boston....WEAN, Providence....CJOR....twice-weekly RASK Reports, SW Florida....WCRB....WCAS....WHER....More.

Television Broadcasts: The Natalie Jacobsen news segment, WCVB-MA....The Joe Hyder Show, WSMV-Worcester...."Morning Break", WDVM-DC....The Chere Avery Show, Ft. Myers....Oprah (2x).... Mid-Day News, WNEW-NYC.... Good Neighbor....Donahue (4x)....Nightly News with Natalie Jacobsen, MA....Action 4, Boston....The Joe Hyder Show, Worcester, MA....Morning Break, Washington, DC....People are Talking, WJZ-Baltimore....Women '79, WBZ-Boston....The Morning Show, Philadelphia....The Pittsburgh 2-Day Show, KIKA-Pittsburg.... Mid-Day, NYC....Sonja, WDIV-Detroit....news segment with Betty Furness, NYC....Nightly News, TX....More.

352

Print Media Interviews: "Lowell Sun," Lowell, MA...."Valley Advocate," Amherst, MA...."Patriot Ledger," Quincy, MA...."Boston Sunday Globe," Boston MA...."Family Involvement," Toronto Ontario...."Boston Herald," Boston, MA...."Parade," NY...."Philadelphia Daily News," PA...."New York Time," NY.... "Wall Street Journal," NY...."Keene Sentinel," NH...."Christian Science Monitor," DC...."Family Weekly," NY...."Good Housekeeping," NY...."Women's Day," NY...."The Courier," NH...."Foster's Daily Democrat," NH...."Family Circle," NY....More.

CAST OFF:
"They called us a danger to the System.
So, we proved them right."

EXPECTED RELEASE: 2014

<u>An Overview:</u>

Just when a '70s housewife perfects her ship in a bottle life on Cape Cod—just when she feels her safest—forbidden memories swamp all she knows. Plunged between layers of time she flounders for one last lifeline: other mothers marooned by state-supported secrets like hers.

With these mothers, she creates a first of its kind band of sisters. As they tread unchartered waters, the women tap their good humor and the best of their nature. They help each other to shed Stepford cover-ups and to discover some of the pride they were denied. They emerge notorious.

Shocked, agents of the state launch their bureaucratic might. They resist changes the women propose and try to force them to surrender, again. But, this time, the women have each other. They stand arm-in-arm on their own beachhead and protest in concert. When their outcry amplifies like keening, resistance divides. Some professionals try to help the women; others to raise their risk.

Some Details:

Lee's personal story continues. With aching restraint, Lee follows Michael's life from a distance. When she learns he's being lied to, she makes an overture to his family. After her reunion with 15-year-old Michael, she convinces Tom of his paternity and is gratified by Tom's family's campaign to meet Michael. Later, she experiences their stunning betrayal. Her post-reunion relationship with Michael becomes an unexpected exercise in push-pull. As early pioneers in a fully-fleshed out reunion with a minor child, everyone has a rollercoaster of a ride. And when the ride is over, there's one more surprise.

Meanwhile, Lee endures a harsh spotlight as she works with members of her organization to reform adoption. Together they break the rules. They create a language that tries to capture who they are and they invent new and controversial ways of being in the world. Through newsletters, educational materials, and research studies, they validate their experience and begin to change a sacred institution for generations to come.

ACKNOWLEDGEMENTS

First and most important, I thank my husband, Parke, who makes love, laughter and all things possible. When my college's paperwork grew into nothing more than excessive busy work, he encouraged me to retire. Now I am able to do my own paperwork in ways that reflect the things I really care about. I couldn't have done this without my Parke.

I also thank E. Wayne Carp who unwittingly provided a kick in the pants. As one of the more self-forgiving people you will ever meet, I'm not normally motivated by guilt. But Wayne's book on the life of my late colleague, Jean Paton, made me ashamed for dumping all my CUB materials. I also appreciate the CUB Board for welcoming me back to CUB as its Curator and allowing me to redeem myself by coordinating the CUB History Project (CHiP). I also appreciate the CUB Board for subsidizing the digitization of many materials that set the record straight and help to support others' projects, too. Special thanks go to CUB Board members Patty Collins and Mary Anne Cohen, my longtime friend and colleague of more than 35 years.

Gail Hanssen Perry, to whom I dedicate STOW AWAY, deserves to lead this paragraph. Gail jumpstarted CUB's archival collection when she escorted more than 50 pounds of CUB materials on the plane during one of her routine trips to Florida to visit me. I think Gail was a little dubious about what I was doing, but she helped anyway, as she always has. It's better than Christmas to have a friend who gifts me with such unconditional faith. I'm also grateful to other early CUB veterans who continue to grace my life: Alison Ward, and Sandy Musser. While we don't have our "old birthmothers' home" yet, we do live in a compound that is spread over three nearby towns.

My local self-publishing guru, James Abraham, his course on writing and his generous mentoring were wind in my sails. Four other women I met in his class continued to meet twice-monthly after the course was over. These Sisters in Stories (SIS) Pam Fricke, Carole Ponzio, Gerry Townsend, Karen Paron, Fredye Cochran, and Carol Dunekirchen became members of my in-town cheerleading squad. They escorted me around many writing blocks.

Two former colleagues in my teaching career were also supportive. Meeting periodically with me over long weekends and day-time writing marathons were Dr. Margaret Desjardins and Natala Orobello, who, as serendipity would have it, were each working on their own writing projects. It was great to re-connect with them in this new way.

My sister Brenda earns special mention. She was unfailingly enthusiastic about whatever needed enthusing. Two of my sons—Scott Campbell and Todd Campbell— kept their confidence alive over several decades that I would someday "do something" with the Journals on which I pounded away during their childhood. Their conviction meant a lot. My daughter-in-law, Melanie, put her PhotoShop skills to work on a previous cover; Norma Bradley helped on that too. Along the way, Sandi Skalkeas exercised her marketing expertise. But it was Bill Cassa, a local artist, who brought the current cover to life. He was an incredibly good sport for giving me so many patient hours. Time and again, he recast the cover as I tried to verbally describe the unformed mud in my mind. Thanks, too, to Jeanette at Buffalo Graffix who PhotoShopped the text on the cover. As for the narrative between the covers, my editor Fran Stewart should take a bow. I'm not detail-oriented but she is, and she was able to catch every freakin' boo-boo. Early readers offered content suggestions and I am grateful to them beyond measure. Suffering through early versions of the manuscript were Patty Collings, Peggy Dawn Moran, Deborah Allen, Pam Fricke and Fredye Cochran.

Last but always first, there's also Michael. I've recently realized that he has put most new people in his life through a litmus test. If they read my 1996 Journal, they could stay on. We will soon celebrate 35 years of reunion, Michael. And, you know what? You are still magical to me. Thanks for sticking with the mother you call "Bear".